LABOR
THEORY

RICHARD PERLMAN

Professor of Economics
University of Wisconsin—Milwaukee

JOHN WILEY & SONS, INC.,

NEW YORK · LONDON · SYDNEY · TORONTO

331
P 45 L

10 9 8 7 6 5 4 3 2 1
Library of Congress Catalog Card Number: 69-19094
SBN 471 680551
Printed in the United States of America

LABOR THEORY

Preface

Although labor theory can still be considered merely an applied branch of micro-and macro-theory, the discipline now concerns itself with a host of new applications. Showing the customary lag that characterizes most advancements in knowledge, general books in the field have not yet given comprehensive treatment to the theoretical aspects of such topics as the negative income tax, human resources, the structural-inadequate demand controversy, the effect of nonmarket labor time on labor supply, wage-price guideposts, and the effect of cyclical changes in the labor force on the Phillips curve.

These topics have not been consolidated into the body of labor theory, and this book does not attempt such a unification. Instead, it incorporates the topics within the familiar elements of labor theory—for example, labor supply, wage structure, and unemployment. My objective here is not a general theory of labor economics nor, hopefully, a mere review and summary of outstanding recent contributions to the field. But my goal is an analysis, a criticism, and a commentary on these additions, along with a restudy of some topics not so new—certainly neither the traditional development of the individual labor-supply curve nor the Keynesian-classical unemployment controversy qualifies as a modern theme.

No claim of comprehensiveness is made; the reader may find his favorite topic omitted. Furthermore, with an almost complete absence of historical or expository treatment of the various themes and ideas, my approach tacitly assumes that the reader has a close familiarity with the standard literature and, in fact, often with the specific writings analyzed.

While the topics share only the common thread of belonging to the area of labor economics, the subject matter falls into definite compartments. At least the work is divided into four broad fields: labor supply and demand, wage structure, unemployment, and the relationship between wages, prices, and unemployment.

I thank those who aided this work. Many helpful criticisms and suggestions for improving earlier drafts were offered by my colleagues Professors Melvin Lurie, Boris P. Pesek, and Manuel Gottlieb, and by

v

Professor Pan A. Yotopoulos and Dr. John E. Maher. Their careful review of the entire manuscript through several stages gave direction to its revision. The Graduate School of the University of Wisconsin provided financial support for beginning research on the project. I am especially grateful to Miss Joan Brau for her patient and efficient typing of many more drafts than we had anticipated.

Richard Perlman

Contents

LABOR THEORY

PART ONE

Labor Supply and Demand

CHAPTER I

Labor Supply

Unlike the supplier of a commodity, the worker does not incur substantial marginal monetary costs in offering his services to the market.[1] What limits the worker's supply of labor are the nonmonetary costs of time and effort involved in working. Thus, if effort can be translated into time equivalents, the marginal cost to the worker of supplying labor is measured by the value to him of the alternative uses of time foregone in order to work.

In traditional theory, this foregone time has been considered "leisure," a desirable employment of time, while work (the cost of labor supply) is considered the leisure time sacrificed in order to earn wage income. This strictly dichotomous treatment of time has been modified recently in a way that alters the traditional conclusions regarding labor-leisure-wage relationships.

In this chapter, the conventional treatment of individual labor supply will be studied first, before the modifications resulting from consideration of other aspects of time are introduced. This first section, besides discussing characteristics of the individual labor-supply schedule, also lays the theoretical groundwork for the application of this and the other two chapters of Part One.

In the remaining sections of this chapter, modifications of the conventional theory are applied to commuting, consumption time, the labor supply of the household with special reference to married women, and the returns on investment in education.

---

[1] The effect on labor supply of his fixed costs, such as education and training, and of his minor partly marginal costs of commuting and so-called "maintenance costs," such as clothing and grooming associated with work, will be discussed in this and subsequent chapters.

INDIVIDUAL LABOR SUPPLY

Whether an increase in the wage rate will lead to an increase or decrease in the individual worker's supply of work time (that is, whether the labor-supply schedule is forward or backward sloping) has long been recognized as uncertain. The underlying basis for this uncertainty is usually explained with reference to indifference curves, substitution and income effects, and all the familiar terms of modern value theory.

However, an understanding of the nature of the problem can be found in Lionel Robbins' noted 1930 article, written when the economist's tools were limited to concepts of utility and disutility.[2] At that time, there was a prevalent notion that the supply schedule of labor would be backward sloping because, at higher wages and consequent higher income, the worker would wish to "buy" more leisure, along with other goods. Robbins points out that at a higher wage, the price of leisure itself has risen.[3] Here we have the germ of the income and substitution effects.

A higher wage rate allows for higher income, which tends to increase the demand for leisure, if leisure is not an inferior good. On the other hand, with a rise in what Robbins calls the real income price of leisure, the substitution effect of a wage rise leads to a reduced demand for leisure. Thus, whether a rise in wages will lead to a rise in labor supply depends on which of the two effects is stronger—income or substitution.

Note the lack of parallelism between the demand for leisure and that of an ordinary commodity. For the latter, the income and substitution effects tend to move together. A fall in the price of a particular commodity encourages a substitution of that commodity for other now relatively more expensive commodities and has a generally weak income effect—weak because the commodity comprises only a small part of total expenditure. However, the income effect supports the substitution effect (if the good is not an inferior one) because the individual's real income rises with a drop in price in one of the items of expenditure.

---

[2] Lionel Robbins, "On the Elasticity of Demand for Income in Terms of Effort," *Economica,* **10** (June 1930), pp. 123–129, reprinted in *Readings in the Theory of Income Distribution,* The Blakiston Co., Philadelphia, 1951, pp. 237–244.

[3] Writing a little after Robbins, E. H. Phelps Brown, *The Framework of the Pricing System,* Chapman & Hill, London, 1936, p. 148, notes that the assumption of a negatively sloped labor supply curve was based on the view that, with declining marginal utility of money, as wages rose the marginal utility of the last dollar earned at the previous effort was not worth the marginal unit of labor required to earn it. As Phelps Brown points out, this reasoning ignores the fact that with higher wages the marginal unit of labor secures more dollars.

M. Blaug, *Economic Theory in Retrospect,* Richard D. Irwin, Homewood, Illinois, 1962, pp. 291–293, reviews earlier theories of labor supply.

On the other hand, a reduction in the price of leisure—signified by a fall in the wage rate—has a similar substitution effect in that it induces an increased demand for leisure. Expressed differently, less income is lost by selecting a given amount of time for leisure than for work. But now the income effect is not only contrary (if leisure is not an inferior good) but strong. It is contrary because the reduction in wages leads to a fall in income, and strong because wage income can be assumed to be the major if not the entire source of the worker's income.

Indifference curve analysis of labor supply will be used extensively in Part I. Income will appear on the Y-axis, and hours of leisure, measured from left to right, and hours of work, measured from right to left, will appear on the X-axis. Regarding the general slope of the map (if leisure is not an inferior good), higher indifference curves become steeper at any level of leisure, that is, a vertical line drawn from any point on the X-axis cuts higher indifference curves at steeper slopes, allowing for a positive income effect on leisure from higher wages. Furthermore, the curves do not cross either axis. They cannot cross the X-axis because, as Hart wryly remarked, "Man cannot live by X alone,"[4] nor can they cross the Y-axis because, when leisure is involved, man cannot live without some X.

There is asymmetry in the practical limits of the curves. Although it is unlikely that a worker would be so surfeited with goods in general over the relative range of income that he would not prefer higher income with the same leisure, the same is not true of his trade off of income for leisure. He can become saturated with leisure; his indifference curve may become horizontal. In fact, the curve for some individuals bends upward,[5] as hours of work are reduced to the point where the worker's very attachment to the labor force becomes an issue, and work at the margin may become desirable in itself, and added leisure a disutility.[6]

A further quality of the income-leisure indifference map has higher

---

[4] Albert G. Hart, "Peculiarities of Indifference Maps Involving Money," *Review of Economic Studies*, **8** (February 1941), p. 126.

[5] Technically, of course, the curves usually drawn are just a section of a contour line, so that eventually at higher income the curve will become vertical, then bend to the right. [See the basic explanation of R. G. D. Allen, "The Nature of Indifference Curves," *Review of Economic Studies*, **1** (1933–1934), pp. 110–120. But this should occur only at extremely high incomes. What, in effect, is maintained here is that the curve will bend upward along the leisure scale closer to the origin than it will bend to the right along the income scale.

[6] The possible utility of work and disutility of leisure is an old concept, found in Marshall. For an elaboration of the point, see James O'Connor, "Smith and Marshall on the Individual's Supply of Labor," *Industrial and Labor Relations Review*, **14** (January 1961), p. 276.

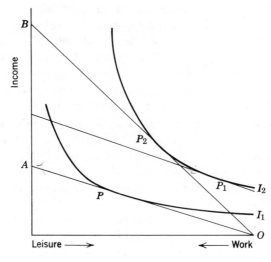

Fig. 1.1

curves becoming flatter for each income level. That is, a horizontal line drawn from any point on the Y-axis will cut through successive indifference curves at flatter points on the curves. This quality, which is derived from the assumption that income, or its equivalent of all-other-goods-except-leisure, is not an inferior (composite) good, leads to the important conclusion that even if the worker's labor-supply schedule is negatively sloped, so that he reduces his supply of labor with a rise in wages, he will not choose to reduce his supply to the point that he reduces his income.[7] In other words, he will take part of the wage gain in the form of additional leisure and part in added income.[8]

Indifference curve analysis explains this result clearly. In Figure 1.1, the increase in wages is shown by the upward movement of the (hourly) wage ray from OA to OB. The income effect of the wage increase is measured by drawing a ray parallel to OA tangent to indifference curve I_2. This ray will be tangent to I_2 at a point higher than P, the equilibrium

[7] K. Rothschild, *Theory of Wages,* Basil Blackwell, Oxford, 1956, p. 43, n. 1, notes that he may reduce his income if income is an inferior good, but points out the improbability of the demand for income taking this form.
[8] There is, of course, the extreme case in which all the gains will be in added leisure. This will be the result if, along with a zero income effect, the marginal rate of substitution of income for leisure at the position of greater leisure is infinite. (Here, the marginal rate of substitution of income for leisure means the rate of change of income with respect to leisure. Thus the greater the MRS, the weaker the substitution effect of income for leisure.)

income-leisure position at the lower wage, under the assumption that "income" is not an inferior good. The substitution effect will move the equilibrium income-leisure level at the higher wage leftward and upward from P_1 to P_2, indicating a still higher income, because the new wage ray is steeper than the old. Thus, both income and substitution effects induce the worker to choose a higher income, even if he also chooses more leisure, when his wage increases.

Notice the difference between the leisure case and that for any other commodity in general, for which the selection of less income (or of other goods) when its price falls is not unusual. This is simply the case of an elastic demand for the product. For the good, just as in the case of leisure, the normal income effect will be for the worker-consumer to buy more of other goods. But in this case the substitution effect leads him to buy more of the commodity whose price has fallen, so that the resultant effect might find him choosing to increase his expenditures on the good and reducing his purchases of all other goods.[9]

The general shape of the indifference map will serve as reference for criticism of the conventional textbook presentation of the backward-bending individual labor-supply curve. It is concluded that while the curve will tend to bend backward at some point, it will also have forward-bending segments, so that the curve that evolves may be one with many bends.

There are three strands to the theory of the backward-bending curve, each of which has weak threads. These can be designated as the appeal to authority, the concept of the reservation price, and the attraction of simplicity.

APPEAL TO AUTHORITY. Before Lionel Robbins' ingenious conversion of labor supply into a demand schedule of income in terms of effort, earlier theorists were not certain whether the labor-supply curve was positively or negatively sloped. Marshall considered it to be negatively

---

[9] Note that for the worker to buy less of the good as its price falls (the so-called "Giffen paradox"), the good must not only be inferior, with a negative income effect, but this income effect must outweigh the substitution effect, which induces him to buy more of the good.

On the other hand, for the worker to choose to reduce his leisure when its price rises, that is, for him to supply more hours of work when his wage increases, indicating a positively sloped labor supply curve, does not require unusual conditions.

In this case, while the income effect of the wage increase may induce the worker to take more leisure and offer less work, which would be the case if leisure were not an inferior good, the substitution effect leads him to "buy" less leisure and choose more of other goods (income.) Thus, for labor supply to increase with the wage increase, the substitution effect need only outweigh the income effect.

sloped for "the more ignorant and phlegmatic of races" who, in terms of indifference curves, experience a strong income effect but weak substitution effect from a wage rise. On the other hand, the curve would be positively sloped for those "whose mental horizon is wider, and who have more firmness and elasticity of character, and work the harder and the longer the higher the rate of pay which is given to them,"[10] that is, those with a strong tendency to substitute leisure for income relative to their increased desire for leisure as wage income rises. Thus, while Marshall notes that individual labor-supply curves may be either backward- or forward-sloping for different workers, he does not consider that the curve for the same worker can follow both directions for different wage levels.

Robbins is on firm ground when he criticizes the untested assumption of earlier theorists that the labor-supply curve is negatively sloped, but he then proceeds to make equally arbitrary assumptions of a supply curve of a different type (the backward-bending one) in his drawing of a curve for quantity of effort, related to income, which rises and then falls. This curve, along with his conventional downward-sloping demand curve for effort in terms of income, serves as the origin of the standard labor-supply curve, showing labor supply increasing with wages up to a point and then falling with further wage increases. For those who are uncomfortable with a bending supply schedule, Robbins offers a conventional demand curve for income, in terms of effort, that has an elasticity greater than one in its upper reaches and less than one as it approaches the X-axis, that is, with first an increase and then a decrease in effort as wages rise. But could we not just as easily draw a demand curve for income in terms of effort to fit another pattern of labor supply with, say, an elasticity greater than one over its relevant range, leading to a negatively sloped, unbent labor-supply curve?[11]

The standard version of labor supply combines the conclusions of Robbins and Marshall, with supply increasing and then decreasing with rising wages, and with the turning point dependent on the level of economic development and on the range of tastes and acquaintance with goods, being at a higher wage the more advanced the economy.[12]

---

[10] Alfred Marshall, *Principles of Economics,* 8th ed., Macmillan, New York, 1948, p. 528.

[11] Robbins, *op. cit.,* pp. 238–239. In fairness to Robbins, it should be noted that he stated that his curve was only one among an infinite variety of possible curves. But the one drawn became the basis of conventional theory.

[12] For example, Milton Friedman, *Price Theory,* Aldine, Chicago, 1962, p. 204, describes the individual supply curve in this manner.

   Harold G. Vatter, "On the Folklore of the Backward Sloping Supply Curve,"

CONCEPT OF RESERVATION PRICE. Regardless of the path of the supply curve at high wages, the assumption that it will be positively sloped for relatively low wages implies the presence of a reservation wage, a minimum wage established by custom or law below which the worker will not or cannot offer his services, with this minimum at or above the subsistence level. Without this operating minimum, the worker would be willing to toil many hours to reach a subsistence standard at wages significantly below this level, no matter how much leisure it cost. He would then be in a position in which he would be susceptible to the trading of some of his potential increase in income from a rise in wages for added leisure.

In his study of African labor, Berg concluded that the individual supply schedule for low-paid labor was negative, even considering the substitution that could take place between market goods and home-produced goods,[13] although market supply schedules were positively sloped as more workers offered market labor in place of home labor.

But what relevance does the African case have to American labor with its high reservation price, either established by the worker himself[14] or by society operating through its customs or laws in the setting of a social minimum wage—to use Reder's term[15]—which prevents the worker from offering his services below a certain wage even if he wished to do so? It can be argued that at whatever minimum wage the American

---

Industrial and Labor Relations Review, **14** (July 1961), pp. 580–582, argues that the supply curve for the typical worker in an advanced economy does not bend backward until an unrealistically high wage is reached, but the bases of his argument have been subjected to penetrating criticism by T. Aldrich Finegan, "Comment: The Backward Sloping Supply Curve," *Ibid.,* **15** (January 1962), p. 230.

[13] Elliot Berg, "Backward Sloping Labor Supply Functions in Dual Economies—The African Case," *Quarterly Journal of Economics,* **75** (August 1961), p. 476.

Jacob Mincer, "Labor Force Participation of Married Women: A Study of Labor Supply," *Aspects of Labor Economics,* National Bureau of Economic Research, Princeton University Press, Princeton, 1962, pp. 63–105, advances and supports the argument that the substitutability of market work for homework tends to make the market-supply curve for married women forward-sloping, since an increase in market labor need not result in an equal reduction in leisure time. (Mincer's work will be discussed in more detail in the next section.) The labor supply discussed here is that of men or in general terms, those whose nonmarket labor potential is slight.

[14] Vatter, *op. cit.,* p. 583, n. 12, claims, somewhat idealistically, that even in the absence of alternative opportunities or the application of legal or traditional minima, the American worker himself will establish a reservation price if on no other basis than on his integrity as a human being. (Does this mean that in the absence of alternative opportunities for income he would choose to starve?)

[15] Melvin Reder introduces this term in "The Theory of Occupational Wage Differentials," *American Economic Review,* **65** (December 1955), pp. 833–852.

worker enters a particular labor market, this wage will determine his subsistence, if not his survival, income. He will work as many hours as necessary to reach this minimum target.[16] Under the assumption of a target income for the low-wage worker, his labor supply curve would be backward-sloping until such a wage income were reached that his consumption goals became importunate but indefinite and until he responded positively to further wage increases by offering more labor.[17] Thus, while the American worker's reservation price is relatively high, his (partially) socially determined minimum income needs are also high, tending to make his relevant labor-supply curve begin in a negatively sloping direction.

But for the present argument it is not necessary to hold that the supply curve must begin in a backward-sloping phase. It is only maintained that over some realistic wage range the curve bends forward and moves from a negative to positive response to wage increases, to contradict the theory of the (single) backward-bending curve. For a curve with many bends, the response to increases in very low wages could be either positive or negative for a forward bend to occur at some intermediate wage. Perhaps the reason that the usual view sees the curve as bending only backward rather than forward is that it is easier to explain why a positively sloped curve must eventually bend backward rather than vice versa. The view held here is not to deny that the curve bends backward, but to claim that it will also tend to bend forward over relevant ranges of wage income, thus possibly leading to a curve with many bends.

ATTRACTION OF SIMPLICITY. Under conditions of a positively-sloped curve, the worker increases his income and reduces his leisure under the influence of rising wages. As this practice continues, added income becomes less important and the sacrifice of leisure more important. In more formal terms, the equilibrium points, where wage lines are tangent

---

[16] The American worker has his reservation price increased by whatever resources he commands outside of his wage earnings and by the promise of social assistance if he does not work, but it is assumed here that for the low-paid worker, neither of these supports is sufficient to bring his reservation price to a level such that he could achieve what he would consider a subsistence income without much labor. The effect of subsistence payments on labor supply is discussed in Chapter III.

[17] As Hicks noted, the consumption patterns of a rich man are less stereotyped than those of a poor man. John R. Hicks, *The Theory of Wages,* 2nd ed., Macmillan, London, 1963, p. 99.

For some inexplicable reason, this observation has gone unheeded by those who postulate the simple backward-bending supply curve. Hicks overstated the argument. It is enough for the curve to bend forward that consumption become less stereotyped as income rises from any level.

to indifference curves, move northwesterly on the worker's income-leisure indifference map. At higher wages they meet increasingly steeper indifference curves above points moving to the left on the leisure axis (stronger income effect on demand for leisure) in the range where the slopes of the curves are steep (weaker substitution effects of income for leisure, with so much income and so little leisure). Eventually, the locus of the equilibrium points moves to the right—the backward bend to the labor-supply curve—when the income effect finally outweighs the substitution effect.

No such obvious balancing forces are at work in the backward-sloping portion of a labor-supply curve, for here the worker increases his leisure as well as his income. For the curve to turn around and move in a forward direction, as both income and leisure expand, the drive for added leisure must become weaker than the drive for added income. But, as noted above, this is just what tends to happen. The income-leisure indifference curve tends toward the horizontal in the range of little work and much income. But it is not necessary to argue that the leisure saturation point must be reached before a backward-sloping labor-supply curve bends forward. Certainly the reason that a farm laborer, who at very low wages may offer less labor as his wages begin to rise, may have a forward bend to his supply curve is not that he is surfeited with leisure. For the curve to bend forward, it is only necessary that the desire for added income significantly outweigh the desire for added leisure. Again, in indifference curve terms, as the locus of equilibrium points moves northeasterly on the income-leisure indifference map, the curves above any point on the leisure axis may still become steeper but decreasingly so.[18] Meanwhile each curve is in a relatively flat range, indicating a willingness to sacrifice increasing amounts of leisure for added income. Eventually, the substitution effect outweighs the income effect, and the labor supply curve bends forward.

But the curve may not have ended its tortuous course. After rising forward with higher wages, income goals might again become more like targets than indefinite yearnings for higher consumption standards, so that the curve may soon bend backward,[19] and so on.

[18] It need not be claimed that leisure becomes an inferior good, but that the income effect depends on the amount of leisure, as well as on the amount of income, becoming weaker at any level of income further removed from the Y-axis. The demand for leisure is somewhat independent of the level of income. Tibor Scitovsky, *Welfare and Competition*, Richard D. Irwin, Chicago, 1951, p. 88, makes this point.

[19] Whether the consumption goal is a trip around the world or command over a pitiful assortment of basic goods that form the survival standard, or attainment of a given subsistence level when income goals are fixed, the short run labor-supply curve tends to be negatively sloped.

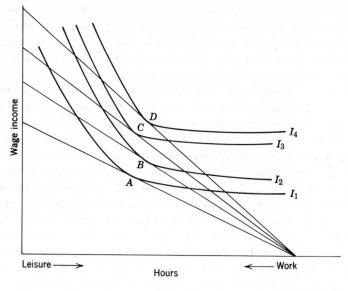

Fig. 1.2

Figure 1.2 shows the income-leisure indifference curve and wage lines that lead to the supply curve with many bends.

Figure 1.3 shows the supply curve related to the wage line—wage-income-leisure indifference map of Figure 1.1.

What may evolve is an individual labor supply schedule which has the worker's labor offer curve winding in and out upward, with no set period, amplitude, or even axis.

For those who shrink at the spectre of a supply curve winding about a labor demand curve yielding numerous equilibrium points, there is

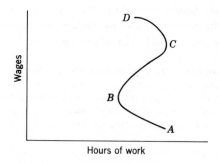

Fig. 1.3

the comforting thought that as individual supply curves are summed from a market-supply curve, the result may be a well-behaved monotonic forward-sloping market curve that meets the demand curve at one unequivocal point. Since individuals differ in their reservation price, as the wage moves upward, total supply may increase even though those who had been in the labor market previously may have reduced their labor supply.

But this macroeconomic harmony may obscure much individual turmoil. In the absence of a smooth adjustment of fewer hours offered by some and new effort by others, in response to a general rise in wages, rigidity of work schedules may lead to an increasing number of workers who would prefer either to work more or less than the standard schedule. In the next chapter, supply schedules of these workers will be discussed with reference to overtime and moonlighting.

MODIFICATION OF CONVENTIONAL SUPPLY SCHEDULES—LEISURE, WORK, AND TIME

The usual income-leisure analysis oversimplifies the relationship between individual labor supply and the wage rate. The primary shortcoming in the analysis lies in the implicit assumption of a strictly dichotomous relationship between the time spent in gainful employment and leisure[20] or, alternatively, the implication that all time not spent on the job yields satisfaction, and that all time not spent in "pleasurable leisure" represents time spent in gainful employment. Furthermore, all time spent on the job represents leisure foregone. Failure to recognize that there exists a range of activities constituting neither gainful employment nor pleasurable leisure leads to overstatement of the possibility of a negatively sloped labor-supply curve.

In the following analysis, it is assumed that this third category of time is similar to work time in that it represents a use of time that reduces the amount available for pleasurable leisure. In fact, work time might be more unpleasantly spent than nonleisure, nonmarket work time, but one can think of activities that are even more dissatisfying than labor time. The oversimplification introduced by equating the disutility of both classes of time .should not alter the general conclusions of the

[20] This expression parallels Jacob Mincer's criticism of the derivation of the backward-bending labor-supply curve based on the assumption that the only alternative uses of time are for work or leisure. "Market Prices, Opportunity Costs, and Income Effects," *Measurement in Economics,* Stanford University Press, Stanford, 1963, p. 71.

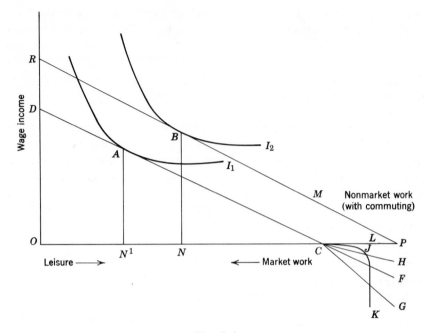

Fig. 1.4

analysis. As a first example of how the individual labor-supply curve tends to be forward-sloping when nonlabor, nonleisure time (to be called nonmarket work) is introduced, the relationship of commuter time to labor supply will be studied.

COMMUTER OR TRANSPORTATION TIME RELATED TO LABOR SUPPLY. Workers travel relatively long distances to their jobs for a variety of reasons. But if it is assumed that commuting comprises nonmarket work, the worker pays for this preference in the form of either less market work (and income) or less pleasurable leisure.[21]

Figure 1.4 shows this loss graphically. If the worker did not travel at all to get to work, with wage line PR, he would be at equilibrium point B on indifference curve I_2 working PN hours per week, and enjoying ON hours of leisure.[22] Now, if he travels back and forth to work,

---

[21] Part of the commuting costs may be transferred to the employer in the form of higher wages to secure the service of workers who choose to commute.
[22] At this stage of the analysis, all leisure hours are assumed to yield equal satisfaction.

a total of PC hours, his wage line, under the assumption that commuting yields as much dissatisfaction as work, becomes in effect CD. His new equilibrium wage-income point is at A on indifference curve I_1. He has a less satisfying combination of income and leisure, $N'A$ and ON', respectively, than without commuting, but this, presumably, is offset by his preference for his present residence over one closer to his work.[23]

By commuting, he has a lower wage income and less leisure. The result of eliminating the commuting time—without cost—would be to shift him to a higher, but parallel, wage line. In other words, the downward movement of his wage line because of commuting creates a negative income effect, which makes the worker choose less leisure.

Although it is clear that without commuting, the worker would choose more leisure, it is not at all obvious that he would also supply more market work than he would if he had to spend time in transportation. What needs demonstrating is that NP is greater than $N'C$ or that CP is greater than $N'N$. This is the same thing as saying that B on I_2 cannot lie below A on I_1. But this is simply an example of the income effect on leisure, discussed above and noted in Figure 1.1, with reference to a wage increase. Then it was explained that the effect of a potential income rise would lead the worker to increase his income, in this case by supplying more market labor, as well as increase his leisure by reducing his nonmarket work time more than he increases his market labor time. Only in the exceptional case for which "income" was an inferior good would he reduce his market labor time.

But just because a worker would choose to supply more market hours at a given wage as his commuting time was reduced (without cost) does not necessarily indicate that he would tend to have a forward-sloping supply curve, increasing his offer of market labor as his wage rose, because of the presence of transportation time in his work setting. This tendency relates to the costs involved in commuting.

If commuting time is reduced without cost because of improved technology in transportation—faster conveyors or better organized traffic flows—the commuter receives an obvious gain as his wage line shifts to the right from CD towards PR. But this case is not interesting. If

---

[23] Apart from the psychic income of open spaces, cleaner air, better (?) schools, suburban living (?), etc., there might be actual financial benefits of lower land values, housing costs, and lower living costs in general. The combined influence of the gains to income, psychic and monetary, must be to shift the worker's effective wage line above RM, with M the point on RP above C if, behaving rationally, he commutes because he gains by doing so. The analysis is not affected by treating only the negative aspects of commuting, because we shall be dealing only with offsets to them, not to the gains of living far from work.

there is a cost associated with a reduction in commuting time—private car instead of public transportation, train over bus, bus instead of foot—then the decision to speed up commuting depends on the relationship between the cost of reducing commuting time and the wage rate.[24]

In Figure 1.4, assume that the cost of reducing (unwanted) transportation by one hour is uniformly equal to the wage. Then, continuing the assumption that transportation time is exactly as unpleasant as work time, the opportunity to reduce commuting time by added expense would be described by a continuation of DC to F. The worker would be indifferent to a reduction of commuting time, as he could not gain any additional income by substituting market work time for nonmarket work time.

If it cost him more than his hourly wage to reduce his commuting time by one hour, he would certainly not choose to make the substitution of work time for commuting time. In Figure 1.4, the line drawn parallel to DC from any point along CG would move the worker to a lower wage line than DC. On the other hand, if it cost uniformly less than an hour's wages to reduce commuting time an hour, it would pay the worker to reduce his commuting to zero because the wage line drawn from H would place him on the highest possible wage line.

Putting a little realism into the analysis (and we would be talking of minutes for wages and commuting time in this case), it would be impossible to reduce commuting time to zero. Furthermore, the cost for reducing commuting time would tend to increase for each minute's reduction. Expressing these adjustments graphically in Figure 1.4, the extension of DC downward to represent the trade off between nonmarket work for market work by paying the extra costs associated with reducing commuting time would take the form CJK dropping vertically after K, never reaching a point below P. When CJK crosses CF, the point is reached where the cost of reducing commuting time by CL, where L is the point along CP lying directly above the intersection of CJK with CF, just equals the wages that could be earned by transferring the saved nonmarket work hours into market labor.

Nothing would be gained by this transfer. An equilibrium position would be reached where the wage line drawn from a point along CJK would lie furthest to the right of DC. Such a point would be J, where the marginal cost of saving an additional minute of commuting time just equaled the wage rate, that is, where the slope of CJK equaled that of the wage line.

---

[24] For another analysis of the relationship of wage rates, transportation costs, and time to the decision on mode of commuting, see Leon N. Moses and Harold F. Williamson, Jr., "Value of Time, Choice of Mode, and the Subsidy Issue in Urban Transportation," *Journal of Political Economy*, **71** (June 1963), pp. 247–264.

With every increase in the wage rate, the extension CF rotates clockwise, becoming as steep as the new wage line. This movement would make the equilibrium point along CJK (where the marginal cost of reducing transportation time equaled the wage rate) shift to the right to lie directly below a point along CP further removed from C. In other words, the shift from nonmarket work to market labor would be encouraged.[25]

Thus the effect of transportation time on labor supply in response to wage changes becomes clear. Without commuter time being involved in the worker's labor-leisure decision, the worker would respond in a certain way to a rise in his wage level, either increasing or decreasing his work time, with opposite effect on his leisure time. With transportation time included, a rise in the wage rate tends to push his wage line further to the right. Such a movement increases his market labor time, as was demonstrated in the description of the effects of the movement from A to B, equilibrium points on their respective wage lines. In effect, then, the reduction in commuting time creates a force tending to make the worker's response to a wage increase show a positive change in his market labor supply.

The effect might be insignificant for the example used (commuter time) because the total amount of time involved may be slight and, further, because the cost of reducing commuter time might follow a sharply increasing path. But the analysis related to Figure 1.4 has other more significant applications, such as the labor supply schedules of married women, to be discussed below. One application, which shows the effects of travel time more clearly, is the case of the choice of air over train travel.

Mincer notes that studies which find a high income elasticity of demand for air travel overestimate the income influence by neglecting a price effect.[26] Higher income people tend to travel by air, partly because the opportunity cost of spending an hour in transportation is greater for those having higher income per time unit. Assuming point C represents the transportation time using a train, with extension below C indicating the added cost of plane over train, C would lie much further to the left of P than would be the case for typical commuting time.

With uniform higher plane cost per unit of time saved, whether a worker would choose a plane instead of a train would depend on the relationship of the added cost per time unit saved by plane to his wage rate, the decision being positive if the latter exceeded the former. The

---

[25] Note that this adjustment results from the fact that transportation costs do not change with wage levels.

[26] Mincer, "Market Price, Opportunity Costs, and Income Effects," pp. 69–70.

higher the wage rate, the more likely then that the savings in travel time translated into market labor would more than compensate for the added cost of air over rail travel.

But even in the case of air travel, the price aspects of the demand for air travel have only limited effects on individual labor supply. For relatively low wages, the increase in demand for air travel as incomes rose would certainly partially reflect the increased opportunity cost of taking cheaper but slower transportation and, in effect, reflect a response to the price of labor foregone. But after a wage level was reached at which it paid to substitute market labor for nonmarket transportation time, any further increases in wages would not affect the (positive) decision to choose air travel. Although, thus, the upward movement of wages would have only a once-and-for-all effect on the individual decision to travel by air (and the same could be said of the effects of *uniform* transportation costs in general), for the market as a whole, as wages moved upward while the travel cost difference increased at a slower pace, the total market demand for air travel would rise.

CONSUMPTION TIME. In accordance with the analysis of Figure 1.4, a rational man might choose to pay to shorten his commuting time; he would, however, never pay to lengthen it. Yet studies show that workers do actually choose to travel a longer time over the same distance at higher travel cost. For example, a highway study reports that many users take toll roads, which are more expensive, even considering gas savings and, what is more significant, take a longer time than off-high-way streets to reach their destination.[27] Discounting the possibility of irrational behavior, why do workers choose transportation facilities that cost more and take longer than alternate means? For these highway users the answer must lie in the lower negative satisfaction associated with riding on less crowded (?) smoother-riding highways than with travel on congested streets where frequent stops are required.

Translated into the previous analysis, if the added comfort and general satisfaction of riding the toll road outweighs the added cost in time, then using the highway in effect reduces the nonmarket work associated with commuting. Travel time involves less nonmarket labor. In terms of Figure 4, translating effort into time, just as for a pure reduction in transportation time, nonmarket labor time moves from C towards P and for this movement the worker might pay the price of added transportation costs depending on the relationship of these costs to his

[27] *Road User Benefit Analysis for Highway Improvements,* American Association of State Highway Officials, Washington, 1960, pp. 76–77.

earnings per time unit. If the cost for the preferable transportation method followed a straight path such as CH or CG in Figure 4, then the worker would tend to choose the more expensive, slower means of transportation the higher his wage.

If it seems illogical to argue that the worker would choose a slower means of transportation the higher his wage, and thus greater potential loss in income, it is because the fact is overlooked that a less painful means of commuting may have the effect of reducing his nonmarket labor time, translating effort into time, allowing for more time to be spent at market work.

More realistically whatever benefits are associated with easier commuting should be considered limited. More specifically and, more importantly, on the positive side, where time spent is for pleasure and not simply on less painful nonmarket labor activities, the benefits from time spent in the enjoyment of any consumption good do not yield constant but rather declining satisfaction. The satisfaction from additional time spent in any pleasurable leisure activity would yield decreasing marginal satisfaction, so that it would begin competing at a disadvantage with other forms of leisure.[28] This competition would be keener for the higher income (wage) individual than the worker with a low earnings potential, because he would have more alternatives for consuming goods and services which also contained a pleasurable time element. Thus the fact that the satisfaction associated with any particular form of leisure tends to decline with the time spent on it would act to deter him from spending too much time on one form of leisure because of alternative more satisfying (at the margin) uses of leisure in consumption.

Gary Becker introduced the concept of consumption time,[29] which refers simply to the time spent in consumption. Much of consumption time is undesirable and can be considered nonmarket work time in accordance with the analysis of Figure 1.4.

Waiting time in general is probably a nondesirable form of "leisure," especially time spent on lines. But some waiting time is pleasurable and counts as true leisure, such as much of the time spent in fishing. It makes sense, though, for high-wage workers to fly to fishing sites if the time associated with getting to the location is not pleasurable but nonmarket work time.

---

[28] H. Gregg Lewis, "Hours of Work and Hours of Leisure," Proceedings of the Ninth Annual Meeting of the Industrial Relations Research Association, 1956, pp. 9–10, and p. 10, n. 7, defines lack of homogeneity in leisure hours as a diminishing marginal rate of substitution of one kind of leisure for another.

[29] Gary Becker, "A Theory of the Allocation of Time," Economic Journal, 75 (September 1965), pp. 493–517.

An interesting example, which shows many of the aspects of consumption time, is the use of motorized golf carts. One theoretical reason for using them is that all golfing time and effort not actually spent in swinging the club in nonmarket work, thus making their use related to commuter time and a function of the wage rate, since their use involves a cost. This would make a large part of the consumption time in playing golf an element making for forward-sloping labor-supply curves. Considering the pleasures associated with open-air exercise and the good fellowship of golf companions (and assuming that walking is also pleasurable), this reason for their use can be assumed to be of minimal significance.

A second possibility is that, although all golfing time is pure leisure, the golfer has a forward-sloping labor supply curve and, with higher wages, substitutes market work time for leisure. The golf cart in this case, by reducing his golfing time, represents a cost enabling him to substitute work for leisure.

A third possibility is that, although pure leisure, the marginal satisfaction of leisure time spent in golfing is less than that spent in undertaking some other consumption activity requiring time. The competition of other consumption activities that require time is a function of the income potential of the golfer.

Thus the golfer in a hurry may be a person who only likes to play the game itself, a person who prefers to use much of the time saved to work, or a person who prefers to spend his leisure time on other consumption activities that take time. For the first two classes, the move to a golf cart would provide an element leading to a forward-sloping market supply curve; the third would be just a reflection of higher income. Thus it is impossible to tell from the behavior of workers with regard to their consumption time in reaction to a wage increase whether they have a forward-sloping supply curve. Direct study of the market labor supply in response to wage changes is required. On balance, though, consumption time is a factor leading to a forward-sloping curve.

As a final note to this discussion of consumption time, it should be emphasized that different kinds of leisure yield different degrees of satisfaction for equal rates of consumption.[30] For example, when shipping lines advertise that "getting there (and back) is half the fun," assuming that more time is usually spent on land abroad than in traveling there by ship, if the marginal rate of substitution of sea travel leisure for land leisure were constant, and the consumption cost of an hour of each

---

[30] Lewis, *op. cit.*, p. 10, n. 7, points out the need for this qualification when satisfaction for *each* type of leisure declines with time.

were equal, if the advertisement were correct, the rational vacationer would choose the slowest ship.[31]

The two-factor indifference curve cannot treat differences in leisure satisfaction adequately. For example, the different satisfaction derived from different hours of leisure explains the need to pay higher rates for the same amount of Sunday or night work as for regular daytime hours. What makes the marginal rate of substitution of income for an hour of Sunday work greater than that for say, Tuesday work, is not that it is more unpleasant to work on Sunday, but that Tuesday's leisure is not as satisfying as Sunday's. The typical indifference curve wage-line presentation only yields an equilibrium position when the wage equals the marginal rate of substitution of income for some average type of leisure. When the leisure to be foregone is above average, such as an hour of Sunday's customary time off, the wage that would draw the marginal hour's work would have to rise above the level required to take away an ordinary hour of leisure.

Household Supply of Labor and the
Labor Supply of Married Women

Before applying Figure 1.4 to the case of the labor supply of married women, aspects of family labor market behavior will be noted. The labor force behavior of wives differs from that of unmarried females in that all the former and only some of the latter contribute labor as part of a household unit, in which decisions regarding work income and leisure depend on the earning potential of other family members.

Mincer notes that when labor is supplied as a family unit, the possibility of individual negative supply curves is reduced. An individual household member may, in isolation, tend to have a negatively sloped supply curve, reducing his labor effort with a rise in wages. But, taken in the family context, a rise in his wages may enable him to substitute more labor for that of another household member whose wages have not changed. This possibility leads Mincer to conclude that "Even the assumption of a backward-bending supply curve would not justify a prediction of a decrease in total hours of work *for the particular earner*, if wages of other family members are fixed."[32]

---

[31] In fact, he would choose never to land. With a rising marginal rate of substitution of sea travel leisure for touring leisure, he would choose a slower ship if the marginal rate of substitution were less than unity at existing levels of sea and land time, other conditions remaining unchanged.

[32] Jacob Mincer, "Labor Force Participation of Married Women," p. 66 (italics in original).

Nevertheless, this substitution of effort among individual family members has its limitations. Mincer exaggerates the effect in claiming that rational family decisions will always encourage greater market labor input by the worker whose wage has increased,[33] with implied gain of greater added leisure for other members. If the husband, who performs little homework, receives wage increases, a point will eventually be reached as he offers more labor at higher wages, reducing the labor market contribution of other members while family income is maintained, when a rational family decision will lead to a reduction in his work effort.[34] Although individual family members may share in the use of family income, independent of their contribution to it, leisure cannot be pooled.

Mincer has resolved the paradox of conflicting behavior of labor force participation of wives revealed by cross-sectional and time series studies. Cross-sectional studies have demonstrated a clear tendency for the labor force participation of wives to be lower, the higher their husband's income. But, over time, labor force participation of wives has increased while family incomes—and that of husbands—have risen. Mincer explains this seeming contradiction in terms of the resultant force of two conflicting influences. The presence of high income for husbands acts as a depressing influence on the labor force participation of wives. The extent of the negative effect of the husband's income depends on the size of that income, since his income acts on his wife's labor-supply schedule as if it were nonwage income at zero effort.

More than offsetting the negative effect of the husband's earnings is the positive response of the wife's labor supply to her own income potential (wage rate). Mincer found this positive element a much stronger force than the negative effect of husband's earnings. Cross-sectional data tend to reveal only the negative influence because of the loose relationship between earnings of husbands and their wives. If the earning potential of wives were randomly distributed, when classified by husband's income, then at each level of husband's income, the average wife's income would tend to be the same. Thus the influence of wives' earning potential on their work effort would not appear in studies of the relationship of husbands' earnings to this effort; only the negative correlation between husbands' earnings and wives' participation would be felt. The correlation between wives' earning potential and husbands' income is not zero, but Mincer found the positive relationship too weak

---

[33] *Loc. cit.*

[34] There will, of course, still be some reduced participation of others because the husband would not cut back his effort to the point where he earned less, if it is assumed that the goal is constant family income.

to offset the negative effect of husbands' earnings on wives' labor force participation.[35]

To explain the strong tendency for wives' labor force participation schedules to be positively related to their wages, Mincer, in effect, considers the relationships among work time, leisure, and nonmarket work time, that is, work at home. Mincer explains the strength of the effect of the nonmarket (home) work on labor supply in terms of the substitutability of other facilities—such as appliances, domestic servants—for wives' time in homework. The more substitutable these factors, the more likely the wife will be able to exchange market work for homework.

In much the same manner, the analysis of Figure 1.4, in which time spent on homework would substitute for commuting time along *CP*, would express the effect of homework on market labor supply in terms of the *cost* of substituting other facilities for homework time of the wife. In keeping with this previous analysis, the higher the wife's wage, the more likely she would choose to pay the costs of substitutes for her time in homework and the more likely the market labor supply schedule of the wife would be forward-sloping.[36]

In a thoughtful comment on Mincer's paper, Clarence Long wonders why the labor force participation of Negro women (wives?) has not behaved the same as that of white wives.[37] While wages of Negro women have risen substantially, their labor force participation has declined over time. But for Negro *wives*, participation has increased, although at a much lower rate than for white wives.

The racial difference with respect to wives' work force participation can be explained theoretically in terms of the analysis of Figure 1.4. For one thing, although wages of Negro wives have risen more, they are substantially below those of white wives. This suggests that, even with wage increases, Negro wives cannot afford the costs of substitutes for their home labor. In terms of Figure 1.4, *CJK* would still lie to the left of the downward extension of the wage line of many Negro wives.[38]

---

[35] Mincer also found transitory and permanent income weakly correlated, so that wives' participation, which is strongly inversely correlated to the algebraic difference between transitory and permanent income, was strongly inversely related to husbands' income at any moment in time.

[36] Mincer does not study labor supply in time of hours per working wife, but in wives' labor force participation. Thus the tendency for market work that is substituted for homework to be limited for the individual worker does not affect the tendency for the market labor supply of wives to be positively sloped.

[37] Clarence Long, "Comment on 'Labor Force Participation of Married Women,'" *Aspects of Labor Economics,* pp. 103–109.

[38] Less extremely, *CJK* would cut the higher but still low wage line only slightly to the right of *C*.

Furthermore, the tendency for doubling up in Negro housing may account for less time used in homework by Negro wives at any wage. In terms of Figure 1.4, this means that the distance between C and P would be less for Negro than for white wives, indicating a smaller potential for more Negro wife labor force participation in the substitution of market work for homework in response to wage increases.

In addition, considering discriminatory restrictions on Negro consumption expenditures and the difficulty of reaching higher socioeconomic levels, Negro family labor-supply schedules would tend to have a greater probability of being backward-sloping than those of white families. Thus the negative income effects of higher husbands' incomes on wives' labor force participation would be stronger for Negro women than for white women, thereby more forcefully dampening the positive effects on their market labor supply of higher wages.[39]

Costs, Income Foregone, and Returns to Education

Almost all students of the returns to education argue that a substantial part of the costs of education consists of income foregone in order to attend school. Contrary to this view, John Vaizey holds that foregone income should not be counted among costs, mainly because, if it were added to education costs, income foregone from other nonmarket activities (work of housewives, voluntary work, etc.) should be counted as costs too.[40] If Vaizey's reasoning were correct, then, of course, estimated returns to investment in education would be greatly increased. Becker, however, points out that, indeed, foregone earnings of these other activities should be counted as costs or reduction in the potential level of national income.[41]

Treating income foregone as a cost in investment in education, the purpose here is not to review the methods of calculating income foregone for the individual student[42] but, instead, to analyze the factors that

---

[39] The effect of these and other variables in explaining the racial difference in wives' labor force trends has been studied statistically and analytically by Glen Cain, *Married Women in the Labor Force,* University of Chicago Press, Chicago, 1966. In addition, Clarence Long, *The Labor Force under Changing Income and Employment,* Princeton University Press, Princeton, 1958, p. 108, notes that labor force participation of Negro women has been historically large and that there has been much Negro migration from the South, where participation rates were high, to the non-South, where they are lower.

[40] John Vaizey, *The Economics of Education,* Glencoe, New York, 1962, pp. 42–43.

[41] Gary Becker, *Human Capital,* National Bureau of Economic Research, Columbia University Press, New York, 1964, p. 74, n. 5.

[42] Theodore W. Schultz, "Capital Formation by Education," *Journal of Political Economy,* **68** (December 1960), pp. 573–577, estimates foregone weekly income

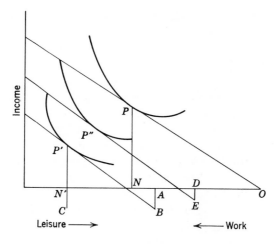

Fig. 1.5

determine the investment costs to him of education and, consequently, the returns to education. This involves study of the relationship between direct and opportunity costs, investment and consumption aspects of education, and income and leisure preferences.

Although much has been written about the consumption benefits of education, little note has been made of the consumption elements in being educated. According to Schultz, the issue is clear: going to school is a form of work. He writes, "Students study, which is work, and this work, among other things helps create human capital. Students are not enjoying leisure when they study . . . ."[43] Schultz's statement can be explained by Figure 1.5, which shows the relationship between income foregone and direct costs and indicates the total costs of education.

If the (college) student did not attend school, he would work *ON*

of a student as the amount earned on average by nonstudents of the same age. He adjusts for unemployment and acknowledges that some students work while attending school, although he does not count for the latter element. Becker, *Human Capital,* pp. 74–75 and pp. 169–171, estimates that college students earn about one-fourth of what high-school graduates of the same age earn, and uses this amount in calculating income foregone. For approaches similar to Schultz's, see Rudolph C. Blitz, "The Nation's Educational Outlay," *Economics of Higher Education,* edited by Selma J. Mushkin, U. S. Government Printing Office, Washington, 1962, pp. 155–156 and Appendix B, and W. Lee Hansen, "Total and Private Rates of Return to Investment in Schooling," *Journal of Political Economy,* **71** (April 1963), pp. 130–131.

[43] Schultz, *op. cit.,* p. 573.

hours and earn income NP.[44] OA, which is similar to PC in Figure 1.4, represents the number of hours per week he attends school, since none of this school time represents leisure but only nonmarket work time. AB represents the total direct costs of attending school, which include not only tuition, books, etc., but also "maintenance costs" such as transportation and travel costs, amusement costs, better clothes, etc.[45] Since he derives no consumption satisfaction from these expenses, which represent his direct costs of education, their effect is to give the student worker a negative income equal to this amount.

According to the income-leisure schedule suggested in Figure ·1.5, the student will work AN' hours, earning CP' income. But CN' of this income is used to pay the direct costs of education. Therefore, while PN-$P'C$ represents income foregone, the larger amount PN-$P'N'$ represents his total costs of education.

Certain relationships among the variables should be noted. The student is subject to two conflicting forces acting on his labor supply. The negative income effect imposed by the direct costs tend to make him work more than if he didn't go to school, while the nonmarket labor time spent in school tends to reduce the time he will offer for market work.

He might choose to work more as a student than if he did not attend school, so that AN' would exceed ON; and CP' would exceed NP, indicating a negative foregone income. This would be the case if his non-school expenses were relatively fixed and therefore difficult to reduce. But in any case, total costs of education would be positive, that is, P' would lie below P except, again, for the unusual case in which income was an inferior good.

An increase in direct costs would increase total costs and thus reduce the rate of return on education. Point B would then lie further below

---

[44] The rigor of the analysis is weakened by the assumption that his tastes would be the same as a student or as a nonstudent worker.

[45] The concept of "maintenance costs" is introduced by Harry G. Shaffer, "Investment in Human Capital: Comment," *American Economic Review,* **51** (December 1961), pp. 1029–1030, but applied only to these special costs of already educated people. Certainly, they can be applied to students as well, and would consist of the extra incidental consumption expenses associated with going to school.

The techniques used by Burton A. Weisbrod, "The Valuation of Human Capital," *Journal of Political Economy,* **69** (October 1961), pp. 425–436, for offsetting returns from education by all consumption costs of educated workers could be applied to the extra consumption costs of students as well.

Obviously, these costs would vary from individual to individual, and their variability would bedevil attempts to measure rates of return to education, since these rates would vary inversely with these incidental costs.

This problem is raised by Boris P. Pesek and Thomas R. Saving, *Money, Wealth, and Economic Theory,* Macmillan, New York, 1967, p. 270.

the X-axis and, again, although market effort might increase over AN', income net of the higher direct costs would be below P'.

But the initial assumptions that no part of school time represents leisure or that none of the school costs represent pleasurable consumption expenditure are unrealistic. Considering the opportunities for social life at school and campus activity in general, some school time represents leisure. There might even be some few students who enjoy the learning process itself. The effect of leisure time associated with schooling would be to shift nonwork time to the right of A and to reduce the investment costs of attending school.[46] OD and DE represent the new values for nonmarket labor time of school attendance and direct costs, respectively.

The student would tend to work less because his negative income is reduced, since some of his school costs are now for consumption, but would tend to work more because his nonmarket labor effort has diminished, since part of school time represents leisure. Whether he would work more if all of his school time represented work is uncertain. But in any case he would increase his income, net of school expenses, over the level he would have earned if all school time were nonmarket work; his total of direct costs and income foregone would be less, and his return to education would rise.

In the extreme case, if all school time were leisure, the total costs of education would be zero and the rate of return on education infinite. Nonmarket work time would fall to zero, so that no income would be foregone and he would work the same number of hours, earning the same income as he would were he not a student. Similarly, his direct investment costs would fall from DE to 0, since these costs would not represent a negative income but an expense for consumption purposes.

In summary, the total costs (and rate of return) of education depend on the income-leisure preferences of the student, the amount of direct education costs, and the importance of the consumption element in education. Income foregone will be less and the rate of return on education greater for the individual student, the less flexible his noneducational income goals, the lower the direct costs of education, and the greater his consumption benefits in being educated.

For the unlikely case of the student for whom all school time represented consumption time, acting rationally, with an infinite rate of return on (zero) investment in education, he would seek more education to

---

[46] Vaizey, *op. cit.*, p. 43, claims that indirect school costs should be adjusted downward by an estimate of benefits incurred while being educated. Becker, *Human Capital*, p. 74, n. 5, seems to be critical of Vaizey's suggestion when he notes that direct costs should also then be subject to partial exclusion from the investment costs of education. The argument here is that they certainly should be.

bring the rate of return down to the level of alternative investments. But there are obvious discontinuities in consumption, or investment, benefits from education. During a given time period a student carries through a given program of study. It would be unrealistic to assume that he would derive almost the same benefits from adding another school program on to his current one during the same period.

Thus, calculating average rate of return to education by use of the average income foregone obscures the fact that students who derive consumption benefits from the education process gain more than the average. Strictly, speaking, if only economic factors determined the choice of education or alternative investments, at equilibrium the rate of return on education for the student, for whom all time spent on education represented work time, would equal the rate of return on other investments. All other students, assuming a sharp discontinuity in benefits from additional education during a given time period, would enjoy a higher return because the consumption elements in education resulted in lower direct investment costs and more time spent in market work while going to school. Thus, at equilibrium, the *average* rate of return on education would be above the rate on alternative investments.

CHAPTER II

Topics in Labor Supply and Demand

In this catch-all chapter, several topics in labor supply and demand are treated. No claim of unity is made. No simple thread binds the subjects. Some are of practical concern relating to current economic problems; others are mainly of theoretical interest.

If, at least, order in presentation is to be maintained, the first topics apply the analysis of the previous chapter to special aspects of labor supply. Then, two elements in labor demand are treated. Finally, exploitation, which has both demand and supply elements, is discussed.

The first subject deals with the effect of social security payments on labor supply. That the system of benefits reduces labor supply of older workers is demonstrated formally. Even in cases in which equilibrium individual labor supply without benefits yields a wage income that exceeds maximum benefits, the tendency for the benefit system to reduce labor supply arises. The relationship between pension benefits and labor supply in some way parallels the impact of assured minimum income on labor supply, a subject to be treated in detail in Chapter III.

In the next two sections the subjects of overtime and moonlighting elements in labor supply are discussed. The conditions under which workers will refuse overtime and engage in moonlighting are examined closely. These reactions are found to require that workers involved be at less than their optimum wage-income-leisure position at their established work schedules.[1]

On the subject of labor demand, the relationship between overtime, fringe benefits, and employer decision between working an existing force overtime or hiring additional workers is studied. Although overtime penalties greatly exceed fringe benefits associated with employment, the

---

[1] An exception occurs when a moonlighter receives a higher wage rate on his second job than on his first.

decision may be in favor of paying overtime if the employer must bid up wages to hire additional workers.

The final topic in labor demand deals with the complications introduced into conventional (marginal productivity) theory of the "economy of high wages." When physical productivity varies, directly, with the wage rate (income) the labor demand curve may become forward-sloping through part of its range.

On exploitation, the analysis traces the effects on wages and employment of attempts to eliminate exploitation by the establishment of uniform wages. Limitations to this elimination process are stressed.

One important current topic in demand theory not treated here concerns the complication introduced by the investment aspect in labor. Equilibrium employment for the firm does not depend on the equality of *current* marginal cost and marginal revenue when the labor in question embodies investment costs to the firm. Although not analyzed in this chapter, the issue appears in the discussion in Chapter IV on the cyclical movements in the skilled-unskilled wage differential and in Chapter VIII on the differential cyclical volatility of unemployment between trained and untrained workers.

SOCIAL SECURITY

The system of social security benefits acts to reduce labor supply. Since up to a certain annual income, $1200, most recently, the worker would receive full benefits, it is obvious that if without benefits he were at a work schedule that yielded less than $1200 he would choose a lighter schedule because of benefits. This follows since the benefits would merely serve to provide him with a fixed nonlabor income, and his additional income per unit of effort would equal his wage, without benefit. In effect his wage line would be raised and the negative income effect of the nonlabor income would reduce labor supply, under the usual assumption that leisure is not an inferior good. But the system of social security payments ties benefits to the amount of labor income earned, in order to reduce benefits in steps as earned income rises. This procedure follows the program's aim of providing *retirement* income. The degree of retirement, in effect, is measured by the amount of income earned through work, the two being inversely related.

The current retirement test requires the worker to forfeit one-half of every dollar of benefits for every dollar earned between $1200 and $1700. Accordingly his wage line would in effect bend to a slope one-half its previous level in the annual wage-income range between $1200 and

$1700. Above an annual income of $1700, the worker would forfeit a dollar of pension benefits for every dollar earned. This means that his wage line, including benefits, would be flat for a range of effort at earnings of $1700. This range would extend until the labor supplied yielded $1700 plus remaining benefits in wage income alone. Further effort would then yield a return per unit of effort equal to the wage rate, that is, the wage line including benefits would follow the wage line without benefits for the rest of its path.

As an example, a worker with maximum annual benefits of $2000, at an hourly wage of $2, could work 600 hours for a total annual income of $3200 ($2000 benefits plus $1200 labor income). For every additional hour worked, he would lose $1 in benefits up to $1700 earned. Thus, if he worked 850 hours, he would receive a total of $3450 ($1750 benefits plus $1700 in wages). For each hour worked beyond 850, he would receive no extra income, his benefits being reduced as much as his additional earnings, until his benefits were reduced to zero. This would occur after 875 more hours of work, or a total of 1725 hours. Thus, after 1725 hours of work and $3450 of earned income, his earnings would follow the same path as if there were no benefit program.

Figure 2.1 shows the wage line without benefits along with that following the social security pension system for the worker with $2000 maximum benefits and a $2 hourly wage.

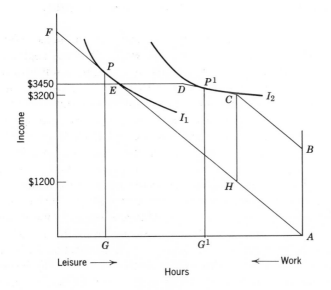

Fig. 2.1

The bent line $BCDEF$ represents the composite wage and benefit income line in accordance with the social security formula. The horizontal distance between B and C depends on the slope of the wage line AEF. For a wage above \$2 per hour, less effort would be expended before the \$1200 labor income is earned. The same applies to the other bent portions of the composite income line. Thus, E, the point at which the composite wage-benefit line meets the simple wage line would occur at less effort, the higher the wage rate.

As has been mentioned above, if equilibrium effort along the simple wage line, AEF, were recorded at a point directly below some point along range BC on the composite wage-benefit line, that is, along AH, then the labor supply of the particular worker would be reduced under the benefit program, if leisure were not an inferior good, because the system of benefits for such wage incomes imposes only a negative income effect on work. With the same wage and a nonlabor income, that is, the retirement benefit, the subjective marginal rate of substitution of income for leisure would equal the same market substitution rate (the wage) with more leisure and less labor offered because of the negative income effects of the subsidy on labor supply.

If individual labor supply would decline when the same wage were added to a fixed benefit, as would be the case when equilibrium had been reached on AEF at a point below H, it would also certainly fall if equilibrium effort were at hours of work directly below a point on the range CE on the composite wage-benefit curve, that is, between H and E.

In this case the social security recipient, for the same effort, would receive a higher income at a lower net wage. Thus the negative income effect of the subsidy would be joined by a negative substitution effect as well. He would no longer choose to work as much as without the subsidy, but would sacrifice some income for more leisure.

This decision is not dependent on the nature of his labor supply schedule, whether positively or negatively sloped. Even if he would choose to work less at higher wages, without benefits (the negatively sloped case), he would still choose to work even less at a lower net wage that still resulted in a higher income, as would be the case under discussion. For a negatively sloped supply curve in general, the negative substitution effect (on labor supply) of a wage reduction would be more than offset by the positive income effect that resulted from the reduced income potential of a lower wage. But in this case, both substitution and income effect operate in the same direction, negatively, in that the income effect on labor supply is also negative, since the effect of the lower, marginal wage between C and E to reduce income is outweighed by the income-raising effect of the social security benefits. Thus, whenever total income is higher at a lower wage, labor supply would fall below its previous equilibrium level.[2]

If the non-benefit equilibrium labor supply for the worker were at a point along *EF*, on both income lines, then the pension plan might have no effect on labor supply. This would be the case if to the right of the equilibrium point, when the wage line was tangent to his income-leisure indifference curve, the worker were unwilling to sacrifice much income for added leisure, that is, if the marginal rate of substitution of income for leisure were low. On the other hand, if the marginal rate of substitution were high and the equilibrium labor supply were along the *EF* portion of the nonbenefit wage line, *AEF*, the benefit program might serve to reduce labor supply.

For example, in Figure 2.1, without benefits, equilibrium would be at *P* along indifference curve I_1 with *AG* hours worked at wage income *GP*. But because, with fewer hours worked, income would not fall by the product of the hours reduction and the wage rate, under the pension program, a higher indifference curve could be reached and equilibrium attained, as depicted in curve I_2 with hours worked AG^1 and total income G^1P^1.

Whether work incentives will be reduced by the benefit program, when nonbenefit equilibrium income and leisure is along the segment *EF*, depends on the size of income and the MRS of income for leisure at that income. The higher the equilibrium level of income, that is, the further removed from *E*, and the lower the MRS of income for leisure, the more likely it is that the benefit program will have no effect on work incentives.

In summary, the benefit program tends to reduce the incentive to work. In fact, a high enough assured pension would eliminate work incentive entirely. This would occur if benefits were raised to the degree that the slope of the indifference curve meeting the wage line at point *B* on the *AB* axis was steeper than the wage line. In any case, whether incentives were eliminated entirely, a rise in the benefit program would reduce incentive. Similarly, considering steady rises in the price level, standard of living, and wages, if a policy of constant (negative) effects on work incentives is a desired goal of the social security program, the benefit formula will have to be raised periodically, for these reasons alone.

If equilibrium effort without benefits were at a number of hours that

---

[2] This analysis also applies to some of the conditions of the negative income tax, to be discussed in Chapter III.

permitted all or some benefits, then equilibrium effort with benefits would always fall below the number of hours that would be supplied without them. Finally, if labor supply without benefits extended to the number of hours that, under the benefit program, would make the worker ineligible for any benefits, labor supply might or might not be reduced. Labor supply would only tend to be maintained for workers who could not improve their income-leisure combination by reducing hours to become eligible for benefits.

OVERTIME AND LABOR SUPPLY

The typical worker, in a position of equilibrium wage income and leisure at a given work schedule, would always choose to work overtime hours at premium pay.[3] Furthermore, this conclusion holds even if the worker's labor supply schedule were backward-sloping, so that he would choose to work fewer hours at a higher *straight-time* wage.[4] At equilibrium, the marginal rate of substitution of income for leisure equals the slope of the wage line. The overtime premium, in effect, bends the wage line upward at the equilibrium point. The income effect of the premium is negligible, applying only to the marginal overtime hours and not to the entire work schedule as would be the case of a rise in straight-time wages. The substitution effect, by making the wage line steeper, leads to a substitution of income for leisure through additional hours of work, until the marginal rate of substitution of income for leisure is increased until it is brought into equality with the slope of the new, steeper, wage line.

This characteristic of overtime, to increase the incentive to work, applies to alternative means of payment to achieve the same income from a given amount of work. For example, if overtime becomes customary in a given job, an adjustment in the straight-time equivalent to yield the same income from the same hours of work would reduce work incentives. With customary overtime, equilibrium would be reached at a higher marginal wage than could be provided by the straight-time equivalent. Since the wage line would be flatter with the straight-time equivalent, equilibrium would be reached at a lower wage income, and greater leisure as the marginal rate of substitution of income for leisure, reduced by this process, became equal to the slope of the straight-time equivalent wage line. Figure 2.2 shows this relationship.

[3] This result has long been recognized. Kenneth Boulding, *Economic Analysis,* 3rd ed., Harper & Brothers, New York, 1955, p. 800, demonstrates it graphically.
[4] T. Aldrich Finegan, "Comment: The Backward Sloping Supply Curve," pp. 231–232, makes this point.

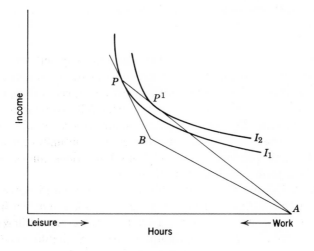

Fig. 2.2

If equilibrium were at P under the overtime arrangement depicted by the wage line ABP, then equilibrium (with greater satisfaction), under the straight-time equivalent, would be attained at P^1, with wage ray AP^1P, such that the same wage income could be attained by straight-time earnings as the amount that would maximize the worker's income-leisure position under the overtime arrangements.[5]

Expressed differently, if the work schedule were not changed when the payment system was switched from wage plus overtime to higher straight-time equivalent, the typical worker would become dissatisfied with the work schedule. He would feel overemployed.

Presumably, the work schedule established in a given situation represents the consensus choice of combination of work—or leisure—and income of the covered workers.[6] Nevertheless, there are workers who are

[5] By similar reasoning, it follows that a program to raise low incomes by raising minimum wages would call forth more labor than a program of subsidy plus unchanged minimum that would permit the attainment of the same income as the equilibrium level under the higher minimum. In this case, the wage line would be flatter under the subsidy program than under the raised minimum where the two wage lines met.

[6] Hicks considers hours of work simply as part of the wage contract the worker makes with his employer which, combined with the wage rate, "determine the degree of benefit he derives from his employment." Hicks, *Theory of Wages,* p. 90.

More pointedly, Friedman argues that in setting conditions of work, the closer the employer establishes work schedules to his workers' preferences, the lower the wage he must offer to attract a desired labor force of a given quality. Friedman, *Price Theory,* p. 205.

dissatisfied with the work schedule—some who would prefer a shorter schedule and others a longer one.

THE OVEREMPLOYED WORKER.[7] While overtime pay will always induce the typical worker to supply hours beyond the standard schedule, there are some workers who would refuse overtime, given the option to do so. These would be part of the group who felt overemployed at the standard schedule. The overemployed might resort to absenteeism as a device to shorten their work schedules to their optimum income-leisure position, but this practice has its obvious limitations for those workers who plan long-term attachments to their jobs.

Figure 2.3 shows the relationship between the indifference map and the wage-line LL of the typical overemployed worker. The work schedule, to which he must comply, is for LA hours of work on indifference curve I_0. At the given wage, his optimum position on indifference curve I_1 would be at a lower income, BR instead of AP, but with more leisure or fewer hours of work, LB. If overtime rates are offered for additional hours beyond the standard schedule, LA, unlike the typical worker, who will always accept overtime, the overemployed worker may or may not wish to work overtime, depending on the rate of overtime pay related to the ratio of his marginal trade off of leisure for income at P. The higher the overtime rate and the less steep the indifference curve I_0 at P, that is, the smaller the worker's MRS of income for leisure at P, the more likely that he will want to work overtime.

This uncertainty arises because, unlike the case for the typical worker, the wage line is not tangent to the indifference curve of the overemployed worker at P. Hence, for overtime hours to be supplied, the wage line must become steeper than the indifference curve to the left of P. Thus the overtime rate must be greater than the rate described by PL^1, the line tangent to I_0 at P, before the overemployed worker will wish to contribute overtime labor.

At higher overtime rate, PL'', he will offer AC additional hours above the standard schedule LA, earn income CS, and reach indifference curve I_2.

Overtime rates would have to reach the level indicated by wage-line PL''', and the worker would have to contribute AD hours above the standard to earn income DT for him to reach the same indifference

[7] Much of the analysis of the relationship of overemployed and underemployed conditions to overtime and moonlighting appears in my "Observations on Overtime and Moonlighting," *Southern Economic Journal,* **33** (October 1966), pp. 237–244. An earlier treatment of these atypical workers was made by Leon Moses, "Income, Leisure, and Wage Pressure," *Economic Journal,* **72** (June 1962), pp. 320–334.

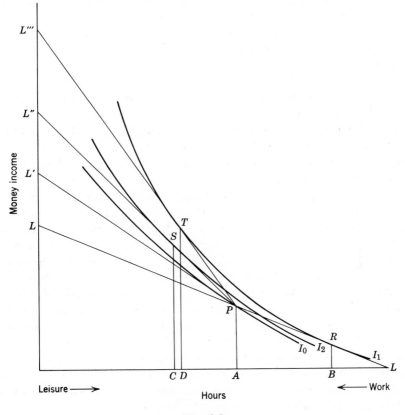

Fig. 2.3

curve he would have attained as his optimum, had he control over his supply of effort and had he worked only LB hours at straight-time wage LL.

Therefore, the overemployed worker, who would prefer to work fewer than the scheduled hours, can only achieve the degree of satisfaction he could have attained under a flexible schedule by upward flexibility in his income, in short, by working longer than the standard schedule at overtime rates.

Thus the response of a work staff to the offer of overtime rates is no indication of the general degree of satisfaction with the work schedule.[8] Included among those who prefer more work at overtime rates are

---

[8] This point is noted by Finegan, *op. cit.*, p. 232.

all the so-called typical workers, some of the overemployed workers—
those for whom the overtime rate is high enough to induce them to
trade leisure for extra income—and all the underemployed workers, to
be studied now, who would prefer to work longer than the standard
schedule even at straight-time rates.

THE UNDEREMPLOYED WORKER.—In theory, those for whom the current
schedule offers less than the optimum hours of work at current wages
should form a small group, since the standard is set with the optimum
of the majority in mind.[9] In practice, however, a bargaining group might
agree to a less-than-optimum schedule as a work-sharing device during
slack periods, a practice that might be favored by the majority of the
workers as a job-protective measure, but which certainly places them
below their optimum offer of work at current wages under conditions
of individually determined schedules. This follows since, if the previous
combination of work and leisure were at the consensus optimum, a reduction in income, even with an addition to leisure, would put the typical
worker at a position where he would prefer to work more hours.[10]

Whether under normal conditions, when the underemployed group is
small or when their number is swelled by a reduction in hours serving
the interests of job maintenance, those who would prefer to offer more
than the scheduled hours at the straight-time wage will, of course, want
to offer more-than-scheduled hours at (higher) overtime rates. But what
is more significant is their willingness to work more hours at rates even
below the established wage. This preference can only be satisfied through
moonlighting—working additional hours on another job.

Figure 2.4 presents indifference curves and wage lines for the underemployed worker.

The work schedule puts him on indifference curve I_0 with LA hours
of work and income AP. His optimum position at this wage is at income
BR with LB hours worked in order to reach indifference curve I_1. He
would prefer outside work at any wage above PL', the wage-line tangent
to I_0 at P.

At wage PL'', below the straight-time rate but above the minimum

---

[9] Technically speaking, it is not the wishes of the numerical majority to which
the schedule is set, but of the dominant group as to influence or preference for
the schedule. Thus the assumption that only a small number will be under-
or overemployed depends on the further assumption that the individual workers will
have a more or less equal interest in the work schedule, or will exert more or
less equal pressure on the employer to set the schedule according to their preferences.

[10] This simply depends on the assumption of a declining MRS of income for leisure
as the ratio of leisure to income rises.

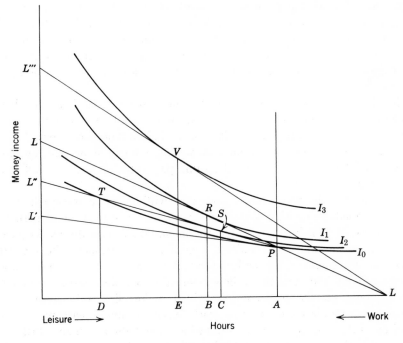

Fig. 2.4

necessary to induce him to offer additional hours, the worker would offer AC hours beyond the standard schedule to earn income CS and reach indifference curve I_2. At any wage above PL, the worker would be earning overtime on his primary job or be in the fortunate position of earning a higher wage on his second job than on his first.

MOONLIGHTING

Although according to Figure 2.4, the moonlighter would be willing to work additional hours at his primary job at a rate substantially below his straight-time wage, it does not follow that he would work on a second job that paid much less. The indifference curves of Figure 2.4 apply to his primary job.[11] Considering the additional costs and effort and

[11] The unreality of the assumption that one set of indifference curves can apply to both jobs of moonlighters is underscored by Martin Bronfenbrenner and Jan Mossin, "The Shorter Work Week and the Labor Supply," *Southern Economic Journal,* **33** (January 1967), p. 324.

problems of adjustment to a new work setting, it might be assumed that it would require a second-job wage somewhat higher than PL', the minimum rate at offering extra hours on his first job, to induce the underemployed worker to moonlight. Thus moonlighters might not be expected to accept significantly lower pay rates on their second job than on their first one.

On the other hand, some moonlighters get more satisfaction from their second jobs, which are not their primary jobs only because they pay lower wages or, more likely, offer only limited hours of work.[12] The sketchy data available on second-job income tend to show that, on balance, moonlighters earn about the same pay rates on their second jobs as on their first.[13]

The shorter the work week, the more willing is the moonlighter to accept secondary employment in settings that require a rigid, perhaps even full-time schedule. Currently, the moonlighter typically works part-time on his secondary job under a flexible self-determined schedule. He tends to moonlight in agriculture, retail trade, or in the service and finance fields. This practice follows from the marginal nature of under-employment on the primary job, which makes flexibility in hours a second-job requirement. If the work week in manufacturing should decline substantially, many would-be moonlighters might look to this field, characterized by inflexible schedules, for their second job. In 1965, the 4.9 percent of manufacturing jobs held by moonlighters was close to the all-industry 5.2 percent average.[14]

Note that in Figure 2.4, the worker at wage PL'', somewhat below his first-job rate, would reach an improved position between income and leisure from confining his activities to one job if he worked any amount less than AD hours on his second job and received less than DT income. He would accept a second full-time job at slightly under AD hours, not in preference to part-time work at AC hours, but because of the absence of part-time opportunities.

If the underemployed worker is the exception in most industries or

---

[12] Of course, if the second job pays more than the first, "typical" and some over-employed workers, as well as the underemployed, would moonlight.

[13] In the May 1962 survey week, male dual job holders averaged $106 per week in full-time wages on their primary jobs and $35 on their secondary jobs, on which they spent about one-third as much time. "Multiple Jobholders in May 1962," *Monthly Labor Review*, **86** (May 1963), pp. 521–522.

[14] "Multiple Jobholders in May 1965," *Monthly Labor Review,* **89** (February 1966), p. 151. The trend in manufacturing moonlighting has as yet advanced only slightly. In 1957 when the overall rate was 5.3 percent, the manufacturing rate was 4.3 percent.

occupations, what few (primary) work settings induce substantial moon-lighting? They are settings in which attainable income is very low by any customary standard or in which worker attachment is based on factors other than income. Consider the farm laborer, who meets both criteria with his low income and tie to agriculture as a way of life. Then there are the low-paid government workers, typified by the postal service employee who trades income for job security, and the male school-teacher who prefers the psychic benefits from his work to the more tangi-ble rewards of other jobs.[15]

These three workers have four common characteristics that help to explain their high 1965 moonlighting rates (percent of employed persons in primary job who moonlight), namely, 8.4 percent for farm, wage and salary worker, 11.2 percent for the postal worker, and 16.5 percent for the male schoolteacher,[16] compared to the 5.2 percent level for all employed workers:

1. They have little or no opportunity for extra work, or overtime, on their primary jobs.

2. They have primary-job schedules that allow them to meet the time obligations of their second jobs. The postal workers and schoolteachers have set schedules and shifts that free them for second jobs having a more demanding formal schedule than can be held by workers in other primary fields where uncertain time demands limit their secondary efforts to sporadic self-employment or odd-hour jobs. Farm laborers have flexi-bility in hours, which permits a wider range of second-job attachment.[17]

3. All three groups feel that their incomes are inadequate. Although the first two characteristics provide a background favorable to moonlight-ing, it is the third that drives the worker to seek a second job. For the farm laborer, with day wages at $7.10 in 1963, without board, the feeling of inadequate income requires no psychological explanation.

---

[15] This means that many male schoolteachers prefer the combination of nonincome benefits but lower income from teaching than other jobs that simply pay more. But they would also prefer to augment their teaching income. Similarly, it can be argued that many overemployed workers prefer jobs that give higher pay but require more work than they wish to offer over lower-paying jobs with optimum schedules for the lower pay. However, they would still like to reduce their hours on their preferred job.

[16] The percentage for male school teachers is a 1964 statistic. The estimate for 1965 is about 20 percent.

[17] Flexibility in agricultural hours works two ways to expand moonlighting. Not only does it allow a relatively large number of farmers to moonlight but it induces substantial moonlighting by other workers in agriculture. In 1965, while only 6.3 percent of all workers were primarily in agriculture, 20.9 percent of secondary jobs were in farm work.

Postal workers and schoolteachers consider their incomes inadequate when matched against the spending potential of workers with comparable training and skills, who have not traded income for security or nonpecuniary satisfactions. In short, these workers try to gain both goals of job satisfaction and high income. Having sacrificed income potential for a preferred occupation, they try to recoup the income foregone through moonlighting.

4. Their earnings are not likely to rise substantially in the future. With little opportunity for income advancement through further training, if consumption goals press on income, the need for added income would just as likely be met by additional effort on the part of the breadwinner as by market labor of the wife or other family member. Although current income is close to permanent income for these workers, usually indicating that extra household effort would not be expended, as would be the case with current income well below permanent income, these workers experience chronic deficits in their consumption budget. What counts in leading toward moonlighting, then, is that there would be little future income gain if the extra effort were not provided by the family head, as would be the case if he were preparing for a career.

Moonlighting related to labor supply. The relationship between the extent of moonlighting and the nature of labor supply schedules can be explained with reference to Figure 2.4. At straight-time wage LL, there are AB unfilled hours of work to reach the worker's optimum position. Under a constant schedule of LA hours, the number of underemployed hours at every wage rate above LL depends on the nature of the labor supply schedule whether forward- or backward-bending or, in indifference curve terms, whether the substitution effect of higher wages to offer more labor outweighs the normal income effect to take more leisure.

This can be seen by extending the vertical line AP upwards, to measure the underemployed hours at successive optimum combinations of income and leisure as the wage rate rises (wage ray steepens). For example, indifference curve I_3, the highest attainable at wage level LL''', is drawn to reflect a forward-sloping segment of the worker's labor-supply curve in that there are more underemployed hours, AE, at optimum income EV than the AB underemployed hours at lower wage LL. Had the indifference curve been drawn to reflect a backward-sloping segment of the labor-supply curve, the number of underemployed hours would have shrunk as the wage rose.

At first view, it might seem illogical to argue the possibility of a negatively sloped labor-supply curve for the moonlighter, considering that his primary quest is for additional income. But the crucial determinant of whether the moonlighter's supply schedule on his first job is positively or negatively sloped at a particular wage is the basis of his desire for extra income. If he wishes to fulfill a more or less set consumption pattern, then his schedule will be backward-sloping and his number of underemployed hours will fall with an increase in his first-job wage. On the other hand, if his inability to reach undefined higher income levels with his first-job income leads him to moonlight, his labor-supply schedule will be forward-sloping, and he will have more underemployed hours with higher first-job wages.

The farm laborer might be assumed to have a negatively sloped supply curve if his goal is a fixed broader subsistence than his primary-job income allows. But his consumption goals might widen with the opportunity for higher income.

On the other hand, the male schoolteacher might feel his first-job income inadequate because it does not permit him to reach the higher indefinite and changing consumption standards of those he considers his social peers. If this is the case, his labor-supply curve would be forward-sloping, with his underemployed hours increasing with higher first-job income. But if his unsatisfied income goals were less vague or flexible, he would have a negatively sloped supply curve and would have fewer underemployed hours at higher wage rates on his first job.

A student of moonlighter psychology describes multiple jobholders as workers who feel that "consumption pressures and aspirations greatly exceed their economic rewards"[18] on their first jobs. This description emphasizes the impossibility of forming a priori conclusion on the nature of the moonlighter's labor-supply curve. If at a given first-job wage, "pressures" goad him to seek a second job, his supply curve will be negatively sloped; if "aspirations" lure him, his supply curve will be positively sloped, and his number of underemployed hours would rise with a wage rise on his primary job.

An interesting question on the relationship between moonlighting and labor supply concerns whether a rise in hourly wages with standard schedules reduced so that weekly income remained unchanged, under a work-sharing program, would induce an increase in supplementary, moonlighting, hours to the extent that individual labor supply exceeded its preraise (equilibrium) level. Except for the case in which income were an inferior good, the worker would always choose to earn more income by not taking the full gain of the wage increase in a proportionate

---

[18] Harold L. Wilensky, "The Moonlighter: A Product of Relative Deprivation," *Industrial Relations*, **3** (October 1963), p. 106.

reduction in hours. If the wage on a second job equaled that of the first, allowing for financial and psychological costs, the worker would wish to increase his hours over the preraise level if his supply schedule were positively sloped and would take some reduction in hours if his supply schedule were negatively sloped.

If the moonlighting wage were below the new higher wage on the primary job but above its preraise level, at first view it might seem that if his labor-supply curve were positively sloped, the worker would increase his total labor supply over its preraise level. But such need not be the case for although, at the same total effort, the marginal labor income would be greater at the (moonlighting) wage, total income would be higher at this level of effort than if the moonlighting wage had prevailed for all hours of effort because of the higher primary job wage. Thus the augmented income effect might reduce labor supply, even if labor supply were forward-sloping for any given *constant* wage.

If the moonlighting wage were at the pre-wage level, then surely less total labor would be offered under the higher wage, including moonlighting hours, provided leisure were not an inferior good. The worker would choose to cut back his total hours because with the same effort he would be earning a higher income at the same marginal wage. If he were at equilibrium before, with the lower primary wage, he would not be at the same effort, assuming the negative effect of higher income on effort.

If the adjusted wage on his second job were below that of his preraise first, the worker again, would never choose to demand enough supplementary hours to leave his total labor supply unchanged from its previous level. This conclusion follows since, if he worked additional hours at a rate below the preraise wage, his income at the previous equilibrium number of hours would be higher, but the wage rate lower. With the usual assumption that leisure is not an inferior good, the negative substitution effect on labor supply of a lower marginal wage would be joined by the negative income effect of a higher potential income, to cause the supply of supplemental moonlighting hours to fall short of the amount required to restore total supply to its preraise level.[19]

But all of the above assumes that the worker did not moonlight at the lower primary wage. If he had done so, then whatever the moonlighting wage, his total labor supply would be reduced at the higher rate for his primary job. Now at the same effort as before, he would receive the same marginal (moonlighting) wage—assuming that the change in his primary job rate has no effect on his moonlighting opportunities—at

[19] This case is analogous to the negative effect on labor supply of declining social security benefits.

a higher income. With leisure not an inferior good, such a condition always results in reduced labor supply.

Bronfenbrenner and Mossin tacitly assume that the worker did moonlight at the lower wage level in their conclusion that a policy of maintaining primary job income at a higher wage and fewer hours would, when leisure is not an inferior good, always result in lower total labor supply, including moonlighting hours, than at the lower primary job rate.[20] The power of their conclusion lies in the realism and applicability of the assumption. When the moonlighting wage is at or below the preraise level, whether the worker would have worked on a secondary job when his wages were lower does not affect the issue under discussion; in either case total labor supply would be reduced at a higher primary wage. When the moonlighting wage is above the preraise level, total labor supply might increase (depending on the amount of the moonlighting wage) at the higher primary wage level, *but only if the worker did not moonlight at the lower wage.* But for the typical worker, and even many "overemployed" workers, this latter condition would be inconsistent with maximizing behavior, since the moonlighting wage would be similar to an overtime wage above the base level. Thus, under the condition for which the assumption that moonlighting occurred at the lower primary job rate matters in the determination of whether total labor supply will be reduced, when the moonlighting wage exceeds the former level of the primary job, the assumption is realistic. Consequently, it can be concluded that with leisure not an inferior good, a system of higher wages and income maintenance (though shorter hours) on the primary job would tend to reduce individual labor supply from its previous level. This means that raising wages and shortening hours to spread out existing work would reduce total hours of work supplied. This suggests that the process would not be self-defeating as an unemployment reducing measure.

But all of the above refers to the case under which income is maintained through a proportionate wage rise as hours are shortened. To generalize for all types of wage adjustment when hours are shortened,[21] the issue depends on whether the combined income at the higher primary wage plus constant moonlighting wage lies above or below the combined income at the lower wage for the same total hours worked. If it would lie above, then the composite of a higher wage and shorter week would result in a reduction in total hours offered, with opposite results, if it fell below.

[20] Bronfenbrenner and Mossin, *op. cit.,* p. 330.
[21] The following generalization appears in my "Moonlighting and Labor Supply—Reply [to Roger Sherman and Thomas D. Willett]," *Southern Economic Journal,* **35** (July 1968), pp. 82–84.

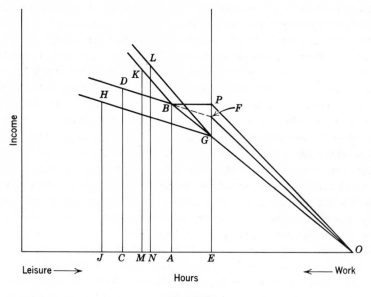

Fig. 2.5

This general conclusion can be derived from Figure 2.5.

Assume that the moonlighting wage is less than the primary wage. With work schedule OA and primary wage-ray OB, assume that the moonlighter's choice between income and leisure puts him at equilibrium with OC hours of work and income CD. Assume that the work schedule is reduced to OE and extend the moonlighting wage-ray BD to meet the vertical extension of E at F. Then if the primary wage were raised to OF so as to enable the worker to earn the same income as before with the same total effort, there would be no change in equilibrium income and labor supply. There would, of course, be an increase in moonlighting hours. If the primary wage increased by more than OF, total effort would decline, and if the primary wage increased by less than OF, total effort would rise (provided that leisure were not an inferior good) since, with a constant moonlighting wage, only income effects on effort would apply at the margin. In short, if the primary wage were raised to a level where the former full-schedule earnings would be reached by moonlighting, labor supply would remain unchanged. A greater rise in the primary wage would reduce labor supply, and a lesser rise would increase it. If the moonlighting wage were above the primary wage, then for total income not to rise above its previous level at the same amount of total effort, and thus for labor supply not to fall, would require a decrease in the primary wage, since BF would be steeper than OB and would cut the vertical extension of point E below G, where it is cut by OB. That is, with a moonlighting wage above the primary wage level and with a shorter schedule, the income earned up to the former full schedule of hours through moonlighting would exceed the former full-schedule income unless the primary wage fell.

If it is assumed that the lower limit to the wage of any labor agreement that reduced the work week was the current wage, then it could be concluded that labor supply would fall for all cases in which the moonlighting wage were above the primary wage, assuming that leisure were not an inferior good. This follows, since at any realistic new wage—at least at the level of the old—and at unchanged total effort, the worker would be at a higher income but would receive the same marginal return per unit of additional effort (the constant moonlighting wage).

Consider finally two extremes to the wage change. If the primary wage were unchanged, then from Figure 2.5 it can be seen that if the moonlighting wage were below the primary wage, such as DBF, the worker would labor more hours than before because he would be at a lower income at OC hours than he was before with the same marginal return per unit of additional effort. Equilibrium would be at, say, income HJ and hours OJ. There would be an increase in hours and a reduction in income, provided that neither leisure nor income were inferior goods.

On the other hand, if the moonlighting wage were above the primary wage, shown by moonlighting wage-ray KB or LG, labor supply would fall from, say, OM[22] to ON and income would rise from KM to LN, under the assumption that leisure and income are normal goods. Thus, with the wage rate unchanged at the reduced schedule, labor supply would rise if the moonlighting wage were below and would fall if it were above the primary wage.

Bronfenbrenner and Mossin treat the extreme case in which the primary wage is raised by a percentage equal to the percentage reduction in the work schedule, so that full-schedule income would remain unchanged. From Figure 2.5, it is easy to see that total labor supply would be reduced at any positive moonlighting wage if leisure is not an inferior good, the conclusion to which Bronfenbrenner and Mossin's analysis leads them. In this case, the new primary wage ray becomes OP. Thus, at

---

[22] That OM is less than OC has no particular significance to the analysis. It merely reflects that the equilibrium points assumed a negatively sloped labor-supply schedule with respect to the moonlighting wage. With a constant moonlighting wage, the labor-supply schedule, whether positively or negetively sloped, will not determine whether more or less labor will be supplied if hours are reduced and the primary wage increased.

any moonlighting wage above *BP*, or zero, total income at the same total effort, as before the primary-wage rise and work-schedule reduction, would lie above the previous level, with the marginal income per unit of additional effort unchanged. In short, then, total effort would be reduced.

OVERTIME AND LABOR DEMAND

An interesting aspect of labor demand arises from the fact that the supply of labor will increase if, instéad of a uniform wage, an overtime system is established such that the same weekly wage is paid with a lower straight-time wage with overtime rates for the latter hours of the weekly schedule. In reality, this type of condition is quite stilted. The employer usually does not have the option of paying his current work staff a lower base wage with built-in overtime.

But in tight and competitive labor markets, he might have the choice of working his existing work force overtime or getting additional hours of labor from his workers by raising the average hourly pay. Then, to secure the same effort, the wage cost to him would be higher if he raised the wage than if he paid oertime. This conclusion can be explained by assuming that the employer receives his desired number of work hours with the lower base plus overtime arrangement and comparing that equilibrium with the labor supply offered under the higher straight-time wage form of payment, which would make average hourly wages the same under both plans.

As has been noted previously, less labor would be forthcoming under the straight-time wage plan because, although wage income would be the same under both payment plans, the marginal return per unit of effort would be higher for the lower-wage plus overtime formula. Thus, to increase the labor supply to the equilibrium level achieved by the wage-plus-incentive method would require paying a still higher straight-time wage, thus raising the average hourly wage and wage bill to the employer to get the same labor force.[23]

---

[23] This conclusion does not depend on the assumption of a forward-sloping supply schedule, although this case deals with the demand side of a tight labor market in which the employer must bid up his wages in some manner in order to get more labor from his workers. Even under the noncompetitive labor market conditions assumed here, he would lose his work force by paying lower wages. Thus the choice of increasing labor supply by reducing the current wage, as would be the theoretical move under a backward-sloping supply curve, is not open to him. What counts is that he would always get less hours along the wage line

Thus, to work the existing work force a given number of extra hours, it would increase the wage bill less to pay overtime than to raise the straight-time wage bill. But an employer need not secure extra hours of work from his existing staff to expand his effective work force. He can hire additional workers. Thus a more important question to the employer is whether he would not follow an even cheaper program by hiring additional workers instead of paying his existing force overtime. Abstracting from other factors unrelated to the issue here of whether an overtime policy would be cheaper, such as the length of time for which the additional labor is needed, and the irregularity of production flow, the answer depends on the availability of additional labor or degree of competition in the labor market. If labor can be hired without raising the wage rate, that is, if the employer hired labor in a perfectly competitive market, then clearly it would be cheaper to hire more workers than to pay overtime.

One complicating element in this simple criterion, however, arises from the fringe benefits and other costs—hiring, laying-off, recalling—related to employing additional workers. In a statistical study comparing the added cost of overtime to hiring new workers, involving additional fringe benefits and other employment related cost, Garbarino concludes that with overtime premiums at 50 percent of the base rate, the employer would more likely prefer the option of hiring additional workers, since additional costs add much less than 50 percent to the base rate.[24] However, Garbarino's analysis makes the "dubious assumption,"[25] that hiring additional workers will not raise the wage rate. But if wages must be raised, that is, if the labor market is not perfectly competitive, then the question of which method would be preferred depends on the addition to the wage bill of hiring more workers—and, of course, any rise in wages will add much more to the wage bill than the wage increase because the wage rate for all will be raised—plus the associated employment costs, compared with the overtime costs. Thus, in tight labor markets, if higher wages must be paid, the magnitude of fringe benefits and other

---

that met the lower wage-plus-overtime line at the equilibrium supply along that bent line, as was shown in Figure 2.2.

This same conclusion, namely, that the average hourly wage would be lower with a wage plus overtime than with a straight-time equivalent is found in Frederic Meyers, "The Economics of Overtime," *Hours of Work,* edited by Clyde E. Dankert, Floyd C. Mann, and Herbert R. Northrup, Harper & Row, New York, 1965, pp. 95–110.

[24] Joseph W. Garbarino, "Fringe Benefits and Overtime as Barriers to Expanding Employment," *Industrial and Labor Relations Reviews,* **17** (April 1964), pp. 426–442.
[25] *Ibid.,* p. 434.

employment costs may play a determining role in the decision to choose the overtime option, even if these costs are substantially less per worker than the overtime premium.

In summary, under perfectly competitive labor market conditions, although it would cost the employer more to pay his *existing* work force a straight-time wage that would yield him as many hours of work as could be derived from a lower wage plus overtime, this condition would not influence his decision whether to offer his current staff overtime. Since he could get additional workers without raising wages, despite the costs associated with expanding his personnel, it would be cheaper to hire additional workers than to work his present staff overtime, at premium rates, to meet his expanded labor requirements.

On the other hand, under noncompetitive labor market conditions, the decision of whether to pay his existing work-staff overtime rates, or hire additional workers, is a real one. A rise in straight-time wages might expand his labor supply, both from the offer of additional hours of his present force and the attraction of new workers, so that his total wage bill might not be greater than that for the same effective supply as could be secured from overtime alone. But the additional payroll costs associated with the rising number in the work staff might act as a marginal cost element tipping the employer's decision in favor of overtime over employment expansion.

THE ECONOMY OF HIGH WAGES

One interesting case, with application to poor countries in which the marginal productivity theory may not apply to the demand curve for labor, concerns the phenomenon called "the economy of high wages." The conventional downward-sloping, short-run, real-wage demand curve for labor relates wages to employment under the implicit assumption that physical productivity of labor is determined only by uniform worker efficiency, the amount of supporting factors, and their technical relationship to labor in production. However, worker efficiency might be a function of the wage rate itself. When this is the case, in which efficiency rises with the wage level because of, say, greater energy and improved health resulting from raised consumption standards associated with higher wages, the labor-demand schedule relating wages and employment demanded becomes confused.

Rothschild notes that conventional labor-demand curves need adjustment when productivity becomes a function of the wage rate itself, but his method of dealing with the problem can be improved upon. He considers that the demand curve shifts to the right with each increase in wages, since the marginal product of each worker rises with the wage.[26] In reality, the demand curve does not shift at all; a shift implies that at each wage, productivity rises, while a condition of the economy of high wages is that productivity rises with *higher* wages.

What is needed is a reconstruction of a single demand curve taking into account improved efficiency at higher wages. Then to conclude whether the marginal productivity theory, when applied to labor demand, yields more than one possible equilibrium position will depend on whether the demand curve derived will be conventionally negatively sloped or positively sloped over part of its range, therefore possibly cutting a (positively sloped) supply curve at more than one point or not at all.

Leibenstein, in his ingenious paper on disguised unemployment treats this problem and derives a demand curve for labor taking improved efficiency related to higher wages into account. His demand curve is nothing more than the locus of the equilibrium points between wages and marginal productivity, with a different marginal productivity schedule for each wage.[27]

Before examining the nature of these different schedules to see whether they yield a conventional demand schedule, it can be concluded at once that in any case there will at least be a tendency for the demand curve to become more inelastic because of the added efficiency factor. As with any short-run labor demand curve, as wages rise the employment fall is retarded by increasing marginal productivity of labor as fewer workers operate with a given capital supply. A further check to the decline in marginal productivity is the increase in physical efficiency of the remaining workers. Similar reasoning, *mutatis mutandis*, can be applied to the employment effects of a wage decline, making for only a slight increase in labor demand in response to a fall in wages.

Looking now at Leibenstein's demand curve, Figure 2.6 presents three marginal productivity schedules for different wage levels in the manner he has drawn them. Note that the curves at higher wage levels fall more steeply and that each successive higher curve crosses its immediately lower curve to the left of the intersection of that curve with its immediately preceding lower one.

Leibenstein explains the steeper decline for higher wages on the grounds that a high-wage productivity curve is subject to two conflicting forces. One conflicting force arises because of increasing marginal productivity

[26] Rothschild, Theory of Wages, pp. 29–31. For a textbook repetition of this slip, see Paul Samuelson, *Economics,* 7th ed., McGraw-Hill, New York, 1967, pp. 556–557.
[27] Harvey Leibenstein, "The Theory of Underemployment in Backward Economies," *Journal of Political Economy,* **65** (April 1957), pp. 91–103.

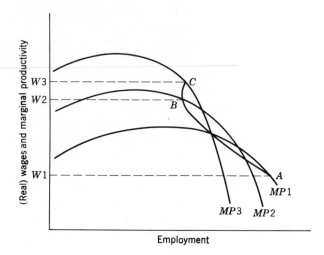

Fig. 2.6

in that, at higher wages, each worker adds more efficiency units to production. The other contrary force arises in that this added efficiency only hastens the onset of diminishing returns, which is really based on the ability of labor to work with supporting factors, not on the number of workers hired. Workers, that is, are assumed to be of equal efficiency at the same wage level, but this uniform individual efficiency rises with the wage level.

Leibenstein states that "beyond some point we expect the declining marginal productivity of work to become more important than the fact that each man does more work."[28] Thus the higher-wage marginal productivity schedule will cross a lower-wage schedule and this intersection will be to the right of the point of diminishing returns on the lower curve. The key to this conclusion is that diminishing returns constitute a continuously growing negative element, while the efficiency aspects of a higher wage comprise only a fixed additive to output for each worker hired.

The effect of this combination of influences in making successive curves steeper can be seen by comparing the marginal products of two sets of workers, one with a higher wage and consequently with an efficiency factor, k, so that a higher-wage worker can add

$$(1 + k)MP_1$$

[28] Leibenstein, *op. cit.*, p. 98.

to output, where MP_1 represents the marginal physical product of a particular worker at a lower wage.

Let a and b equal the marginal product of workers *1* and *2*, respectively, at the lower wage. Then at the higher wage, worker *1* would add

$$(1 + k)a + [1 - (1 - k)]b$$

to output.[29]

This result needs correction. No term can be greater than 1, since such a value signifies that the efficiency units are so great as to cut into what would be the production of the next worker at a lower wage. Hence the adjusted productivity gain of the first worker at the higher wage becomes

$$a + kb$$

At the lower wage, the second worker would contribute b to output and, at the higher wage, he would add

$$(1 - k)b + (1 + k)c - (1 - k)c = (1 - k)b + 2kc$$

where c would be the contribution to output of a third worker at the lower wage. If k exceeds ½, this second worker would cut into what

Table 2.1 Addition to Output of Two Workers at Different Wage Levels

Worker	Marginal Product, Lower Wage	Marginal Product, Higher Wage
1	a	$a + kb$
2	b	$(1 - k)b + c + (2k - 1)d$

would be the addition to output of a fourth worker at a lower wage, to the extent of $(2k - 1)d$. Thus the addition to output of the second worker at the higher wage would be

$$(1 - k)b + c + (2k - 1)d$$

A comparison of the marginal products for the two workers employed after diminishing returns have set in, at different wage levels, is shown in Table 2.1.

Table 2.1 indicates that the marginal product at the higher wage falls

[29] For simplicity, it is assumed here that k is less than one. If it were greater than one the first worker would cut into what would be the production of a third worker at a lower wage. This would not affect the analysis but only clutter the equation.

more rapidly than that at the lower. With one worker the marginal product is greater. With two workers at the lower wage the marginal product falls from a to b. At the higher wage, since d is less than b, and k exceeds $\frac{1}{2}$, the terms $(1 - k)b + (2k - 1)d$ must be less than kb. Further c is less than a by a greater amount than b is from a, so that the total drop in the marginal product is greater for the higher wage when diminishing returns set in for each successive worker. (This result does not require that k exceed $\frac{1}{2}$.) At some point then, the marginal product falls below that for the lower wage. Since it is assumed that at each higher wage, k becomes smaller, that is, the gain in efficiency from the higher wage decreases with each wage income, the higher marginal productivity curve cuts its immediately lower one to the left of the intersection of that wage's marginal product curve with its next lower one.

But all of this says nothing about the relation of the equilibrium points at successive wages. These points determine the labor demand curve. Leibenstein has drawn his demand curve to follow the conventional negatively sloping pattern. But the reason for this is that his equilibrium points, where wage equals marginal product, at each wage lie to the right of the intersection of the next higher marginal product curve with the curve in question. Since the lower curve is flatter than the higher one at these points, the intersection of the higher wage with its marginal curve must always lie to the left of the lower one.

Thus, in Figure 2.6, with MP_1 corresponding to the MP for W_1, equilibrium employment at W_1A lies to the right of the intersection of MP_2 with MP_1. Hence, W_2B, which represents equilibrium employment at W_2 and corresponding marginal productivity schedule MP_2, must be less than W_2A, describing a conventional backward-sloping labor demand curve.

But it is not a necessary condition for equilibrium that the equilibrium wage cut its appropriate marginal productivity schedule to the right of the intersection of the next higher marginal productivity schedule with the curve in question. As long as the marginal product falls for both curves before they intersect, it is quite possible that the necessary condition for stable equilibrium, under the conventional marginal productivity theory, that the (real) wage equal marginal productivity after diminishing returns, still holds, while wages cut the marginal product for successively higher curves to the left of the intersection of the marginal product curves.[30]

---

[30] This condition is not meant as criticism of Leibenstein's analysis, since he notes repeatedly that his presentation represents only one of alternative possibilities.

If such is the case, then the demand curve can have a positively sloped range. Thus, in Figure 2.6, W_3C, equilibrium employment or labor demand for wage W_3, exceeds that of the lower wage W_2.

The demand curve connects the equilibrium wage and employment points. Demand curves, then, under "economy of high wage" conditions can take many forms. They can still be negatively sloped for all wages, but they can also be positively sloped for part of their range, as in ABC of Figure 2.6.[31]

They cannot be positively sloped throughout their range, though, given the condition of diminishing returns and declining efficiency gains from higher wages. As the efficiency effects of higher wages become negligible and approach zero, the marginal productivity curves for successive higher wages tend to coincide, and the labor demand curve at higher wages becomes identical with the conventional curve, which takes no account of the efficiency factor.

Thus the possibility arises for a partially positively sloped labor-demand curve. Just as the backward-bending supply curve, such a schedule would confound the theorist looking for stable supply and demand equilibrium.

It remains to question how important is the "economy of high wages," how much is efficiency increased by higher income potential. Of course, when the increase actually permits greater physical well-being as in the case of the poorest countries, the gain is direct and obvious. In advanced countries, though, it can be argued that even at the lowest wages there is great doubt as to whether higher incomes would actually affect physical efficiency. But the psychological pressures for higher incomes might affect worker efficiency. The environment of higher consumption standards might be such as to lead to improved attitudes and performance with higher wages.[32]

Higher wages might assuage labor unrest and even make the firm a pleasanter place for management to operate, itself a consideration that weakens the application of marginal principles to industry. Higher wages will help retain a work force, reduce turnover, perhaps reduce

---

[31] Pan A. Yotopoulos, "The Wage-Productivity Theory of Underemployment: A Refinement," *Review of Economic Studies,* **32** (January 1965), pp. 59–65, presents an alternative reason for uncertainty regarding the slope of the demand curve. He notes that a necessary condition for equilibrium in Leibenstein's model is that profits increase for each higher wage. There is no particular relationship between this condition and the special points of equilibrium drawn by Leibenstein required to yield a negatively sloped demand curve.

[32] These pressures add to the purely mental ones of the "nerve-racking atmosphere of modern factory life," which Rothschild, *op. cit.,* p. 31, cites as being somewhat mollified by higher wages.

lateness and absenteeism and contribute to greater efficiency in many subtle ways.

The question of efficiency wages also confuses the issue of whether higher pay attracts more efficient labor. Studies show that higher wage firms have more efficient labor. Where efficiency is relatively easily measured by testing before hiring, a firm can gear its wage scale to efficiency levels. But perhaps the reverse path is also possible, where higher wages bring out more of the worker's potential efficiency.[33] As an example in point, perhaps the "economy of high wages" principle may have application as a dampener of the harmful effects of a rise in the minimum wage. In this case there might be some slight positive effects in direct improvement in physical well-being and consequent industrial efficiency of the lowest paid workers. Added to this are the possible psychological spurs to activity initiated by higher wages and consumption possibilities.

EXPLOITATION

The generally held definition of exploitation as the payment of a wage below labor's marginal revenue product[34] implies not only that exploitation results from the monopsonistic nature of the labor market, but also that it must always exist when the supply of labor to the firm is not perfectly elastic.

[33] Studies show only the former causal relationship—that workers of high quality tend to be paid more. See Robert Evans, Jr., "Worker Quality and Wage Dispersion: An Analysis of a Clerical Labor Market in Boston," *Proceedings of the 14th Annual Meetings of the Industrial Relations Research Association*, 1961, pp. 246–259, and Eaton H. Conant, "Worker Efficiency and Wage Differentials in a Clerical Labor Market," *Industrial and Labor Relations Review*, **16** (April 1963), pp. 428–433.

Both writers used a priori indications of efficiency—experience or test score results. For examining the latter causal relationship, it would be interesting to find whether wages and actual efficiency were correlated. Of course a high correlation would just as well indicate that high efficiency led to higher wages as that higher wages induced greater efficiency, but at least the latter would be a possibility.

[34] At least this definition represents Bloom's acceptance of Chamberlin's criticism of the Pigou-Joan Robinson view that the term should include the lower wage that results from monopoly as well as monopsony, since they consider the value of the marginal product as the wage to be paid if exploitation is to be avoided. Chamberlin explains that under imperfect product market competition all factors, not just labor, receive less than the value of their marginal product.

See Gordon Bloom, "A Reconsideration of the Theory of Exploitation," *Quarterly Journal of Economics*, **55** (1940–1941), reprinted in *Readings in the Theory of Income Distribution*, Blakiston Co., Philadelphia, 1946, p. 246, and Edward Chamberlin, *The Theory of Monopolistic Competition*, Harvard University Press, Cambridge, Mass., 1947, pp. 181 ff.

But this does not mean that efforts to make the labor-supply curve infinitely elastic by, say, the establishment of a minimum or union wage must raise both wages and the level of employment. As a step toward explaining this conclusion, consider the typical presentation of the monopsonistic firm, as shown in Figure 2.7.

The firm pays wage NA, and under the accepted definition, labor is exploited because the wage is below the marginal revenue product, NB. But just because labor is exploited does not signify that the firm is earning more than normal profits.

Consider first the case in which the firm is earning only normal profits. Assuming, for simplicity, a competitive product market, the equilibrium wage would be NA. Any attempt to establish a uniform wage NB such that at the same employment the wage would equal MRP, thus eliminating exploitation, would result in economic losses and an eventual close-down of the firm. Whether firms, which can only survive by paying wages below MRP, should be encouraged to survive is not the issue here. What is argued is that if firms can only make normal profits when these profits are the result of monopsonistic exploitation, then any attempts to eliminate or reduce exploitation will not raise employment in the firm but eliminate it.

In Figure 2.8, with labor the only variable factor and with normal profits earned, the firm would operate at output OA. At a uniform wage established at NB in Figure 2.7, the new marginal cost curve to the firm, MC', would be less steep than the old MC because it would rise only under the influence of diminishing returns and not also because

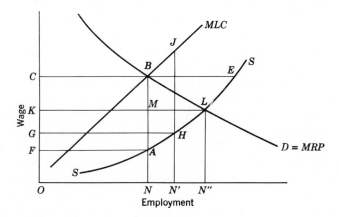

Fig. 2.7

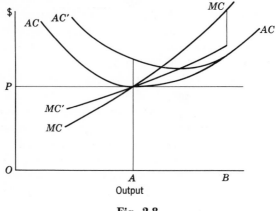

Fig. 2.8

of increasing wage rates as more labor were hired, as would MC. But MC' would lie above MC up to output OA, corresponding to employment ON in Figure 2.7, since CB would lie above the marginal labor-cost curve until employment ON were hired. Similarly, MC' would lie below MC between employment CB and CE because CBE lies below MLC for this employment range. MC' would become vertical and continue along MC at and beyond output OB, corresponding to employment CE in Figure 2.7, because beyond point E, more labor would be hired only if wages rose along the supply curve SS. Similarly, AC' would lie above AC, the average cost curve corresponding to labor-supply curve SS, because of the higher wage paid until employment CE at output OB. Afterward, AC' follows along AC as CBE continued along the old labor-supply curve in Figure 2.7. Although equilibrium output would again be reached at OA, where MC' equaled price, production would be at an economic loss and would not long be continued.

Thus, if the firm could only earn normal profits at wage NA, it would be impossible to raise the wage by introducing a minimum wage or a union wage into the system that would make the labor supply to the firm more perfectly elastic over part of its range, to leave short-run equilibrium employment unchanged without causing the firm to operate at a loss. Labor would be "exploited" under these conditions because the wage fell short of MRP. But in this case the term "exploitation" does not imply that workers could improve their wage-employment condition with the firm by measures to reduce their exploitation. In this case, employment *with this firm* depends on being taken advantage of.

Consider next the case in which monopsony profits were earned at wage NA. Then labor would be exploited. The wage would not only be below marginal cost and marginal revenue product but, in addition, a rise in (uniform) wages could be achieved with an increase in employment. However, in a move to eliminate exploitation, establishment of a uniform wage as high as NB might again cause the firm to suffer economic losses.

Assume that excess monopsony profits could be eliminated by the establishment of a minimum wage $N'H$ in Figure 2.7. At this new wage level, the firm would be operating at an equilibrium position because any further employment beyond ON' would raise marginal cost above $MRP;$ the new marginal cost curve, GHJ, would rise vertically to reach and follow the old MLC at and after J.[35] Exploitation would still exist because the wage was below MRP but, again, any additional uniform wage increase to eliminate exploitation would be self-defeating in that the firm would suffer economic losses and eventually shut down.

Joan Robinson notes that the function of a trade union in removing exploitation lies in its artificial establishment of the conditions of perfect competition in the labor market by bringing infinite elasticity to the labor-supply schedule. But she further argues that exploitation is impossible, in the Chamberlin-Bloom sense, when labor supply to the individual firm becomes infinitely elastic, so that the wage equals the marginal cost of labor.[36]

There is no automatic process, though, by which a uniform union wage exactly eliminates all exploitation. If the wage is set too high to cause economic losses, the firm will not be able to operate. If set too low, below $N'H$ if that level represents the wage that would eliminate excess monopsonistic profits, employment could be increased by raising wages. If the minimum wage is set at $N'H$ in Figure 2.7 and if above normal monopsony profits still existed, exploitation could only be eliminated by cutting the upward sloping supply curve beyond H by setting a higher uniform wage. Finally, if wage $N'H$ eliminated above normal monopsonistic profits, the union could only raise wages to that level without causing unemployment, but exploitation would still exist. In short, Mrs. Robinson's formulation does not allow for a uniform wage being set below the level that would eliminate excess monopsonistic

---

[35] In other words, average cost and price would be equal at output, corresponding to employment ON'. AC would fall, and excess monopsony profits would be earned if more labor beyond ON' were available at wage $N'H$. This follows, since MC wage is below MRP at ON'. But no more labor is available at that wage.

[36] Joan Robinson, *Economics of Imperfect Competition*, Macmillan, London, 1933, p. 282.

profits, nor for the possibility that the wage would not be raised to the level that would eliminate exploitation but cause unemployment.

One explanation for a uniform wage being set too low, that is, below the level that would eliminate excess monopsonistic profits, say, by collective bargaining, might be that the collusive power of the firms involved, if more than one, was effective in establishing low wages. Bloom considers this power a potential source of exploitation, but discounts it on the grounds that no matter how low the wage is set, it would always pay the employers to hire labor until the (now horizontal) marginal cost curve crossed the marginal revenue product curve. Thus, he concludes that "competition among employers is not needed to assure that labor gets its marginal revenue product."[37] He carefully points out that a necessary condition for this to occur is the pressure of a sufficient pool of labor for employers to hire as many as they can at this same low price.

But this condition is precisely the one that does not exist in monopsonistic markets. Bloom's argument is consistent, but his premise is unrealistic. Because employers can succeed in setting low wages does not guarantee that abundant labor will be forthcoming at this wage. If the work force available at depressed wage $N'H$ is fully employed at ON' in Figure 2.7, and above normal profits were earned, then the individual firms could only secure more labor by bidding against each other. If they agreed not to do this, then the amount of labor available to each firm would fall short of the desired goal of employing workers, to the point where the marginal cost curve crossed the marginal revenue product curve.

A conclusion that labor is not exploited when it receives a wage depressed by the collusive power of employers, because the wage equals the marginal labor cost, is not consistent with the concept of exploitation. If a collusive wage $N'H$ is maintained, such that more workers could be hired at a higher uniform wage, then labor is considered exploited. The crucial point in this argument is that the identity of marginal cost and wages over part of the range of the labor-supply curve does not necessarily assure a maximization of the wages-employment combination consistent with profitable operation. But labor would also be exploited if excess monopsony profits were absorbed at a uniform wage level such that the marginal cost fell below MRP.

Suppose all excess monopsony profits are not eliminated until the establishment of a uniform wage at $N''L$ in Figure 2.7, which cuts the supply curve at its intersection with the employer's labor demand curve.

---

[37] Bloom, *op. cit.*, p. 271.

Then, under the accepted definition, exploitation is eliminated because the wage equals the marginal revenue product. Wages could still be raised higher, but only at the cost of reduced employment.

In fact, uniform wage $N''L$ must eliminate both all monopsony profits and exploitation. If any above-normal profits remain to the firm, they could not result from the monopsonistic character of the labor market beyond L. This follows, since any higher wage would lead the firm to move back along its labor-demand curve, so that the range of the labor-supply curve beyond L would not be relevant to the firm's employment decisions.

Any economic profits remaining after wage $N''L$ was set would represent monopoly profits resulting from imperfection in the product market or short-run competitive (disequilibrium) profits. A wage above $N''L$ could transfer these profits to labor, but only at the cost of a reduction in employment.

EXPLOITATION AND UNEMPLOYMENT. In the typical presentation of monopsonistic conditions of Figure 2.7, it is usually noted that a union could bargain for wage NB without any reduction in employment, thereby making the area ALB a bargaining range, with the location of the actual wage within that range a measure of the union's power to gain concessions from the employer. Having discussed the flaws in this picture of the bargaining range, should extra monopsony profits be entirely absorbed at a wage lower than $N''L$, let us assume that it takes wage $N''L$ to absorb these profits and thus eliminate exploitation.

But the term "bargaining range" implies a wage range over which the bargaining group will at least maintain its level of employment that would prevail at the lower limit of the range. Clearly, at any wage between NA and $N''L$, this condition would be met.

At any wage above $N''L$, though, unemployment may arise among the original bargaining group. At wage NB, for example, there is excess labor supply of BE. Consider first the case in which the union group is fixed at ON. Unless the union can restrain the firm from hiring non-union labor, there is no guarantee that the firm's labor force would not include new workers drawn to it, indicated by the rising supply curve, in response to the rise in wages. If this restraint cannot be exercised and, under today's labor laws, it is likely that it could not be, then unemployment would tend to arise among the original group. At first, the firm might have no incentive to change its work force, but over time as operations and products change, the presence of excess labor supply poses a constant threat to the job security of the original membership.

Consider next that the union expands its membership in accordance with the labor-supply schedule. Then at wage NB, union employment would be maintained, but unemployment BE among union members would arise.

Thus the wage range AB loses much of its significance as a bargaining range, if that term implies a wage interval over which the union can raise wages without harmful employment effects. Whether workers wish to risk unemployment by seeking a wage above $N''L$ is another matter and has nothing to do with monopsony or exploitation. Instead, it forms the central issue in the setting of union wage goals.

CHAPTER III

Alleviating Poverty—the Negative Income Tax and Labor Supply

This chapter treats only one aspect of the problem of poverty—the effect on labor supply of efforts to raise family income above the poverty line. To assure the removal of poverty requires the guarantee of a minimum income. For those in full-time employment, this income could be provided by upward adjustment in minimum wages. For removing poverty in general, though, without regard to employment or labor force participation, a direct government guarantee of a minimum income is required.[1]

One policy for achieving this goal, which has received wide publicity and discussion, is the imposition of a negative income tax. The (negative) effects of this tax on labor supply are studied. Although no value judgments are made as to the social effects of reducing labor supply, the varying degrees of impact on incentives to work for different forms of the negative tax are analyzed. A negative tax system is presented which, under certain conditions, will not reduce work incentive. Before this study of the negative income tax, the comparative effects on labor supply of those who work, of raising minimum wages, and of providing direct subsidies will be discussed.

---

[1] This chapter deals only with measures to alleviate poverty at a moment in time. Whether the incidence of poverty can be reduced over time by education and training of the poor or by expanded growth in national income is another issue. Apart from popular writings on the ineffectiveness of the latter policy, see Lowell E. Gallaway, "The Foundations of the 'War on Poverty,'" *American Economic Review,* **55** (March 1965), pp. 122–131, and W. H. Locke Anderson, "Trickling Down: The Relationship Between Economic Growth and the Extent of Poverty Among American Families," *Quarterly Journal of Economics,* **78** (November 1964), pp. 511–524, for statistical studies indicating that as income rises the effect of the increase on reducing poverty declines.

HIGHER MINIMUM AND SUBSIDY COMPARED

Poverty strikes those who work as well as those who receive no income from contributing to production. In effect, there are two methods to raise those currently earning below-poverty incomes above the poverty line. One way to guarantee a minimum income level would be to raise the minimum wage; another would be to supplement income earned with additional money provided by the government.[2] For those who do not work, the entire income would consist of government subsidy. The second alternative reduces the labor supply more than the first.

Consider the worker who reaches an equilibrium position with the higher minimum wage; his subjective marginal rate of substitution of income for leisure just equals the rate of exchange of income for leisure—his wage. Offer him now the alternative consisting of his original wage rate, combined with supplemental income high enough to yield the same income as above. He could earn the same weekly wage with the same effort, but will he do so? In this case the marginal return from his last hour of work will be less than in the case of the higher minimum wage. Thus, his position will no longer be one of equilibrium in that his wage would be less than his marginal rate of substitution of income for leisure. Consequently, he will not offer the last hour of work and will choose more leisure than in the previous case. Therefore, to induce the worker who receives a direct subsidy to supply enough labor to cross the poverty line requires a larger subsidy than that which would lead him to the poverty line if he worked as much as under the minimum wage.

The above relationships are explained diagrammatically in Figure 3.1.

Originally, before the application of the alternative methods to raise minimum income, the worker who faced the wage line OA supplied OH hours and earned HP income. With a higher minimum wage, depicted by wage line OR, the worker increases his effort to OH' hours,[3] in order to earn socially desirable minimum income $H'P'$.

[2] Note the analogy to agriculture. The alternatives could be called the wage-support program and the subsidy plan. The wage-support program, of course, is available only to those who work. But it is interesting to note that in 1962, about 70 percent of poor families (those with incomes of less than $3000), then a widely held estimate of the poverty line, had at least one income earner. *1964 Annual Report of the Council of Economic Advisors*, Washington, 1964, Table 4, p. 61.

[3] The labor supply curve is positively sloped in this diagram. But the analysis is not affected by the nature of the labor-supply schedule. Of course, with a positively sloped curve, though, a smaller rise in the minimum is required to induce the worker to earn a certain minimum income than if his supply curve were negatively sloped.

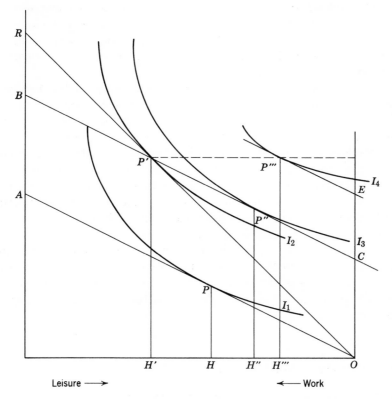

Leisure ⟶   ⟵ Work

Fig. 3.1

With a subsidy OC such that the minimum income could be earned with the same effort, the original labor supply would not be forthcoming. In fact, supply would be reduced from OH to OH'', but income would only be $H''P''$, below the poverty line goal. To assure that the minimum income would be earned, the subsidy would have to be raised to OE, with the worker then supplying only OH''' hours of work. There is always the risk that the indifference curve, which touches the vertical axis at zero hours of work, and income $H'P'$ will be steeper than a line parallel to OA at this point. Translating this geometry into terms of labor supply, there is the possibility that under the subsidy program the worker might not choose to work at all.

But the above analysis implies nothing about the relative costs of alleviating poverty through a higher minimum wage or a subsidy program. The question of relative costs is not only affected by the influences on supply but also on demand. A rise in the minimum might increase labor supply, but it will likely reduce demand as some workers are priced above their value to employers. To satisfy the goal of alleviating poverty, these unemployed workers then would have to be brought up to the poverty level entirely through a subsidy.

The main operational fault with either procedure, higher minimum wage or subsidy program, is that it establishes a uniform formula for individuals with varying supply schedules for the attainment of a particular goal. For example, consider a worker with a less positively sloped supply schedule than that presented in Figure 3.1. He would choose to earn less than the socially desired minimum income with minimum wage OR. Should he be paid a higher minimum than the worker of Figure 3.1?[4] The same shortcoming appears for the subsidy program. Should the worker with the least inclination to work be paid the highest subsidy to guarantee a minimum income for all workers?

The question arises as to whether any system of income guarantee can be devised without weakening the incentive to work of those who earn less than this minimum and of those who earn slightly above this level. These questions will be studied within the framework of the negative income tax.

THE NEGATIVE INCOME TAX

Perhaps the most widely considered proposal to eliminate poverty is the negative income tax. This plan, attributed to Milton Friedman[5] but not spelled out by him in detail, aims to build up the income of low-income recipients by federal grants, negative taxes, based on the relationship of the individual's income to the upper poverty limit. Presumably, the family that earned nothing would be awarded the full poverty income as a negative tax.

A system, whereby an individual (or family) was guaranteed a mini-

---

[4] This weakness in the plan appears even if the minimum were raised to the point that would assure him a poverty income at labor supply OH. Then those with a negatively sloped labor supply schedule would choose to earn less than the poverty income.

[5] Milton Friedman, *Capitalism and Freedom,* University of Chicago Press, Chicago, 1962, pp. 191–194. Actually, the idea of a negative income tax as an antipoverty device was proposed much earlier. George Stigler, "The Economics of Minimum-Wage Legislation," *American Economic Review,* **36** (June 1946), reprinted in *Labor and the National Economy,* edited by William G. Bowen, Norton, New York, 1965, p. 48, makes this suggestion but is even more vague about details than Friedman.

mum income whether he worked or not, that reduced the subsidy and implemented this guarantee in equal step with earned income would destroy all incentive to work of those who earned less than the minimum. Furthermore, it would cause discontent among those who earned slightly above the minimum and who received no subsidy. More relevant to the current issue of the effect on labor supply, it would reduce the labor supply of those a little above the minimum level who could earn almost as much income by not working at all. One aspect of public assistance programs that leads to negative labor supply effects is their policy of subsidizing income only up to a certain level. To minimize the effect on work incentives, it would be necessary to subsidize incomes so that total earnings could be above the minimum level. This would also require some support for those whose work earnings alone were above the minimum. Of course, such a policy contradicts the principle of public assistance. Little public support could be found for a direct payment program that gave money to those not in need, but a negative income tax might be so designed.

Friedman worries about the effect on work incentives and claims that, although the negative tax would reduce incentives "like any other measure to alleviate poverty," it would not eliminate incentive entirely, "as a system of supplementary incomes up to some fixed income would. An extra dollar earned always means more money available for expenditure."[6] Friedman has in mind a simple graduated income tax.[7] Examination of such a plan leads to the conclusion that its implementation would certainly weaken work incentive for low-income groups.

THE CONVENTIONAL GRADUATED NEGATIVE INCOME TAX. Following the principle of eliminating poverty through the tax system, a negative tax of the entire poverty-limit annual income, say, $3000, would be guaranteed to every household, with adjustments for differences in family size, special needs, etc. Then the negative tax could be gradually reduced on incomes earned above zero. But the graduation must not only permit total earnings above $3000 for those earning some income below $3000,

---

[6] Friedman, op. cit., p. 192.

Stigler, op. cit., p. 48, is also concerned about work incentives, and, in relation to the analysis of this chapter, wrote, "If the negative rates are appropriately graduated, we may still retain some measure of incentive for a family to increase its income." The purpose here is to present a model for "appropriate graduation" to achieve not only this goal, but in addition possibly to retain most, if not all, work incentive.

[7] For another formulation of the simple graduated plan, see Robert J. Lampman, "Approaches to the Reduction of Poverty," American Economic Review, Papers and Proceedings LV (May 1965), pp. 526–527.

but must also permit positive benefits to those earning $3000 and slightly above this level, if an attempt is made to protect the work incentives of these earners.

Establishment of a satisfactory formula faces serious difficulties because of the need to follow three goals that, to some extent, conflict with each other. The three objectives of a successful program are to eliminate poverty, to preserve work incentives as much as possible, and to maintain equity in the (low) income structure, with equity defined as the maintenance of the ordinal ranking of earned income. In short, this last objective is achieved if the system operated so that those who earned more also received more.

Table 3.1 presents a hypothetical progressive tax schedule that is con-

Table 3.1 Hypothetical Tax Schedule

Earned Income	Negative Tax	Composite Income	Marginal Tax Rate (Percent)
$ 0	$3000	$3000	
1000	2800	3800	20
2000	2500	4500	30
3000	2100	5100	40
4000	1550	5550	55
5000	850	5850	70
6000	0	6000	85

sistent with the first and third goals, eliminating poverty and allowing for greater total income for those who earn higher incomes through market effort.

To study the effect of the tax program on labor supply, conventional indifference curve analysis will be used. Figure 3.2 shows the effect for the $1000 earner.

For reasons that have become familiar, from the analysis of the social security program, the effect of the tax formula to eliminate poverty would reduce labor supply. Equilibrium income and work was assumed to be at P for the worker without the tax assistance. On the higher composite income line, including wage earnings and negative tax, the income effect alone, if leisure were not an inferior good, would move P' to the right of P. But, in addition, the marginal income gain from an hour's work is reduced up to the work schedule by the tax formula. (Note that the composite line becomes even flatter after the former work schedule because of the progression in the tax plan.)

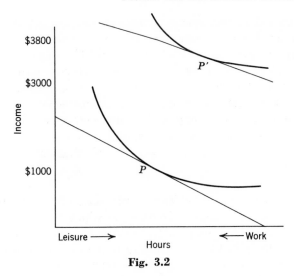

Fig. 3.2

In fact the worker might not choose to work at all. This would be the case if the indifference curve, which cut the zero work point at the $3000 income level, were steeper than the composite wage-income line.[8]

The above analysis also applies to those who earn income above $1000. In fact, the negative effect on labor supply is more pronounced for these workers in that the marginal returns on a unit of effort near the full schedule is more sharply reduced because of the progression in the tax schedule.

Closer study of the reasons for the necessary drop in labor supply under the above conditions provides the key to the essential requirement for a system that would not necessarily reduce work incentives. Two effects influence the worker's changed attitude toward work and leisure,

---

[8] In an interesting study of the effect of general assistance payments on labor supply, C. T. Brehm and T. R. Saving, "The Demand for General Assistance Payments," *American Economic Review*, **54** (December 1964), pp. 1003–1006, note that in theory and practice people work, even though they add nothing to their total income, by not receiving all their income in general assistance payments because of the "stigma" attached to this form of income. One purpose of the negative income tax, though, is to remove the stigma attached to the usual assistance payment. Thus, there is no need to adjust Figure 3.2 to account for unwillingness to receive income from a government support plan of this type. Christopher Green and Robert J. Lampman, "Schemes for Transferring Income to the Poor," *Industrial Relations*, **6** (February 1967), p. 123, claim that a well-administered, impersonal, negative tax program would avoid most of the stigma of being "on relief."

which can be called the income effect and the wage effect. The income effect, resulting from the assurance of some income whether he works or not always acts to depress his labor supply. The wage effect, therefore, must act to enhance his preference for work in order to offset the negative income effect for it to become possible that he retain his work incentive. Under the above plan, the worker's composite income line was flatter than the nonsubsidy wage line, which only aggravated the negative income effect. Thus the worker's composite income line must be made steeper by the negative income tax for the wage effect to offset the income effect.

AN ALTERNATIVE NEGATIVE TAX PLAN—RELATING TAX BENEFITS TO LABOR SUPPLIED. The simple technique by which the composite income line could be made steeper involves tying the negative income tax formula not only to earned income but also to the amount of work supplied.

Thus, for the worker who could earn $1000 at a full schedule, composite income could exceed $3000 for the first hours worked, with the negative tax declining at a decreasing rate as more hours were offered, that is, with the marginal tax rate decreasing.[9]

Finally, the decline in the subsidy would be halted and then would be turned into an increase until the total income of $3800, as under the simple graduated plan, were attained at the normal work schedule. The effect of this tax system would be to curve the worker's total income line from the very beginning of his hours worked. Furthermore, the last hour in the schedule would yield a greater return than the wage without subsidy, since the negative tax would be higher than for the previous hour.

Table 3.2 presents a hypothetical tax schedule for the worker who would earn $1000 at a full schedule, under both a constant marginal tax rate plan and a plan that ties his negative tax to his supply of labor, allowing for greater increments to total income as more labor is supplied.

Note that in the $500–$600 range of earned income, or 50 percent to 60 percent of the work schedule, the rate of increase of total income at $80 is the same as under the simple graduated plan. Further, after 70 percent of the schedule, or earned income over $700, the marginal tax rate became negative and the subsidy increases, so that the rate of increase in total income exceeds that from earned income alone.

Figure 3.3 presents the composite wage lines for the $1000 full-time

---

[9] The marginal tax rate is defined as the ratio of the reduction in subsidy, or negative tax, to the increment of earned income.

Table 3.2 Hypothetical Schedules under Constant and
Decreasing Marginal Tax Rate Plans

Income Earned	Constant Marginal Tax Rate Within $1000 Earnings Ranges			Alternative Plan		
	Negative Tax	Composite Income	Marginal Tax Rate (Percent)	Negative Tax	Composite Income	Marginal Tax Rate (Percent)
0	$3000	$3000		$3000	$3000	
$ 100	2980	3080	20	2930	3030	70
200	2960	3160	20	2870	3070	60
300	2940	3240	20	2820	3120	50
400	2920	3320	20	2780	3180	40
500	2900	3400	20	2750	3250	30
600	2880	3480	20	2730	3330	20
700	2860	3560	20	2720	3420	10
800	2840	3640	20	2730	3530	−10
900	2820	3720	20	2760	3660	−30
1000	2800	3800	20	2800	3800	−40

earner under the two plans, the simple graduated plan A and the
adjusted plan, which ties the tax benefit to the proportion of the full
schedule worked. At P, the slope of the curve under B equals the slope
of line A. That is, at P total income under B rose by $80 per $100 earned,
the constant rate under A.

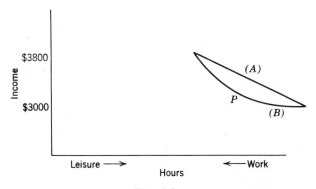

Fig. 3.3

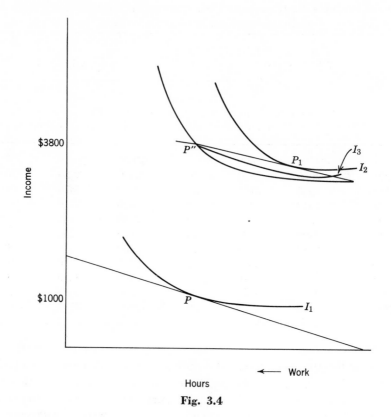

Fig. 3.4

On the surface, it appears that plan *B* might have a regressive quality. It may seem contrary to the purpose of an antipoverty program to grant larger subsidies to higher incomes, as would be the case under this plan. But closer examination reveals that the higher subsidy is not going to workers with higher earnings potential, but as a reward to the same worker for more effort. The maximum attainable subsidy declines with rising full-schedule income, thereby retaining the progressive nature of the tax structure.

Figure 3.4 presents the wage-income schedules and indifference curves for a case in which work incentives can be retained for the $1000 worker, who was assumed to be in equilibrium with his work schedule without the subsidy.

The composite wage-income lines under both plans are presented, along with the wage line, without the negative tax.

Note that under plan *B*, although the highest indifference curve that the worker could reach would find him working the full schedule, he would be on a lower indifference curve than under plan A in which he would choose a lighter schedule. This follows because under plan A he would have the opportunity of higher earnings at hours below the normal schedule than under plan B.

At first view it might seem that point P'' is not an equilibrium position for the worker under plan B because although I_3 is the highest indifference curve he can reach under plan B, the composite income curve is not tangent to this curve at P''. It seems as if he could get on a higher indifference curve by working more hours. But it should be noted that P'' is a corner solution. For an earned income over \$1000 the subsidy would fall, so that the composite curve to the left of P'' would move towards the horizontal, allowing P'' to be an equilibrium position, even though the bow of the composite income curve were steeper than the indifference curve at P''.[10] The effect is directly opposite to that of the usual case for overtime, for which more labor would always be offered as premium rates were paid beyond equilibrium hours. Here the negative substitution effect of a reduced marginal income potential from an extra hour's work makes the fact that, at the point where the curves meet, the worker would offer more labor at the *same* marginal return from effort irrelevant.

However, although a plan of eventually increasing negative tax returns with hours worked is a necessary condition for maintaining work incentives, it is by no means a sufficient condition. It is quite possible for the effect of such a plan to reduce the amount of labor offered even more than would be the case for the constant rate plan. The necessary condition for P'' to be an equilibrium point is that the path of indifference curve I_3 to the right of P be less steep than the bow of the income line.

It is possible for the labor supply to be greater under plan A than under plan B because higher incomes would be earned at less than full schedules under A, and it is possible that under either or both plans no labor would be supplied. But, relevant to the present discussion, plan B is the only one under which full pretax labor supply could be maintained.

All of the above, though, relates to the effects on work incentives of alternative negative tax plans for low income earners. For those earning more money, but still receiving a subsidy in accordance with Table 3.1, say, the \$4000 earners, two new elements enter the analysis. First,

---

[10] For P'' to be an equilibrium position, it is necessary that the slope of the extension of the bow be less than the slope of I_3 to the left of P''. This would be the case if the subsidy declined for overtime hours.

the $3000 poverty-line income can be earned with much less effort, thus reducing the likelihood that under either plan the worker would choose not to work at all. Second, the fact that the subsidy declines with increasing income levels flattens out the composite income line under plan *A*.

In fact, if the worker were at equilibrium income and effort without the negative tax, the effect of negative tax plan *A* would be always to reduce his labor supply. This follows because the program would always put him on a higher income level at a lower marginal rate of income per unit of extra work-time supplies. If he were at equilibrium at the lower income, derived only from earnings, then he would work less at the same wage at a higher income level, leisure assumed not to be an inferior good[11], and would certainly choose to work less at a higher income level and lower wage—marginal return comprised of wage offset by smaller negative tax.

The effect of plan *B* is to allow for the possibility of choosing to work the full schedule by increasing the marginal rate of income growth above that of the straight wage payment for hours of work (income) close to the full schedule.

At first view it might appear that the composite income curve under plan *B* can have only a slight bow for higher incomes, making it unlikely that the composite curve would be steep enough at the higher composite income to allow for maintenance of work incentives, because the curve cannot cross the wage-income line from earnings alone. The curve does not cross this line because to do so would signify that, under a subsidy

---

[11] If leisure is an inferior good for those receiving a negative income tax, then it is possible for work incentives to be maintained, or perhaps strengthened, even under plan A because a lower marginal increment to higher income levels would no longer necessarily signify a reduction of work effort. Leisure may be an inferior good for the lower income earners if the subsidy puts them in a position to strive to attain a higher socioeconomic level. Furthermore, increased income from very low levels may lead to new amplified consumption patterns and goals. On the effect of leisure as an inferior good on the work incentive question, see John Conlisk, "Simple Dynamic Effects on Work-Leisure Choice: A Skeptical Comment on the Static Theory," *Journal of Human Resources,* **3** (Summer 1968), pp. 323–326.

In addition, even if leisure were not an inferior good, work incentives would not be reduced under plan A for poor workers who were underemployed, as the term was described in the last chapter. The disincentive to work under plan A might merely reflect a reduction in surplus hours potentially offered at existing schedules, rather than a reduction in actual hours. James N. Morgan, "The Supply of Effort, The Measurement of Well-Being and the Dynamics of Improvement," *American Economic Review,* Papers and Proceedings, **58** (May 1968), pp. 31–39, contends that those at lowest income would characteristically supply more labor if it were demanded.

plan over a certain income range, the worker would be earning less with the aid of a negative tax than he could earn without it.

But, on the other hand, the bow can still be pronounced because the plan permits a higher wage worker to receive less total income, wages plus subsidy, than a low-wage worker, if he works a smaller part of his full schedule. Referring to Table 3.1, the $3000 worker, who could only earn $3000 by working his full schedule, would receive a total income of $5100. The $4000 worker could earn $3000 by working only ¾ of his schedule. But this does not mean that he would receive a total as high as $5100 for this lesser effort. The equity principle of giving those who earn more greater total income would not be violated if he received less than $5100, as he would under graduated plan B which, in effect, favored hours of work close to the schedule. In short, the equity principle applies only with equality of effort. This qualification then permits the bow of the composite income curve for the higher income earners, who receive the negative tax, to be pronounced, so that perhaps work incentives may be maintained under the subsidy plan, as the marginal return for extra effort near the full schedule exceeds the basic wage.

The practical shortcomings of applying plan B are obvious. But they should be enumerated lest the unwanted impression be created that what has been presented above is any more than an exemplification of a principle, so that work incentives may be maintained under a system that paid subsidies—negative taxes—in accordance with hours worked as well as with potential income earned.

In the first place, any program that paid negative taxes in line with hours worked would be difficult (expensive) to administer. Apart from record keeping, there would be the need for constant adjustment in payments as hours of work related to schedules varied. This is to say nothing of the monumental problem of establishing and applying a formula for those who did not work fixed schedules. Then there is the question of adjustment for those who work less than a full schedule because of illness. In addition, a program would have to be devised that would provide adequate coverage for those who customarily work part time, and would have to include downward adjustments in subsidies for those of very low income but substantial assets.

Apart from administrative and procedural difficulties, the program suffers from potential long-run damaging effects on desirable work incentives. While the incentive for an individual to work his full schedule may be maintained, the incentive for a worker to upgrade his skills, among low-rated jobs, would be reduced, perhaps seriously. Note in Table 3.1, for example, the smaller increment in addition to net income from each $1000 of earned income, compared to the increment without the subsidy plan. Thus, either negative tax plan has the harmful effect of weakening incentives to invest in education and training, even though work incentives on current (lower skilled) jobs may be maintained.

SUMMARY. Any subsidy plan for supplementing low incomes tends to reduce labor supply to the extent that leisure is not an inferior good by raising incomes over what they would be from earnings alone. Reinforcing this negative tendency, under a uniform subsidy plan, is the fact that as long as a certain minimum must be guaranteed, the marginal income gained from an extra hour's work would be less than that for an hour of earned income. The only possibility for maintaining labor supply would come about through a technique of making marginal income received above that received from earnings without a negative tax. This would require not only that the subsidy be graduated but graduated in such a way that the extra amount received increase with the number of hours worked near the full schedule for those receiving a subsidy.[12] This technique would not be regressive, since the plan refers to the income path for the individual worker; those with lower full-time income potential would still receive larger subsidies than those whose income rate was higher, *for the same effort*. It is not higher income earners as such who would be given preferential awards, but those at whatever income potential who chose to work longer, up to a full schedule.

Even under such a graduated program, it is by no means certain that work incentives would be maintained and labor supply not be reduced. The stronger the worker's preference for income over leisure, the more likely it is that such a plan would be successful in its goal to maintain labor supply. Even if work incentives are maintained, any plan that adds to the earnings of low-income workers dulls the incentive to invest in education and training.

[12] In a review of alternative negative tax rate schedules, Christopher Green, *Negative Taxes and the Poverty Problem,* The Brookings Institution, Washington, 1967, pp. 126–128, notes that work incentives would be reduced less if the reduction in allowance fell as the poverty line were approached, under what he calls a regressive allowance plan, than if the reduction increased as income rose toward the poverty line, under a progressive allowance plan. But the argument here is that if incentives are to be maintained, not just reduced less, it is not enough for subsidies to slow their decline as the poverty line is approached through work; they must in fact increase.

PART TWO

Wage Structure

CHAPTER IV

The Skill Differential

According to the competitive model, wage differences between occupations should be "equalizing." That is, skilled jobs should pay more than unskilled jobs by an amount necessary to cover the costs involved in acquiring skill—training costs and income foregone—plus a surplus allowing for a return on investment in skills equal to the return attainable on alternative investments.[1] Thus, changes in occupational wage structure can be explained without deviating from competitive assumptions, primarily through changes in direct and indirect costs associated with training and changes in the rate of return on capital in general, with the wage structure narrowing if related costs decline and/or alternative returns fall.

Two phenomena, working through the competitive model, affecting the relative labor supply of skilled and unskilled are changes in immigration from abroad and migration from agriculture to industry. For the United States, in the past the growth in immigration and also the out-migration from the farms tended to swell the unskilled labor supply. Thus, even as relative labor supply under the competitive model adjusts to changes in training costs and returns on alternative investments, these independent sources of increases in supply of unskilled workers operated against any tendency of the skill differential to narrow; that is, they served as widening forces, keeping the rate of return on investment in education relatively high. In more recent years, this migration has slackened with reverse effects on the skill differential.

Finally, two monopolistic, or noncompetitive, forces affect the occupational wage structure. One set of forces relates to the concept of noncompeting groups, the other to institutional measures that affect the wage structure. As for the former factor, interoccupational wage differences exist and persist that reflect an amount more than that attributable

---

[1] This abstracts from differences in unpleasantness of jobs, etc. discussed by Adam Smith as sources of wage differences within the competitive model.

to costs and returns from training. Barriers, whether social, economic, or personal—related to inability and lack of opportunity to acquire skills—have widened wage differences beyond the amount determined by competitive labor market conditions.[2] Reduction of these barriers would tend to narrow the occupational wage structure.

Institutional forces operating outside the market framework can affect the skill differential. Government measures to validate growing egalitarianism through establishment and elevation of minimum wages, for example, tend to compress the occupational wage structure. Unions might affect the structure by exerting unbalanced wage pressure on behalf of the skilled or the unskilled. When these noncompetitive forces are effective, they, of course, affect relative employment as well as wages.

In the first section of this chapter, the historical movement in the skill differential will be examined with reference to the above competitive and noncompetitive forces affecting relative labor supply and occupational wage differences.[3] Specifically, these forces will serve to explain the long-term compression of the occupational wage structure and the leveling off of this trend that seemed to set in since the early 1950's. Then the hypothesis that the narrowing of the absolute real differential, which results when all wages rise by an equal percentage, serves as

---

[2] In a study of 1939 wage data, Kenneth M. McCaffree, "The Earnings Differential Between White Collar and Manual Occupations," *Review of Economics and Statistics,* **35** (February 1953), pp. 20–30, concluded that not all of the wage differences between the two groups examined represented compensating differences. He speculated that a small part of the difference was attributable to differences in ability and financial resources among workers, making white collar workers a noncompeting group for some unskilled workers.

[3] In the long run, the differential is affected by changes in supply, or changes in adjustment of supply to changing demand conditions. Confusion and uncertainty describe the theorizing on the direction of relative demand for skills under changing technology. There are probably more writers on automation who claim that the new technology creates greater demand for skilled workers than those who think labor demand shifts toward the unskilled. As for the old technology, or mass production and wider application of machinery, there was probably an illogical bias toward thinking that machines substituted for skilled labor while they increased the productivity of the unskilled. For example, Lloyd G. Reynolds and Cynthia Taft, *The Evolution of Wage Structure,* Yale University Press, New Haven, 1956, p. 357, explain the narrowing of the skill differential on the grounds "that many skilled occupations are becoming less skilled, arduous, and responsible, with the improvement of mechanical equipment. . . ."

On the other hand, Harry M. Douty, "Union Impact on Wage Structure," Proceedings of the *Sixth Annual Meeting of the Industrial Relations Research Association* (December 1955), pp. 67–68, claims that the increased mechanization of unskilled labor and consequent increase in its productivity has been a factor narrowing the skill differential.

an independent force acting to reduce percentage differentials will be examined critically.

In the second section, two theories which explain the characteristic cyclical pattern of narrowing wages differentials during prosperous periods and widening during recessions will be examined. The theories offer alternative but not necessarily conflicting explanations. Finally, the importance of inflation as an independent narrowing force will be studied.

SECULAR CHANGES IN THE SKILL DIFFERENTIAL

Trends and Forces Affecting the Skill Differential

There are two customary ways of measuring changes in interoccupational wages. Changes in dispersion in the whole structure or movements of the ratio of the highest (skilled) to the lowest (unskilled) wages serve as the measure of occupational wage changes. The first relationship refers to the occupational structure, the second to the skill differential. This chapter deals mainly with the latter relationship, for which more statistical and theoretical studies have been made. Although the skill differential compares the extremes of the wage structure, it applies to many workers in that the customary method of measurement involves not just the few workers earning the highest and lowest wages, but the average wage of a group of highly paid skilled workers and the average wage of a large number of unskilled workers.

In any case it should be stressed that changes in the skill differential need not parallel changes in the structure. Statistically, it is obviously possible for the coefficient of variation of a group of occupational wages—a good measure of structural changes—to decline, while the ratio of a group of highest to a group of lowest wages—usual measure of the skill differential—remains stable or increases.

Economically, the divergence can be explained with reference to the concept of noncompeting groups. Assume a steady growth throughout the occupational structure in the demand for training and education for its own sake, not in response to the economic variables of a relative decline in training costs or in a relative rise in income potential for trained workers, but in response to social pressures or increased consumption benefits of education. Both the occupational wage structure and skill differential would tend to narrow under this influence because the supply of skilled labor would increase and the supply of unskilled labor would decrease, autonomously, as labor upgraded its capacities all along the line.[4] But assume that changing technology makes greater demands on the breadth and intensity of acquired skills. Then the desire to upgrade skills meets a capacity or ability barrier for the higher skilled jobs. The end result of the flow of labor upward can then be a rise in the unskilled wage relative to the semiskilled wage, as greater autonomous increases in training of the unskilled swell the ranks of the semiskilled; but a fall in the wage of the semiskilled relative to the skilled occurs as the flow upward from the semiskilled is reduced by the barrier of incapacity to acquire the highest skills. This barrier leaves a wage gap between the semiskilled and skilled larger than that attributable to the discounted costs and returns of attaining the highest skills. The wage structure narrows under this process because of the relative growth of the semiskilled group even though the skill differential remains more or less constant. The process assumes finer gradations of job differences in the lower to middle job classification than from the middle to upper steps; it assumes missing rungs near the top of the skill ladder.

Data on Skill Differentials

Whether changes in interoccupational wages are measured by changes in the occupational structure or by relative movements in the skill differential, the data point strongly to a narrowing trend over the first half of this century.

Keat's comprehensive study of structure changes shows an annual rate of decline in the coefficient of variation of 114 American manufacturing occupational wages of over 0.5 percent from 1903 to 1956.[5] Studies by Ober and Kanninen show a narrowing of the skill differential (skilled relative to unskilled wage as an index) in manufacturing from 205 in 1907 to 155 in 1945–1947 to 137 in 1952–1953.[6]

Since the mid-fifties, though, there has been an unmistakable stabilizing trend in the differential. This trend is discernible not only in the

---

[4] This assumes that opportunities for the upgrading of skills are more limited for the highly skilled than for the unskilled, a reasonable assumption in the short run, during which techniques and processes of production are more or less fixed.

[5] Paul G. Keat, "Long-Run Changes in Occupational Wage Structure, 1900–1956," *Journal of Political Economy,* **68** (December 1960), pp. 584–600.

[6] Harry Ober, "Occupational Wage Differentials, 1907–1947," *Monthly Labor Review,* **71** (August 1948), pp. 127–134, presents the data through 1947, and Toivo Kanninen, "Occupational Wage Relationships in Manufacturing," *Monthly Labor Review,* **76** (November 1953), pp. 1171–1178, presents the 1952–1953 data. However, when Kanninen's data are adjusted to Ober's method of calculation, the 1952–1953 differential rises to 145, indicating a slighter narrowing trend over the latter years. For the adjustment technique see Richard Perlman, "Forces Widening Occupational Wage Differentials," *Review of Economics and Statistics,* **40** (May 1958), pp. 107–109.

United States[7] but also in other advanced economies such as Italy, West Germany, Switzerland, and the United Kingdom.[8] In these countries, too, recent stability has followed a long period of narrowing.

Explanations of the long-term narrowing trend are easier to find than those of the recent reversal. For the United States, during the period 1900–1950, one need only cite the narrowing influence of the autonomous increase in the demand for education and training,[9] the development of mass production and the declining complexity of skilled work making the skilled category less of a noncompeting group, the drying up of the flow of immigrants into the ranks of the unskilled, and the expansion of egalitarian sentiment reflected in the development and extension of legal minimum wages.[10]

[7] Extending Kanninen's technique to more recent years, a labor department study found that the differential remained exactly constant at 137 over the decade 1953–1962. Donald J. Blackmore "Occupational Wage Relationships in Metropolitan Areas, 1961–1962," *Monthly Labor Review,* **86** (December 1963), p. 1431.

Further statistical evidence of recent constancy in the skill differential is found in Martin Segal, "Occupational Wage Differentials in Major Cities During the 1950's," *Human Resources in the Urban Economy,* edited by Mark Perlman, Johns Hopkins Press, Baltimore, 1963, p. 197. For 16 cities using fewer occupations than in other studies, Segal found the skill index, measured by Kanninen's method of the median of city indices, constant at 146 for the period 1951–1961.

Because the differential widened in 11 of the 16 cities, George H. Hildebrand and George E. Delehanty, "Wage Levels and Differentials," *Prosperity and Unemployment,* Wiley, New York, 1966, p. 285, cite Segal's findings as indicating a widening of the differential. But the method of measurement that compares only the instances of widening with those of narrowing instead of a comparison of overall average changes is inconsistent with the technique of other studies. In their own study of 16 cities for the period 1952–1964, Hildebrand and Delehanty, *op. cit.,* pp. 283–285, claimed they found a narrowing trend because the index of skilled wages rose more than the index of unskilled wages in only 5 cities. But consistent with the method of other studies, the median index of the differentials (skilled earnings index divided by unskilled earnings index) stood at 99 for the latter year, a value in keeping with the constancy of the differential found in other studies.

[8] For the data on recent international changes in the skill differential, see H. Gunter, "Changes in Occupational Wage Differentials," *International Labour Review,* **89** (February 1964), pp. 136–155. In a close study of the British situation, Edwin Mansfield, "A Note on Skill Wage Differentials in Britain, 1948–1954," *Review of Economics and Statistics,* **39** (August 1957), pp. 348–351, found a slowing down of the narrowing trend in the early postwar years, with the index of unskilled wages (skilled wages = 100) rising only from 80 to 83 for the period 1948–1954, compared with a movement from 70 to 79 over the 1939–1946 period.

[9] For an early familiar treatment of the role of expanded education on narrowing the skill differential, see Allen G. B. Fisher, "Education and Relative Wage Rates," *International Labour Review,* **25** (June 1932), pp. 742–764.

[10] For an expanded discussion of most of these narrowing forces, see Earl Muntz,

Also since the mid-fifties, new forces and changes in the old may explain the recent stability in the skill differential. As for the old forces, the decline in flow of immigrants and agricultural workers into the ranks of the unskilled has been taking place for a long time. For the skill differential to narrow because of the influence of migration, it is necessary that this flow fall over time to reduce the stock of unskilled labor at a particular time and thus exert narrowing pressure on the skill differential. Certainly, for immigration, the flow into the unskilled ranks has long since stopped declining; thus, on balance, immigration has at best for some time, certainly since the 1950's, been a stabilizing influence on the skill differential.

As for the autonomous drive for training and education, it has undoubtedly continued to expand over recent years. There is no need to overstate the case for stability in the skill differential. Some forces may act in a narrowing, direction, and it can be admitted that the growing trend toward education and training acts as such a force.

As for new forces, the growth of secondary workers in the work force and increased labor-force participation of women, especially in response to reasonably easy job availability that has characterized the postwar period, serve as modern counterparts to the flow of immigrants and former agricultural workers that kept the skill differential from contracting in the past, prior to about 1920. As Reder notes, increased labor-force participation of women may only reflect increased demand for their services[11] but, at the same time, as homework has become easier, part of the increased supply may be autonomous in response to increased job opportunities if not to actual job openings.[12]

"The Decline in Wage Differentials Based on Skill in the United States," *International Labour Review,* **71** (June 1955), pp. 575–592.

The role of unions as an equalizing force is somewhat questionable. H. A. Turner, "Trade Unions, Differentials, and the Levelling of Wages," *Manchester School of Economics and Social Studies,* **21** (September 1952), pp. 227–282, and "Inflation and Wage Differentials in Great Britain," *The Theory of Wage Determination,* edited by John T. Dunlop, St. Martin's Press, New York, 1957, p. 133, argues that unions on balance have narrowed the skill differential in Great Britain because of the growing influence of unskilled members.

For the United States, though, Reynolds and Taft, *op. cit.,* p. 186, and Clark Kerr, "Wage Relationships—The Comparative Impact of Market and Power Forces," *The Theory of Wage Determination,* pp. 188–189, conclude that unions have played no particular role in strengthening the narrowing trend, which began before their widespread emergence.

[11] Melvin Reder, "Wage Differentials: Theory and Measurement," *Aspects of Labor Economics,* pp. 266–267 and p. 266, n. 12.

[12] See Chapter IX for this distinction.

One new speculative widening force relates to changing technology and changing industrial demand for labor. Although it is debatable whether the new technology, or automation, increases the relative numerical demand for skilled workers, it is reasonable to assume that the complexity of job requirements has intensified over the level demanded by previous technology. In reality, it is the complexity of skilled jobs as well as the number of skilled workers required that partially determines the skill differential.

It is usually argued that during the early stages of economic development the skill differential widens because the increased demand for skilled labor faces a short supply. But what causes the shortage is the inability to transfer skills from old to new technology, an inability perpetuated by relatively high training costs and high returns on alternative investment. It can be argued that mechanization does not require relatively more skilled than unskilled labor than characterized the prior preindustrial labor mix. But because of the difficulty of transferring preindustrial skills into those required by mechanized industry and the comparative ease with which unskilled labor (including workers with obsolete skills) can transfer into unskilled industrial jobs, temporary shortage of skilled labor appears.

This argument suggests that since the 1950's, changing American industrial requirements have created problems in labor supply similar to those facing a developing country. A temporary noncompeting group of skilled labor has been created, not based on the old causes of social stratification posed by Mill and Cairnes when they introduced the concept, but on perhaps temporary barriers of knowledge and ability.[13]

The importance of this speculative widening force is of course questionable, but if it is a valid explanation of recent stability in the skill differential, then the expectation is for a later resumption of the narrowing trend as the economy "develops" and the temporary barriers of inadequate knowledge and capacities are broken, and they will be broken if the autonomous growth in demand for education and training continues.

Human Capital and the Skill Differential

Emphasis on the human capital aspects of labor provides the capitalistic answer to Marxist doctrine by turning it inside out. Whereas Marxism

---

[13] Melvin Reder, "Wage Structure and Structural Unemployment," *Review of Economic Studies*, **31** (October 1964), p. 315, attributes the failure of the differential to continue its narrowing trend in the post-World War II period partly to the slow adjustment of labor supply to more rapidly changing types of skill demanded.

considers capital the embodiment of labor, the "human capitalism" school sees differences in labor quality as the reflection of differential amounts of capital applied.

One interpretation of this investment approach to labor has been the view that the standard practice of measuring skill differentials on a percentage rather than an absolute basis leads to faulty conclusions regarding the direction of forces operating on the skill differential. More specifically, the position is reached that, although percentage differences apply to the explanation of effects on and of relative labor demand for the skilled and unskilled, it is the absolute difference that influences labor supply. That is, supply of skilled workers tends to increase with a widening of the absolute differential (skilled wages minus unskilled), even if the percentage differential (skilled wage as relative to unskilled) should narrow.

The implications of this conclusion, to be criticized in the following discussion, on the long-run pattern of the percentage differential are obvious. Movements in the percentage differential are affected by relative changes in supply and demand of skilled and unskilled labor. Wages in general advance secularly, if for no other reason than because of upward pressures generated by productivity growth. With no change in relative labor demand, the percentage skill differential would remain constant, while the absolute differential widened. If the supply of skilled labor reacted positively to the widening of the absolute differential, then a persistent narrowing influence on the percentage differential, operating from the supply side, would be felt. This upward bias to the supply of skilled workers could thus serve as a forceful explanation of the secular percentage narrowing that took place in the past, and as a basis for arguing that the narrowing trend will be resumed in the future.[14]

Gary Becker, in his path-breaking article on investment in human capital, first presented the view that a widening of the absolute real differential would stimulate investment in training, increase the relative supply of skilled labor, and narrow the percentage differential.[15] This

---

[14] There is nothing in this theory that argues whether the percentage or absolute basis is the correct standard to measure relative changes in welfare for the two groups. While the percentage basis is generally used, and is implicitly applied in this theory, a contrary view is tenable. John Dunlop, "Discussion of Papers on Behavior of Wages," *Proceedings of the Sixteenth Annual Meeting of the Industrial Relations Research Association* (December 1953), p. 82, for example, disputes the wisdom of unqualified use of the percentage criterion.

[15] Gary Becker, "Investment in Human Capital: A Theoretical Analysis," *Journal of Political Economy,* **70,** Supplement (October 1962), pp. 39–41.

Becker carefully notes that the absolute *real* differential and not just the money

conclusion has remained unchallenged.[16] Nevertheless, closer examination reveals that, even for labor supply, the percentage and not the absolute difference determines the demand for training and supply of skilled labor. This conclusion is not in accord with Becker's that the narrowing of the percentage skill differential partially reflects increased supply of skilled labor induced by technological change—which widened the absolute differential. Thus the counterargument presented here supports the more conventional thesis that the supply of skilled labor has increased autonomously, not in response to the economic stimulus of an increased rate of return on skills.

The view that absolute rather than percentage differentials are an important independent determinant of demand for training and supply of skilled labor is based on the undeniable fact that the internal rate of return on investment in skill—defined as the rate of discount equating the present value of lifetime returns to skill, measured by the ratio of the differences between skilled and unskilled wages, over time, to the present value of all costs related to acquiring skill—rises with an increase in the absolute skill differential. This assumes, of course, that an initial change in the absolute skill differential is expected to be maintained over future periods. However, granted that the rate of return on capital invested in training increases with a rise in the absolute spread between the wage of trained and untrained workers, it does not follow that this rise in the internal rate will exceed a concurrent rise in returns to other investments. Moreover, the crucial determinant of whether a change in the internal rate of return on investment in training, r, will lead to an increased demand for training and, consequently, an increased supply of skilled workers depends on the relationship of Δr to Δi, the change in the rate of return on other investments. Thus, to deny Becker's

---

differential is the proper measure. If all prices rose the same amount the money differential would widen but, relevant to his conclusions, the rate of return on investment in training would not change. The difference between real and money differential is more than academic. The absolute real differential can narrow while the absolute money differential widens. The absolute real differential will widen only if the percentage increase in the absolute money differential exceeds the percentage change in prices. For an explanation of the relationship between money and real differentials, see Richard Perlman, "A Note on the Measurement of Real Wage Differentials," *Review of Economics and Statistics*, **41** (May 1959), pp. 192–195.

In this section, when not mentioned, the real differential is implied.

[16] Becker, in *Human Capital*, pp. 52–55, saw no need to change his analysis. Melvin Reder, "Wage Differentials: Theory and Measurement," *Aspects of Labor Economics*, p. 259, accepted Becker's view.

argument that absolute rather than relative movements in the skilled-unskilled wage structure are relevant for labor supply, it is only necessary to demonstrate that for cases in which the absolute difference rises while the relative difference falls, the rise in i will exceed that of r.[17]

Consider the sources of an increase in r. Becker poses the condition of a neutral technological advance in which progress is uniform for all factors.[18] Under constant costs, prices would remain constant while all wages rose by the same proportion. Then the percentage wage differential would remain constant. Absolute wage differences would rise by the same rate as the uniform relative increase in wage rates and r would rise by the same amount.[19] Meanwhile, since progress is neutral with respect to all factors, the rate of return to other investment would rise by the same amount as r. This equal change to all factors leaves no residual in favor of investment in skills to serve as a source of increased supply of skilled labor.

Consider next the case in which progress is not neutral. Assume three factors, capital and labor divided into two subgroups of equal size—skilled and unskilled workers—with technological change such as to increase the demand for capital and labor as a whole equally, but to increase the demand for unskilled labor relative to that of skilled labor. Under these conditions, the increase in the average rate of return to labor as a whole will equal the increase in the rate of return to capital.

[17] In evaluating whether investment in college education has been excessive, Becker himself measures the rate of return on this investment against that of other investments. "Underinvestment in College Education?" *American Economic Review,* Papers and Proceedings, **50** (May 1960), pp. 346–354.

In fact, it may be argued that in equilibrium the rate of return on investment in the human resource must exceed that of investment in nonhuman resources because the owner of the former resource does not have the option of liquidating his investment. This point is made in Pesek and Saving, *op. cit.,* p. **273.** (One can think of exceptions to this general rule; a professor leaving the profession may write a textbook.) This inseparable tie between the human resource and its owner, on the other hand, also explains the reluctance of others to invest in an individual's training. Expressed by Richard S. Eckaus, "Education and Economic Growth," *Economics of Higher Education,* p. **126,** "The ultimate vesting of ownership of his labor with the individual forestalls general reliance on business sponsorship. . . ."

[18] This is the Hicksian form of the term, in which technological progress leaves the ratio of marginal products of factors unchanged. Hicks, *Theory of Wages,* pp. **121–122.**

[19] This is Becker's analysis, which would not be weakened by an adjustment to a rise in productivity that yielded a downward movement in prices, factor returns remaining constant, for then r would rise because of a decline in training costs. This latter adjustment path, however, would not show the relationship between changes in the absolute differential and supply of skilled labor—the issue here.

Expressed algebraically,

$$\Delta i = \frac{sWs_0 + uWu_0}{Ws_0 + Wu_0}$$

with
$$i = \text{rate of return on capital}$$
$$s = \text{rate of increase in skilled wage}$$
$$u = \text{rate of increase in unskilled wage}$$
$$Ws_0 = \text{skilled wage before technological change}$$
$$Wu_0 = \text{unskilled wage before technological change}$$

The change in r, the internal rate of return on investment in skills, takes the form

$$\Delta r = \frac{sWs_0 - uWu_0}{Ws_0 - Wu_0} \text{[20]}$$

Accordingly,

$$\Delta i - \Delta r = \frac{sWs_0 + uWu_0}{Ws_0 + Wu_0} - \frac{sWs_0 - uWu_0}{Ws_0 - Wu_0}$$

which reduces to

$$\Delta i - \Delta r = \frac{2Ws_0Wu_0(u - s)}{Ws_0^2 - Wu_0^2}$$

which is positive when u is greater than s.

Thus, when the unskilled wage increases at a greater rate than the skilled wage (while technology advances neutrally between capital and labor as a whole), the rate of return on invested capital rises more than the internal rate of return on investment in training. Insofar as the decision on whether to undergo training is based on the return to acquisi-

---

[20] The fraction only measures the rate of return due to the wage change. Since technological advance is no longer neutral, all prices do not remain constant. Therefore, the other elements determining r—cost of training including income foregone during training—may vary, depending on the factor components they contain. Since income foregone would probably reflect earnings from unskilled labor, while the skilled and unskilled labor components of training costs are uncertain, it might be argued that the fraction overstates Δr because of the relative rise in unskilled wages.

Even when technological change is neutral, treatment of foregone earnings creates problems. It could be argued that foregone earnings would rise with the increase in unskilled wages, thus offsetting the increase in returns to training brought about by the increase in the absolute wage differential. Becker, "Investment in Human Capital," p. 40, n. 61, argues, though, that foregone earnings would not rise, since neutral technological progress leads to an equivalent increase in the productivity of a student's time. This explanation, however, assumes that every hour saved in school time would be transferred to the labor market—certainly a heroic assumption in view of the discussion of Chapter I.

tion of skills as an investment to be compared with the return on other investments, a narrowing of the percentage skill differential would weaken the incentive to invest in skill and reduce the future relative supply of skilled labor. This conclusion follows even if the absolute rise in the skilled wage exceeded that of the unskilled wage, since the crucial determinant is the change in the relative rates, not in absolute levels.

But what if nonneutral technological change favored labor as a whole? In this case, even though the demand for unskilled labor rose more than that for skilled labor (indicating that new techniques favored the use of unskilled workers)[21] and their wages consequently rose relatively higher than skilled wages, the return on investment in acquiring skills might increase above that of the return on other investments. This condition, however, offers no support to the Becker thesis. What stimulates the incentive to invest in skill in this case is not the change in the absolute level of wage differences in favor of the skilled that might occur, but the relative fall in return on other investments. In fact, if the changes in productive processes weigh heavily enough in favor of labor and against capital, the incentive to invest in training might strengthen, and the future supply of skilled workers might increase even if the absolute wage difference between skilled and unskilled workers narrows, since the returns to capital would have fallen even more than those from investment in training.

In arguing his point, Becker makes the logical assumption of neutral technological advancement but, as has been explained, this type of growth creates no particular stimulus to investment in training, instead of in physical capital, nor favors increasing the relative future supply of skilled workers. In cases in which progress is neutral (with respect to physical capital and labor as a whole) but factor demand favors the unskilled over the skilled, so that wages of the unskilled rise relative to those of the skilled, investment in skills will be discouraged no matter how great the widening of the absolute differential. The adjustment of relative supply of the two types of labor would tend to widen the skill differential to its previous level, tending to equate the returns to investment in human capital with that on nonhuman investment. Whether this equilibrium is ever achieved is, of course, an empirical question.

---

[21] The much debated issue of whether automation displaces the skilled more than the unskilled is relevant here. Although most writers seem to hold that the "new technology" presses hard against the unskilled, Stanley Lebergott, "Unemployment: A Perspective," *Men Without Work*, edited by Lebergott, Prentice-Hall, Englewood Cliffs, N.J., 1964, pp. 29–33, offers statistical support for the view that automation does not particularly increase the relative demand for skilled labor.

The argument that the skill differential still narrowed, even after the inflow of immigrants ceased declining, say from the period 1920–1950, because of a decline in time and real money costs of education[22] is subject to the same criticism as that of the view that a rise in the absolute differential resulting from neutral technology was a narrowing force. Under neutral technological change, the costs of other investments would tend to fall proportionately, assuming that the share of productivity gain taken in the form of lower prices was uniformly distributed throughout the economy. The returns to investment in human capital would tend to rise in step with those of other investments. At the same time, the returns to "undeveloped labor" would rise equivalently, so that there would be no tendency for a relative increase in the supply of factors requiring investment, whether human or nonhuman, over the supply of unskilled labor.

But the skill differential did narrow over a long period, even when the differential was no longer subject to the disequilibrating narrowing force of reduced immigration. To suggest that this narrowing indicates a decline in the average rate of return on investment in education and training,[23] while the rate of return of nonhuman capital was rising, is to assume that decisions to invest in human capital were made without regard to economic elements or that relative supply of the two types of labor was in long-run disequilibrium.

An argument that the skill differential has narrowed autonomously, brought about by an increased supply in skilled labor (not in response to a relative increase in demand for skills but by a change in tastes toward more education and training, perhaps in response to higher incomes), is not inconsistent with a rise in the rate of return to investment in education or training. That is, the skill differential may narrow, while the rate of return on human investment keeps pace with the rising rate of return on nonhuman investment. Increased tastes for education can be translated into greater consumption benefits from education, even if these benefits involve no more than avoidance of the social stigma of not going to school that has arisen as a greater percentage of the population has become educated.

An increase in the consumption element in education increases the pure investment returns for a given expense on education. In fact, the

---

[22] Keat, *op. cit.*, pp. 598–600, offers this explanation.

[23] Becker, "Investment in Human Capital," p. 40, and Theodore W. Schultz, *The Economic Value of Education*, Columbia University Press, New York, 1963, p. 53, claim that analysts have erroneously concluded that the secular decline in the skill differential indicated a decline in the returns to skill. The literature does not appear to disclose this confusion.

narrowing of the skill differential, which tends to occur as the relative supply of educated and trained workers increases, may be an equilibrating force that keeps the rates of return on investment in human capital from outpacing the advance on returns to nonhuman investment.

CYCLICAL MOVEMENTS IN THE SKILL DIFFERENTIAL

Just as differential changes in supply and demand of skilled and unskilled labor can explain long-run movements in the skill differential, so too can these basic economic elements account for the cyclical variations in the relative wages of the skilled and unskilled. The facts to which any theory of these variations must adjust are a widening of the differential and a smaller decline in employment among the skilled during the downturn, with opposite relationships during the prosperity phase of the cycle. Supply and demand changes mainly in the recession will be treated, but the theories discussed apply to the prosperity phases as well, *mutatis mutandis*.

In addition, price changes are often suggested as an independent variable affecting the cyclical skill differential. For variety's sake, the effect of inflation as a narrowing influence during prosperity will be studied.

Returning to supply and demand, alternative theories have either stressed the relative increase in supply of the unskilled or relative increase in demand for the skilled during recessions. The former theory is associated with the writings of Melvin Reder,[24] the latter with the human-capital approach to labor demand, as exemplified by the analysis of Walter Oi.[25]

THEORIES OF REDER AND OI. In Reder's theory, as the economy weakens and the demand for both skilled and unskilled labor falls, hiring and job qualification standards tighten all along the skill ladder. Downward mobility of labor accounts for a relative increase in supply of the unskilled and decline of the skilled, as displaced workers (unable to meet more exacting standards) move to less demanding work. (Even without a tightening of standards, displaced skilled workers could compete with the lesser skilled but this additional expansion in supply of the unskilled, which plays no role in Reder's theory, would only reinforce his conclu-

[24] Melvin Reder, "The Theory of Occupational Wage Differentials," pp. 833–852. Reder offers variations on this theory in "Wage Differentials: Theory and Measurement," *Aspects of Labor Economics*, pp. 269–276.
[25] Walter Oi, "Labor as a Quasi-Fixed Factor," *Journal of Political Economy*, **70** (December 1962), pp. 538–555.

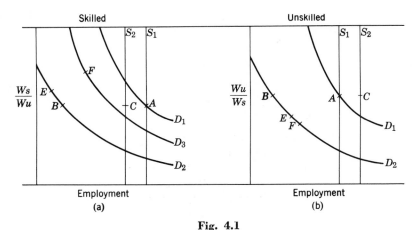

Fig. 4.1

Changes in labor supply and demand during recession.

sions.) Finally, the relative increase in supply of the unskilled acts to lower unskilled more than skilled wages.

Figures 4.1a and 4.1b present the Reder hypothesis in its simplest form. The decline in demand is assumed equal for both types of labor. Supply schedules are fixed after the shift from the skilled to unskilled categories resulting from tightened standards.

Initially there is no change in the skill differential as the wage and employment equilibrium point moves from A to position B on each demand curve after the decline in demand. Employment falls equally, but unemployment increases more for the unskilled than the skilled—BC on each figure.

Because of greater unemployment, there will be greater downward wage pressure for the unskilled than for the skilled, and it is this differential wage pressure that gives rise to the widening of the skill differential. Finally, with the rise in skilled to unskilled wages, position E is reached on both graphs, and the wage differential has expanded from its prerecession level.

Two implied assumptions of the graph need explanation. First, factor substitution of labor by skill must be possible since, no matter how great the relative increase in unemployment of the unskilled, there would be no incentive for these workers to seek a lower wage if they could not narrow the unemployment gap. Second, there must be some inflexibility in wages (of the skilled) to a reduction in the unskilled wage. If skilled workers reacted to protect their employment position at all costs, even if they suffered relatively lower unemployment than the unskilled,

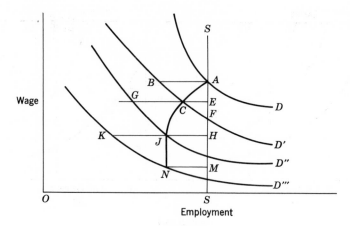

Fig. 4.2

Wage-employment schedule.

then any wage reduction among the unskilled would be met by an equal reduction for the skilled, leaving the skill differential unchanged.[26]

A degree of inflexibility in wage response to unemployment, in turn, implies that, despite its shape, the S lines in Figures 4.1a and 4.1b do not reflect perfectly inelastic supply schedules. Such schedules mean that the assumed fixed supply will offer itself at any wage to reduce unemployment. On the other hand, short-run fixity of supply, depicted here, implies that the amount of labor available at any *established* wage remains constant. The established wage, in turn, depends on the level of employment and unemployment for a particular group of workers.

Consider a decline from full employment for either group resulting from a decline in labor demand consequent to a fall in aggregate demand. Assume a fixed labor supply. In Figure 4.2, the labor-demand schedule falls from D to D'. Because of the fall in employment from A to B and the appearance of unemployment, the fixed supply of labor accepts a wage reduction from SA to SE to increase employment and reduce unemployment to CE. What is crucial to the analysis is that the acceptable wage does not fall to SF. For if it did, then the wage would be completely flexible to a potential rise in unemployment and, to repeat, it would be impossible for the skill differential to widen. Each labor

---

[26] Note that these assumptions are directly opposite to the implied simplified Keynesian ones of lack of factor substitutability and complete wage flexibility, to be discussed in Chapter VII.

class would in effect strive for full employment at whatever wage and, specifically, the skilled would refuse to allow their relative wage to rise at the cost of part of their relatively superior unemployment position.

If demand fell to D'' and unemployment rose to EG, the labor involved would lower its wage to reduce unemployment. The new position would find the wage at H with unemployment at HJ.

Note that J lies to the left of C, indicating that the workers are still willing to increase their unemployment in order not to suffer the full drop in wages required to maintain employment. At the same time, they have reduced their inclination to trade unemployment for the maintenance of wages.[27] At J, however, it can be assumed that wages will be completely flexible, that is, workers will be unwilling to increase unemployment to prevent wages from falling to the extent required to maintain employment.

Then if demand falls to D''', so that unemployment would rise to HK, the wage will fall to SM to reduce unemployment to MN, the same level as HJ.

The locus of points A, E, H, M, etc., would seem to describe a conventional perfectly inelastic short-run labor-supply curve. But the line so drawn does not represent a true supply curve. It does not indicate that OS units of labor will be offered at any wage but, instead, every point along SS corresponds to a particular wage and level of employment. The locus of points A, C, J, N, etc., is certainly not a supply curve either but may be called a wage-employment schedule, showing the resulting wage and employment, as short-run supply schedules shift downward in response to changing demand and unemployment potential. Thus there is not a single supply schedule but, in effect, a family of perfectly elastic curves that shift downward when the fixed quantity of labor offers its services at successively lower wages as the demand for labor falls.

Supply curves of this type can explain the widening of the skill differential as the volume of available unskilled labor increases and that of skilled labor declines, while demand for each type falls equivalently. With a potential relative rise in unemployment for the unskilled, the relative downward wage pressure for unskilled wages becomes effective and the wage differential widens. But if this were all that the Reder hypothesis entailed, it would not fit the facts of cyclical declines. If supply adjustments alone affected the differential, as Figure 4.1 shows, the result would be a decline in employment, if not necessarily a rise

---

[27] The assumption here is of a declining marginal rate of substitution of employment for wages.

in unemployment, for the skilled compared to the unskilled as point E was reached on Figures 4.1a and 4.1b. But, in fact, the usual cyclical pattern shows a slighter reduction in employment of the skilled than for the unskilled.

In effect, though, Reder's theory adjusts to this shortcoming by introducing factors that can explain differential declines in demand for both types of labor as total labor demand declines. Specifically, the demand for skilled labor tends to decline less than that of the unskilled as job standards tighten.

The argument for relative stability in demand for skilled workers relates to the greater variety and complexity of tasks performed by those on the higher rungs of the skill ladder, compared to the job duties of the unskilled. Thus the possible variation in labor quality among the skilled is greater than among the unskilled, so that an employer who tightens standards more or less equally by, say, a method of retaining an equal percentage of the best of all labor classes will find the efficiency of his skilled staff strengthened more than that of his unskilled workers.[28]

Furthermore, during slack periods with particular production runs more sporadic than in good times, there is greater incentive for employers to retain the most qualified, broadly trained workers who can generalize their skills among many operations. In short, although firms will tend to lay off workers all along the skill spectrum, they will have a much greater tendency to use superior overall productivity as a criterion in retention of the skilled than for lesser-skilled workers.[29]

An argument in support of the view that recession demand for skilled workers falls less than that of the unskilled, within the Reder framework,

---

[28] At first view it might appear that the downward movement of displaced skilled workers will serve as a strong independent force raising the quality of the unskilled class, which they temporarily join. Operating against this possibility are two factors. First, movement down the skill ladder is probably made one rung at a time, so that new entries to the unskilled ranks come not from the highly trained but from those only slightly more trained. Second, and more important, there is no reason to assume that those with higher skills perform unskilled work more efficiently than those customarily attached to the unskilled work force.

[29] This argument just reverses that presented by Reder, "Wage Differentials: Theory and Measurement," p. 270, to show that during boom (war) periods there is a greater tendency to hire partially instead of broadly trained skilled workers when particular production runs are continuous. Here, of course, we are discussing depression conditions.

Note that this theory refers to the stability of demand for broadly trained (skilled) workers who can perform more than one operation compared to the demand for unskilled labor. It does not touch on the question of the change in demand for broadly trained workers opposed to that of workers who have received specific training, an issue discussed below.

concerns that part of job performance dependent on experience. Each occupation has a learning curve that reaches a maximum after a certain period on the job. Assuming that the learning curve levels off after a longer period for skilled than for unskilled work, it would take new workers a still relatively longer time to reach the maximum point on the learning curve, when output was sporadic during recession, than for the unskilled. Thus, firms would have a greater incentive to prevent turnover, that is, to retain skilled workers during recession than to keep the unskilled; the demand for skilled workers would fall relatively less than that of unskilled workers.[30] But this argument comes very close to the explanation of cyclical variations in the skill differential based on the human capital approach.

In any case, Reder's theory needs and implies a greater relative stability in demand for skilled labor. In Figure 4.1a, D_3 is drawn not to show an increase in demand for skilled workers from D_2, but as a correction of the curve to indicate that the demand for skilled labor fell less than that of unskilled labor during the recession. With unemployment for them at each wage much reduced at D_3 compared to D_2, the skilled workers would trade some of the employment gain, if they were to seek relative wage E on the corrected demand curve, for a higher wage. Thus F would lie above E, and the wage differential would widen. Unemployment for unskilled workers would consequently fall but, what is most important, the theory would match the data in that employment for the skilled would now exceed that of the unskilled. F would lie further from the Y-axis on Figure 4.1a than on Figure 4.1b.

A much simpler explanation of the widening of the skill differential during business slumps is offered by Walter Oi, who explains the widening exclusively on the basis of a smaller decline in the demand for skilled workers.[31] The decision of whether to retain skilled workers in whom the firm has invested specific training expenses depends not only on current returns but also on the need to amortize these training costs. These costs add a fixed element to labor costs and introduce an element encouraging retention of the skilled even if the returns on skilled labor (current value productivity) did not temporarily cover their variable costs (wage). A weaker tendency to reduce employment of skilled labor could be expressed by a slighter leftward shift in the demand schedule of skilled than unskilled labor for a given fall in total labor demand. This pattern is presented in Figures 4.3a and 4.3b, in which only labor demand is assumed to change.

[30] This theory is advanced by Louis R. Salkever, *Toward a Wage Structure Theory,* Humanities Press, New York, 1964, pp. 140 and 150.
[31] Oi, *op. cit.,* pp. 553–554.

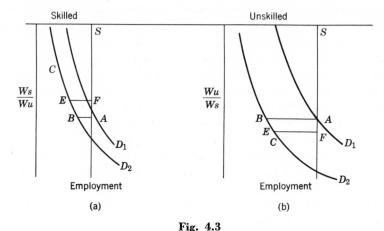

Fig. 4.3

Change in labor demand during recession.

With no change in the skill differential, unemployment at relative wage A would be greater for the unskilled than the skilled. There would be a tendency for the skill differential to widen as the unskilled traded a reduced wage for lower unemployment, while the skilled accepted this trade by increasing their relative wage at the cost of higher unemployment. At point C the volume of unemployment would be the same for both groups.

The equilibrium point, however, would not reach C. Assuming a declining marginal rate of substitution of employment for wages for both groups (see Figure 4.2), with equal unemployment but a relatively higher wage for the skilled than the unskilled, the tendency for the skilled to trade wages for increased employment—reduced unemployment—would be matched by a tendency for the unskilled to trade more employment for higher wages. The downward movement for skilled and upward movement for unskilled along D_2 would stop at point E where the marginal rate of substitution of employment for wages would be equal for both groups. At this point, the wage differential would have widened from its predepression level, and the employment of the skilled would have fallen less than that of the unskilled—EF in each case.

Although it is usual for the skill differential to widen during recessions, the Great Depression of 1929–1933 provides an important exception to this rule. Then the skill differential remained relatively unchanged from its predepression level.[32] Reference to Figures 4.2 and 4.3 can explain

[32] While Ober's data indicated a widening for the shorter period 1931–1932, Philip

this phenomenon. Figure 4.3 shows that with a change in relative labor demand, unemployment at the same wage differential is much less for the skilled than for the unskilled. At first view then, it would appear that the skilled would be willing to trade extra unemployment for somewhat higher wages.

But Figure 4.2 tells us that when unemployment reaches a relatively high level the marginal rate of substitution of employment for wages approaches zero.

Recalling the severity of the Great Depression, it can be assumed that even for the skilled, who suffered a *relatively* slight reduction in demand for their services, the point was reached when they protected their employment at all costs, when they refused to gain any higher (relative) wage at the cost of additional unemployment. Thus, as a result of a deep enough depression, the differential shifts in demand between skilled and unskilled is reflected not in a widening of the wage differential, but only in a difference in employment and annual wages in favor of the skilled, as was the case for the period 1929–1933. This reaction fits either the Reder or Oi theory, in that both contain differential shifts in demand among their explanatory variables.

INFLATION AS A NARROWING INFLUENCE. To explain the narrowing in the skill differential when the economy strengthens, accepting the applicability of the above theories, requires only that the relevant variables change their direction. The supply of skilled workers expands greater than that of the unskilled as hiring and job standards are relaxed and upgrading takes place easily; the relative demand for the skilled increases less than that of the unskilled as less broadly trained workers can fill skilled classifications when output for particular items approaches capacity; demand for the skilled rises relatively less as the time required to reach the maximum point on the learning curve becomes relatively shorter for the skilled when production runs become continuous; the relative demand for the unskilled increases more as these unemployed workers are now needed to collaborate with the skilled who were retained anyway during the downturn because of their fixed-cost element.

In addition, the hypothesis has been advanced that inflation which customarily accompanies prosperity serves as an independent force narrowing the differential. This inflation hypothesis is not new. For example, Hicks has argued that equalitarian sentiment strengthens directly with

---

Bell, "Cyclical Variations and Trends in Occupational Wage Differences in American Industry," *Review of Economics and Statistics,* **33** (November 1951), pp. 332–333, notes the stability of the differential over the longer period.

a general rise in wages, responding to price increases.[33] Knowles and Roberts argue that narrowing takes place "in a fit of absence of mind," mainly because market forces are ignored as flat-rate increases are given to all workers to meet cost-of-living increases.[34] Salkever argues that, since spending tends to be a greater proportion of spendable earnings during expansion and tends to exceed these earnings for the lowest-income groups, the lower-wage workers are under greater pressure to protect their real income from the eroding effects of higher prices.[35]

Whatever its form, the inflation hypothesis is based on the assumption that low-wage workers will fight harder to protect their real incomes from the damaging effects on real income of price increases. One way to look at the isolated influence of inflation is to consider it a type of proportional tax, which affects every income equally.[36] To make the tax progressive requires a higher percentage wage increase for the lower-wage unskilled workers than for the skilled.

But such reasoning requires that wage increases that take place during inflationary prosperous periods are thought of as really constituting two independent elements: a defensive one to offset the negative effects of inflation, and the usual positive one associated with labor's drive to share in productivity and profit gains. If both elements were fused into one wage goal, then the tax aspect of inflation would play no role in wage decisions. That is, if the independent influence of inflation were not considered, the positive goal would be grafted on to an implicit equal percentage increase to all wage earners, equal to the price-level increase.

If inflation acts independently to increase the wage demands of the unskilled over those of the skilled, the effect on wage structure and employment can be studied with reference to Figures 4.2 and 4.3. Figure 4.2 shows the wage-employment locus for a particular group of workers. Under the inflation hypothesis though, this wage-employment curve for the unskilled would shift to the left of that of the skilled during an inflationary period. This reflects the corollary of the inflation thesis, namely, that the unskilled would be more willing to trade unemployment for wages at any given level of labor demand for the group.

---

[33] J. R. Hicks, "Economic Foundations of Wage Policy," *Economic Journal*, **65** (September 1955), p. 397, writes: "It is true that equalitarian sentiments have more power when wages are changing. Especially if the impetus to a wage-rise is derived from the cost-of-living motive, it is recognized that a fall in real wages is a more serious matter for the low-wage than the high-wage groups."

[34] K. G. J. C. Knowles and D. E. Roberts, "Differences Between the Wages of Skilled and Unskilled Workers, 1880–1950," *Bulletin of the Oxford Istitute of Statistics*, **13** (April 1951), p. 121.

[35] Salkever, *op. cit.*, p. 151.

[36] This assumes the same market basket for all.

Translating this reaction to Figure 4.3, assuming that demand conditions and supply availability remain unchanged, the equilibrium point of employment and wage differential for each group would find a narrowing in the wage differential, with unemployment rising for the unskilled and falling for the skilled. This adjustment process leads Reder to demand that the inflation-hypothesis school present data showing differential movements in unemployment rates or in the volume of excess demand in favor of the skilled to substantiate the theory.[37] Since inflation usually accompanies high employment conditions, the test for excessive demand of skilled over unskilled labor is the relevant one. Indications are that this condition does exist in prosperous inflationary periods—witness greater job shortages for the skilled during prosperous periods—but this may be due to other causes, such as short-run limits to the supply of skilled labor rather than to inflation itself.

In any case, tests of the inflation hypothesis have been sparse and inconclusive. Dunlop and Rothbaum attribute a great deal of the narrowing in the skill differential in Italy, France, and the United States, in the immediate postwar years to inflation,[38] but they do not isolate the effect of inflation, so that the narrowing could have resulted from other causes, principally prosperity or supply availability changes. A French study for the same period shows that even under intense inflationary conditions, the skill differential widened for Paris metal workers because of the extreme shortage of skilled workers in this industry in this region in the postwar period. For workers in general, however, narrowing took place in almost every industry.[39] Again, this study does not adequately isolate the effects of inflation on the skill differential.

In a brief study, Robert Evans tries to compare the validity of the Reder hypothesis, emphasizing the differential effects on labor demand and supply, with that of the inflation hypothesis as an explanation of the narrowing of the skill differential during prosperous inflationary periods. Taking three war periods Evans found that the narrowing of the skill differential more closely accompanied rising prices than the tightening of the labor market.[40]

At first view, Evans' findings seem to support the inflation hypothesis against the labor-market-changes school. But for the two world wars, after Evans quite correctly reduces his study to years in which the

[37] Reder, "Wage Differentials: Theory and Measurement," pp. 268–269, n. 20.

[38] John T. Dunlop and Melvin Rothbaum, "International Comparisons of Wage Structures," *International Labour Review*, **71** (April 1955), pp. 347–363.

[39] Francois Sellier, "The Effects of Inflation on the Wage Structure of France," *The Theory of Wage Determination*, pp. 264–277.

[40] Robert Evans, "Wage Differentials, Excess Demand for Labor, and Inflation: A Note," *Review of Economics and Statistics*, **45** (February 1963), pp. 95–98.

labor market was tight—less than 4 percent unemployment—to put the Reder hypothesis to a fair test, the relationships are less clear. In fact, if the years 1919–1920 and 1945–1946 are omitted from their two respective world-war periods, (as they should be), since the unemployment rate rose above Evans' criterion of labor market tightness, (4 percent), narrowing of the differential accompanies *tightness,* if not *tightening,* of the labor market just as much as it does inflation. The italicized words emphasize that Reder's hypothesis does not necessarily relate narrowing of the differential to minor changes in the degree of tightness of the general labor market, but to the condition of a tight market.

For the Civil War period, Evans presents no unemployment data, but claims that this period shows the best results for the inflation hypothesis because, while the narrowing differential in 1862–1863 was accompanied by both tightening labor market conditions and inflation, the further contraction of the skill differential the following year was associated only with rising prices, the labor market loosening somewhat. Apart from the point made above that Reder's hypothesis depends only on tight and not tightening labor markets, his theory could apply if the possibility of lags in adjustment were permitted. When the general demand for labor presses on available supply, shortages appear for both unskilled and skilled labor. The shortage is relieved for the former by new entrants and for the latter by training and upgrading. Assuming that the latter process is more successful in alleviating labor-market tightness, as Reder implicitly assumes, it does take a longer time. Thus, in one year, while both inflation and labor market tightness may accompany a narrowing of the differential, in the following year, even if the labor market is looser but still tight, greater relative expansion of the skilled work force can account for further narrowing of the skill differential.

Considering the various tests of the inflation hypothesis, empirical evidence in its support is by no means conclusive nor convincing. At the same time neither has the theory been invalidated by events. Rather than consider it an alternative to the other theories that emphasize relative changes in demand and available supply, inflation, even if accompanying tight labor markets, can be thought of as an additional narrowing force on the skill differential.

SUMMARY

Whether changes in occupational wages are measured by changes in dispersion of all occupational wages or by a comparison of changes in the ratio of the highest to lowest paid wages—called here the skill differential—the long-term trend, at least until 1950, has followed a narrowing direction. Since the mid-fifties though, the skill differential has stabilized in all countries for which the data have been studied, not just in the United States. It remains to be seen whether this now lengthening period of stability represents a definite reversal of the trend or merely an intermediate-term aberration. A hypothesis offered here to explain stability in the skill differential, while the entire occupational structure narrows, assumes the emergence of a new concept of noncompeting groups based on an abilities barrier.

The past secular narrowing is explainable on grounds of shifting labor supply, strongly affected by autonomous increases in the demand for education and training, operating to narrow the skill differential. Improvements in technology, and concomitant growth in productivity have led to increases in all wages. Under the assumption of neutral technological advances, the absolute real differential widens, while the percentage differential remains unchanged. Widening of the absolute real differential does not act as an independent force inducing narrowing of the percentage skill differential for, although the rate of return on investment in skill would rise, an equivalent rise in returns on other investments would tend to occur at the same time.

Cyclically, the skill differential typically narrows during prosperity and widens during depression. One theory explains this tendency on the basis of differential movements in supply of the two labor groups resulting from tightening and lossening in hiring and job standards as the economy weakens and strengthens, respectively. This theory also implies differential shifts in demand to explain the relative growth in employment, as well as wages for the skilled during recessions, with reverse tendencies during prosperity. An alternative theory explains cyclical movements in the skill differential from shifts in demand only, with the demand for skilled labor less cyclically volatile because of the presence of fixed elements, representing training outlays, in the labor cost of skilled workers. Stability of the differential during the Great Depression fits both theories if it can be assumed that even the slighter fall in demand for skilled labor during that period was great enough to make the skilled workers refuse to trade any more unemployment for relatively higher wages.

Some have argued that inflation serves as an independent narrowing force during economic expansions. Despite the logic of the argument and the accompanying relatively greater intensity of labor shortages for the skilled during inflationary periods, which the theory requires, tests of the inflation hypothesis have been inconclusive. Most studies, which relate contraction in the skill differential to inflation, have failed to isolate the effects of inflation from those of strength in the economy in general. When corrections and adjustments are made to the one study that attempts to measure the relative effects of inflation and tightness in the labor market, there is as much support for the supply-and-demand hypothesis as for the inflation theory as an explanation of the narrowing of the skill differential that occurred during past boom periods.

CHAPTER V

Industrial Wage Structure

Movements in the industrial wage structure are usually studied for the information they yield on the effectiveness of the operation of competitive forces in the labor market. Under competitive conditions, allowing for differences in nonmonetary benefits among jobs and a lack of homogeneity within occupational classifications, workers of the same class should receive the same pay. Disequilibrating forces that lead to pay differences for the same work in the short run should, in the long run, tend to be counterbalanced by mobility within the labor market, which restores wage equality.

Unfortunately, for measuring the strength of competitive forces, changes in average wages within industries, and consequently between industries, are subject to forces other than the movement toward, or away from, equality of wages of the same labor class. Changes in occupational mix and changes in the occupational wage structure may also lead to differential movements of average wages between industries.[1] If we keep in mind these other sources of wage changes, we may then study movements in the industrial wage structure, along with the relationship of these movements to changes in other economic variables to test the power of competition within the labor market in equalizing wages for the same labor class. Both long-run and short-run relationships will be analyzed.

According to the competitive model, the tendency for wage equalization should be greater in the long run. The competitive framework allows for noncompensating short-fun variations in wages for similar work, resulting from the influence of differences in labor demand, derived from variations in productivity and product demand among industries and from the effect of interindustrial differences in the institutional framework within which wages are set. The role of these factors is found to

---

[1] In addition, there are the effects of changes in geographical location of industries, to be discussed in the next chapter.

be important in creating short-run wage differences. But the data do not clearly support the long-run competitive hypothesis, in that there are also many instances in which demand elements are related to differential long-period wage changes.

LONG-RUN MOVEMENTS IN THE INDUSTRIAL WAGE STRUCTURE AND THE COMPETITIVE HYPOTHESIS

The conventional method of considering relationships over a long period of time as an indication of the effectiveness of competition in the long run contains a grave logical error. It results from confusion of a long period of time with the economic concept of the long run. The latter term refers to the extended period of time over which a given economic impulse operates. On the other hand, wages, employment, productivity, and other data over a long period merely reflect the combined impact of impulses felt long ago, *plus* changes in these impulses over time. Thus, if admittedly short-run influences are more important in affecting data than long-run factors, conclusions reached on relationships over a long period of time are dominated by changes in the former forces and do not truly indicate long-run effects.

For example, would the finding for the period 1880–1960, measured by the values at the terminal dates, of no correlation between wage movements and employment among industries support the competitive hypothesis that changes in employment and wages among a group of industries should be unrelated in the long run? (The competitive hypothesis permits employment and wages to rise, relatively, in the short run, in those industries that experience a relative increase in labor demand. In the long run, however, with the tendency for competition in the labor market to equalize wages throughout different industries, differential changes in employment, but not differential changes in wages, would occur in response to relative shifts in demand.) The real test of the long-run hypothesis in this case is whether the relationship that existed between wage and employment changes, if any, in 1880, or—not to overstress the argument—in the early years of the period was still evident in 1960.

But, of course, the data do not permit such a test. The employment changes that are most closely related to relative wage movements in 1960, if these variables are related at all, will be those that occur in the years immediately preceding 1960. The lingering relationship, if any, of the earlier changes, will be swamped by the more recent variations.[2] Thus, because short-run relationships are stronger than long-run relationships, the effect of the distant correlation may not be felt. For example, a long-run relationship may be counteracted by a short-term one giving the impression that there is no long-run association between wage and employment changes if, for example, the industries that grew the most in employment near the end of the period were the ones that were expanding the least at the beginning.

But this confusion of the long period with the long run is not the only error in long-period tests of the competitive hypothesis, of equal pay for the same type of labor. Others will be noted in the following discussion of long-term relationships between the industrial wage structure and economic variables. Before reviewing these long-period relationships, the inability of changes in the structure itself to shed light on the strength of competitive forces will be stressed.

STABILITY IN THE INDUSTRIAL STRUCTURE AND THE COMPETITIVE HYPOTHESIS. One dominating characteristic of the industrial structure itself, found by several investigators, is the long-run stability in the ordinal rankings of industries by their average wage levels.[3]

Average wages in an industry change in response to changes in its occupational mix, in rates of pay for different jobs and in wage movements within job classifications. It is this last that realtes to the competitive hypothesis. In the long run, wage movements within job classifications should be in the direction that tends to eliminate intraoccupational differences. Stability of the structure over time might suggest relative constancy of occupational mix within industries. That is, it might indicate that industries have been subject to more or less neutral technologi-

---

[2] The use of year-by-year data instead of terminal date comparisons does not solve the problem in that the former technique merely yields a series of short-period relationships.

[3] Donald E. Cullen, "The Interindustry Wage Structure, 1899–1950," *American Economic Review,* **46** (June 1956), pp. 353–369, John W. Kendrick, *Productivity Trends in the United States,* National Bureau of Economic Research, Princeton University Press, Princeton, 1961, pp. 196–197, and Sumner H. Slichter, "Notes on the Structure of Wages," *Review of Economics and Statistics,* **32** (February 1950), pp. 88–89, present data showing this stability for long, but somewhat different periods, and for different industry groups.

Pamela Haddy and N. Arnold Tolles, "British and American Changes in Interindustry Wage Structure Under Full Employment," *Review of Economics and Statistics,* **33** (November 1957), pp. 408–414, find the same stability of ranking among broad English industrial categories for a briefer, more recent period.

cal advance, with respect to their different classes of labor. On the other hand, stability in the structure might reflect variation in the skill mix and offsetting changes in the other elements that determine wage levels within industries.[4]

The one systematic long-run element operating on the industrial wage structure has been the narrowing of the skill differential.[5] Thus, if wages within job classifications were uniform among industries at the beginning of a period under study and were again uniform at the end of the period, the wage structure would experience some compression over the period, assuming random changes in skill mix, even if the industries kept their relative position within the structure. In other words, with competition within the labor market equalizing wages for the same type of work at both terminal dates, the wage structure would be subject to the narrowing influence of the decline in the skill or occupational differential. This conclusion rests on the fact that industries paying relatively high average wages have a greater proportion of skilled labor than low-wage industries.

But, except for some narrowing between average wages at the extremes of the distribution, there is no indication of a general compression of the structure over time.[6] At first view, then, it might appear that the competitive hypothesis was challenged because the failure of the inter-industry structure to narrow might indicate differential rates of pay for the same work at the end of the period.[7]

Note, though, that the above test of the competitive hypothesis rests on the assumption of the dominance of competitive forces at both terminal dates. If the beginning of the period were one of labor market dis-

---

[4] Reder, "Wage Structure: Theory and Measurement," p. 282, n. 59, notes that the lack of relationship between richness of skill mix at the end of a long period and industrial wage changes over the period indicates a lack of constancy in the skill mix. This conclusion follows from the fact that if the skill mix were constant, the two variables would be strongly inversely related because of the decline in the skill differential.

[5] This, of course, refers to the historical narrowing, noted in the last chapter, which characterized the skill differential until the 1950's, or the period covered by most of the long-run studies of the industrial wage structure.

[6] Cullen, *op. cit.*, pp. 361–362. Cullen measures dispersion by the interquartile range as a percentage of median average annual earnings for 84 industries.

[7] Reder expresses the view that "Because of the secular decline in skill margins and in regional differentials the competitive hypothesis implies that there would have been a secular decrease in interindustry relative wage dispersion if the skills and geographical mix had remained more or less unchanged," "Wage Differentials: Theory and Measurement," p. 281. Even if skill mixes and geographical location of industries varied, if the variations were more or less random, the narrowing influence of the compression of the occupational structure should have been felt.

equilibrium with substantial random variation in wages for the same type of work, and the labor market at the end of the period were also subject to noncompetitive influences, then the wage structure might narrow even though competitive forces did not dominate in the determination of wages at either terminal date. Again, the only consistent element affecting the structure would be the narrowing of the skill differential. Thus, in this case, the industrial structure would tend to compress even though competitive forces did not determine wage levels within occupations. If the structure had narrowed, therefore, this could have served as evidence of the absence of competitive forces just as much as it could have indicated their presence.

At the same time, the failure of the structure to compress does not necessarily deny the competitive hypothesis, any more than narrowing would have supported it. That is to say, a movement towards equalization of average wages by industry would not necessarily have indicated the full effect of the narrowing skill differential being felt on the industrial structure. As was explained above, if in both terminal years over an extended period wages within occupations were determined by competitive forces, this effect would have operated, uninhibited by relative movements in intraoccupational wages. But if the initial period were one in which wages were determined noncompetitively so that wages varied within occupations, it would not necessarily follow that a move towards wage equalization, as would occur in keeping with the competitive model, would tend to add to or, at worst, have only a neutral effect upon the narrowing influence of the decline in occupational differentials.

Whether the equalization of wages within occupational classifications would act as a narrowing force on the interindustry wage structure depends on the relationship of wage differences for particular jobs at the beginning of a period to the prevailing individual industry wage levels. For example, if wage differences within occupational classes at the beginning of the period were such that workers who received above-average wages for their job classification were in the industries heavily weighted with skilled workers, then a move toward wage equalization within job classifications would reinforce the narrowing tendencies to the industrial structure contributed by the reduction in the skill differential.

On the other hand, if high-wage workers for particular jobs were concentrated in the low-wage industries, those employing a relatively large number of unskilled workers, the drift toward wage equalization within occupational classifications would tend to offset the narrowing impact on the industrial wage structure of the reduction in the skill differential. Thus, in this case, wage changes that followed the competitive path would tend to neutralize narrowing forces and perhaps leave the entire structure as dispersed at the end of a period during which competitive forces operated as at the beginning.

In summary, variations in the occupational structure itself shed no light on the strength of competitive forces in the establishment of occupational wages in the long run. With competition among workers, wages would tend to be equal within occupational classifications. If competition prevailed at both the beginning and end of the period, during which the skill differential narrowed, the industrial wage structure would have contracted. But it also would have contracted in the absence of competition if variable intraoccupational wages were randomly distributed among industries at both terminal dates. Thus, if the structure had narrowed, it could have done so whether or not competition prevailed.

Similarly, that the structure did not contract does not indicate the absence of competition. Under certain conditions, if the initial position were not one of competitive equilibrium, a movement toward wage equalization, in keeping with the competitive model, would act as a narrowing force on the structure, but under other conditions the tendency toward equality of wages for the same type of work would act as a widening force.

If evidence of long-run competition in the labor market, tending to equalize wages for the same type of work, cannot be derived from examination of changes in the structure itself, the relationship between wages and other economic variables can be tested for the strength of their support to the competitive model. The data are by no means conclusive in either direction.

WAGES AND PRODUCTIVITY. Increases in productivity, assuming no changes in product demand, permit an industry to raise wages while maintaining profit levels. Thus, industries experiencing relative gains in productivity may be under short-run pressure from their workers to raise wages. At the same time, competition among firms within the industry would also lead to higher wages. But, in the long run, if there is competition among workers, wage levels for the same type of labor would tend toward equality. Accordingly, any short-run gain in wages to industries experiencing relative growth in productivity would be dissipated in the long run.

Thus, as a check on the strength of the competitive hypothesis with respect to labor markets, there should be no relationship between relative productivity changes among a group of industries and their relative wage movements. Indeed, many studies reveal this lack of correlation.

Fabricant found a rank correlation of only —.05 between changes in unit labor requirements—the reciprocal of output per man-hour—and wages per worker among 38 industries for the period 1909–1937.[8] But when wages per man-hour instead of wages per worker are used, allowing for variation in the work week among industries, the wage output per man-hour correlation rises to +.22.[9] For a 33-industry group over the period 1899–1953, Kendrick's data yields a statistically insignificant correlation of +.28 between changes in average hourly earnings and output per man-hour.[10] Salter's study of American interindustry changes for 1923–1950 reveals a coefficient of correlation of +.22 between output per man-hour and average hourly earnings changes.[11] For English data, Salter finds a coefficient of correlation of only +.09 between variation in output per worker and earnings per worker.[12]

Despite slight variations in the productivity and wage terms used, the above studies indicate a lack of significant relationship between interindustry wage and productivity movements over relatively long periods of time, providing indirect support to the competitive hypothesis. But to cloud the issue, a few studies find a significant relationship between the variables. Dunlop found a rank correlation of +.49 between percentage changes in average hourly earnings and output per man-hour among 35 industries for the period 1923–1940[13] and, for the same period, Garbarino found a rank correlation of +.60 for 34 manufacturing industries.[14]

There are two reasons for not valuing the absence of a relationship between productivity and wage movements very highly as indirect evidence in support of the competitive hypothesis. In the first place, as noted above, statistical studies are not unanimous in their finding of a lack of correlation between the variables.

[8] Solomon Fabricant, *Employment in Manufacturing, 1899–1939,* National Bureau of Economic Research, New York, 1942, p. 105, n. 19.

[9] John T. Dunlop, "Productivity and the Wage Structure," *Income, Employment and Public Policy,* Norton, New York, 1949, p. 350.

[10] This calculation is made from Kendrick's data as it appears in Fabricant, *Basic Facts on Productivity Changes,* National Bureau of Economic Research, Occasional Paper No. 63, New York, 1959, pp. 46–47, Table B.

[11] W. E. G. Salter, *Productivity and Technical Change,* Cambridge University Press, Cambridge, 1960, p. 166.

[12] *Loc. cit.,* pp. 114–115.

[13] Dunlop, p. 350. Extending Dunlop's study to 1947, however, but losing comparability in the process because of a reduction by several industries, Frederick Meyers and Roger Bowlby, "The Interindustry Wage Structure and Productivity," *Industrial and Labor Relations Review,* 7 (October 1953), p. 97, found that the rank correlation fell to +.17.

[14] Joseph Garbarino, "A Theory of Interindustry Wage Structure Variation," *Quarterly Journal of Economics,* 54 (May 1950), p. 298.

In the second place, and more basic to the issue, it is questionable whether a close relationship between productivity and wage movements would follow in the absence of competition within the labor market. Strengthening this doubt on a statistical basis, parallel movements in the variables do not usually occur even in the short run. (This lack of relationship will be documented in the next section.) Thus it would seem illogical to argue on behalf of the competitive model in the long run, on the basis of movements of economic variables that do not act in a manner contrary to the competitive model in the short run. Then there is no issue of whether long-run elasticity in labor supply will tend to create long-run competitive market conditions out of short-run disequilibrating changes.

Without going into a detailed explanation in this long-run section of the reasons behind the lack of relationship between physical productivity and wage changes between industries, even if competitive forces were not strong enough to tend to equalize wages for the same type of work, it is enough to note that many industries might react to a productivity increase with a reduction in product prices instead of a wage increase. Suggesting that the former type of adjustment occurs among some industries does not assume the operation of the competitive model. That is, it is not suggested that all industries act this way, which would lead to the negative relationship between productivity and prices, discussed below. Rather it is argued here that if the alternative adjustments were randomly distributed among industries, with some adjusting wages and other prices to productivity gains, differential wage changes would occur. Any relationship between wage and physical productivity changes that would otherwise have existed would be somewhat reduced by the practice among some industries of lowering prices instead of raising wages in response to productivity gains. In other words, even if wages are paid in accordance with ability to pay rather than in response to labor-market competition, productivity changes are a poor indicator of ability to pay. Over time, firms in some industries might translate their ability to pay higher wages because of productivity growth into the form of lower prices.

But a comparison of wage movements with value productivity changes would eliminate this shortcoming of the wage-physical productivity comparison as an indicator of the degree to which wages react to differences in ability to pay. Value productivity changes measure the combined influence of productivity and price changes. Thus, looking at historical data, considering that some industries might lower prices and others raise wages in response to productivity gains, there should be a significant correlation between wage movements and value productivity changes if wages moved differentially among industries in correspondence with their variations in productivity and product prices, taken in combination. Conversely, the competitive hypothesis would be supported if whatever differential wage changes occurred showed only a random relationship to interindustry changes in value productivity.

Fabricant's data permit this test, but the results are by no means conclusive. Comparing movements in average hourly earnings with output per man-hour for 25 of the 33 manufacturing industries for which product selling price indexes are available, thus allowing for a value productivity-wage study, the rank correlation coefficient is +.25, not significant at the 5 percent level. The wage value-productivity comparison raises the coefficient to +.32, slightly below the 5 percent level of significance.[15] For Kendrick's 33 industries, the value productivity-average hourly earning rank correlation remains the same as the physical productivity-wage value, +.28. The refinement of the productivity measure does not seem to be crucial in these instances in that the data are still not inconsistent with the competitive hypothesis. But it should be stressed that these represent the findings of just two studies.

While the value productivity wage relationship offers only slight support to the competitive model, in that the correlation between long-run movements in the variables was high if not quite statistically significant, substantial support to the model is provided by the close negative relationship between wage and product price changes among industries.

WAGE MOVEMENTS AND PRICE CHANGES. It was noted above that even a partial association among some industries between productivity changes and selling-price adjustments would weaken the tie between wage and physical productivity movements. But if the competitive model operates, this association should not be random but the general pattern among a group of industries. If, in keeping with the competitive hypothesis, wages are not to move differentially among industries in response to factors that affect industries' ability to pay higher wages differentially, then varying productivity changes should be passed on in the form of inverse price changes. That is, industries with a relative increase in productivity should experience relative price declines, with the obvious opposite relationship for industries having relative productivity declines.[16] This means that the gains from relative productivity increases are dis-

---

[15] These calculations are based on Fabricant, *Employment in Manufacturing*, pp. 102–104, Table 8.

[16] This assumes competition among producers and abstracts from differential changes in demand, a theme treated in Chapter X.

tributed to buyers of the product rather than to the factors producing those goods. As Salter views the high inverse correlation he finds between price and productivity movements, ". . . the gains from differential increases in productivity have not been appropriated at their source by strong unions."[17]

Despite differences among industries in the ratio of nonlabor-cost to labor-cost changes and, despite differences in profit rates that may exist at any time among industries, both acting to loosen the tie between output per man-hour changes and price adjustments, all the studies referred to above show a significant inverse relationship between the two variables.[18] The long-run inverse relationship between productivity and price changes indicates a degree of uniformity in wage changes among industries over time. Despite uncertainty over whether the competitive model requires uniformity in wage changes or whether it is denied by a lack of uniformity, expressed above, the model does imply that whatever differential wage changes occur will be random and not associated with any particular economic variable.

It has been noted that this randomness is neither clearly demonstrated in the relationship between physical productivity and wage movements nor between value productivity and wage changes.

In addition there is also evidence of a long-term tie between wage and employment changes among industries, at least for manufacturing industries, serving as further evidence against the applicability of the competitive model of labor markets, which requires that wage changes among industries be uncorrelated to forces that reflect varying changes in labor demand.

WAGES AND EMPLOYMENT. To the degree that varying changes in employment among a group of industries reflect interindustry differences in demand for labor over time, the short-run effect of these changes on wages would tend to raise wages in industries experiencing greater growth in employment more than industries having less employment expansion. In the long run, though, competition within the labor market,

---

[17] Salter, *op. cit.*, p. 169.

[18] Fabricant, *op. cit.*, p. 108, n. 27, found a significant rank correlation of $+.39$ between unit labor requirements—the reciprocal of output per man-hour—and selling-price movements.

Kendrick, *op. cit.*, p. 201, derived a value of $-.55$ for the rank correlation between product prices and total productivity. The rank correlation was $-.76$ between wholesale price movements and output per man-hour for Salter's American data and $-.88$ for the rank correlation between price and output per worker for his British industries. Salter, *op. cit.*, pp. 119 and 168.

expressed by labor mobility toward the better paying jobs, should tend to equalize wage changes among industries.[19]   .

The overall relationship between employment and wage changes among industries in the short run has generally not been found to be statistically significant. As was noted above in the case of the long-run wage-productivity relationship, it would be illogical to test the long-run competitive hypothesis by noting the relationship between variables in the long run that showed no short-run correspondence in adjustments. That is, if the factor does not seem to be related to short-run wage movements, there is no question of a long-run competitive adjustment to this (nonexistent) short-run influence.

In the case of short-run wage and employment changes, though, a tendency toward a relationship has been found, to be noted below, among industries having the greatest and least changes in employment. Thus, separating employment changes into two groups—those having substantially above and below average employment changes—the former industries tend to have the greater wage gain in the short run.

This type of test can be carried out for long-run data. If the relationship tends to exist in the long run, with industries having above-average employment gains tending to have wage increases above the average, with correspondingly lower wage gains for industries having lower employment gains, the competitive model would not be followed. It would be implied that the impact on wages of changes in demand for labor, reflected by changes in employment, would persist into the long run.

For Kendrick's 33 industries, Reder calculated a rank correlation of +.21 between employment and wage changes for the 1899–1953 period.[20] This value in itself is not statistically significant (at the 5 percent level) and, besides, no relationship between the two variables appears when the comparison is made between wage movements at the extremes of the employment distribution. For the 10 industries with the lowest employment change, in this case actual losses, exactly half had wage changes lower than the average (median) change of the 33 industries, and the other 5 had wage changes greater than the average. Furthermore, for the 10 industries with the greatest employment increase, 5

---

[19] To repeat, though, this pattern of operation of the competitive model ignores the effect of changes in the skill mix among industries and the changes in occupational differentials over time, and assumes labor market equilibrium at the beginning of the period from which differential employment changes are measured.

[20] Reder, "Wage Differentials . . . ," p. 278. In his calculation, Reder used Fabricant's computation of indexes of employment (man-hours) and wages (real average hourly earnings) from Kendrick's data. Fabricant, *Basic Facts on Productivity Change*, pp. 46–47.

experienced above-average wage changes, while 3 showed increases below the average, and 2 had exactly the median wage increase over the period. Certainly these findings confirm a lack of long-run relationships between wage and employment changes.

But for the 33 industries, besides the lack of long-run relationship, there was no evidence of a short-run pattern. In fact, for the period 1899–1909, the first short run period for which Kendrick's wage-employment data are presented,[21] the calculated rank correlation coefficient is —.12, with the sign even in the wrong direction. Moreover, for the 10 industries with the greatest employment gain, only 2 had above-average wage increases and for the least employment growth, 5 had below-average wage increases. Thus, for these industries, while there was no long-run relationship, neither did employment and wages vary together in the short run. For this case, then, the absence of a long-run relationship gives no support to the competitive hypothesis in that there was no short-run maladjustment to be corrected by long-run adjustments in labor supply.

When the 20 manufacturing industries are studied separately, the results also fail to confirm the competitive hypothesis. In the short run, for the years 1899–1909, the rank correlating between wage and employment changes was a significant +.48. But in the long run, instead of showing a correction to this relationship, the rank correlation between man-hours and average hourly earnings changes for the 20 industries for the period 1899–1953 even rises to +.52.

Thus, for these industries, the short-run relationship persists into the long run, contrary to the competitive model, under which whatever short-run relationship exists between the two variables should be eliminated by competition within the labor market. In short, for all 33 of Kendrick's industries there is no short-run relationship between wage and employment changes, making a long-run test meaningless while, for the manufacturing industries alone, the significant short-run relationship continues into the long-run, a pattern inconsistent with the competitive hypothesis.

SHORT-RUN VARIATIONS IN THE INDUSTRIAL WAGE STRUCTURE

The competitive model permits the dependence of short-run variations in individual industry wages on factors that affect the demand for labor

[21] Kendrick, *op. cit.*, pp. 218–222 and Appendices.

differentially. In fact, test of the long-run hypothesis requires that these factors, which relate to short-run inelasticity in labor supply to demand-induced relative wage changes within occupational classifications, affect the wage structure in order to differentiate long-run adjustment from short-run effects. This is not to deny that if an element does not affect the structure in the short- or long-run, the competitive model receives support from this resistance of the structure to disturbing forces.

In this section, though, to differentiate the two time-period classifications, factors that do affect the structure in the short run will be documented.

WAGE STRUCTURE AND VALUE PRODUCTIVITY. In the discussion of the long-run relationship between wage and productivity changes, it was noted that adjustment to productivity gains by opposite price changes would tend to weaken the wage-physical productivity change correlation. An additional factor loosening the tie between changes in the variables relates to differences in product market experience among the individual industries.

Industries enjoying relative growth in product demand will in the short run tend to raise prices and bid up wages relative to other industries. If productivity gains are randomly distributed with respect to changes in product demand throughout industries, the relationship between physical productivity and wage movements would be somewhat weakened but still apparent if the isolated relationship between the variables were strong. On the other hand, if productivity gains tend to occur in the relatively declining industries, in the short run, as these industries strive to compensate for dwindling product demand by greater stress on efficiency in production, wages would not be expected to rise with productivity gains. The sequence of adjustment would run from a relative decline in product demand, a relative fall in price and wages, and a concomitant improvement in efficiency and productivity that would tend to offset the wage fall. In this case there is no question of the sharing of productivity gains, but a productivity increase would be in response to factors that tended to depress wages.

Substitution of value instead of physical productivity changes tends to restore the influence of productivity changes on wages. In the above example of relatively declining industries, wages would tend to move in response to the conbined impact of product market (price) and physical productivity changes, as would be the case for all industries, insofar as wage changes in the short run followed differences in the individual industries' ability to pay.

In fact, the data tend to reveal a significant short-run relationship between changes in value productivity and wages.[22]

Unfortunately, though, for the sake of clear-cut evidence in support of the view that value productivity changes relate significantly to wage movements, all the data do not point to this direction. Using a large group of English industries (113), Brown and Browne found no relationship between changes in male average hourly earnings and in gross value output per worker for the period 1948–1954.[23]

Thus the short-run relationship between wages and value productivity does not exist for all cases. Another short-run element in ability to pay, differential profits for individual industries, also tends to show a close relationship to interindustry variation in wage movements.[24] There is no long-run study of the relationship between profit levels and wage

[22] Richard Perlman, "Value Productivity and the Interindustry Wage Structure," *Industrial and Labor Relations Review,* **10** (October 1956). pp. 35–37, found a rank correlation of +.68 for the period 1939–1947 and +.58 for 1947–1953 between changes in average hourly earnings and sales per man-hour—the value productivity measure used—for 18 large manufacturing industry classifications. This source also discusses the advantages of using the value instead of the physical concept for the productivity variable, pp. 29–31.

Slichter, *op. cit.,* p. 87, calculates a rank correlation of +.83 between wage levels of male unskilled workers and value product per man-hour for 13 manufacturing industries in 1939. But this study compares *levels* in a moment-of-time cross-sectional approach and is thus not directly comparable to the above-cited study.

David G. Brown, "Expected Ability to Pay and Interindustry Wage Structure in Manufacturing," *Industrial and Labor Relations Review,* **16** (October 1962) p. 52, in another cross-sectional study found a correlation of +.47 between average annual earnings and value added per man-hour for 81 manufacturing industries for the average of the values over the period 1951–1957. Significantly, though, Brown found only a low (+.093) partial correlation between the variables suggesting that value added was not an independent determinant of wage levels, but related to other factors that affected ability to pay.

[23] E. H. Phelps Brown and M. H. Browne, "Earnings in Industries of the United Kingdom, 1948–1959," *Economic Journal,* **62** (September 1962), pp. 538–539.

[24] Harold M. Levinson, *Postwar Movements of Prices and Wages in Manufacturing Industries,* Study Paper No. 21, Joint Economic Committee, Congress of the United States, Washington, 1960, pp. 3–4, found a significant partial correlation between wage changes and profit levels, output and employment changes held constant, for 19 manufacturing industries between the period 1953–1958. The partial correlation was positive but not significant at the 5 percent level for the period 1947–1953. As Reder, "Wage Differentials . . . ," p. 292, points out, Levinson's study is partly cross-sectional in that wage changes are related to average profit levels. But the competitive model would still be denied if industries having high profit levels over time paid higher wages over a given period than low-profit industries. Reder, however, warns that the wage data may obscure changes in labor quality such that the high-profit industries employ higher paid and more productive labor, a condition, if prevalent, that would not contradict the competitive hypothesis.

changes to test whether the competitive model is denied by a persistent tendency of high-profit industries to raise wages more than other industries.

Wages and Employment Changes. In the previous section, it was noted that calculation of Kendrick's data revealed no significant relationship, long-run or short-run, between employment and wage changes for a mixed group of industries, cutting across broad industrial classifications. But when the data were studied for manufacturing industries alone, significant long-run and short-run correlations were calculated. There are many other studies of the wage-employment relationship, running a range of results from close to insignificant correlation.[25]

Such varied results indicate either that in many cases competitive forces in the labor market operate quickly to correct any tendency for differences in employment changes to affect the structure, or that employment changes themselves are poor measures of differential movements in labor demand, among a group of industries. As for the latter possibility, an increase in productivity may tend to raise wages but, in itself, if not accompanied by a proportional growth in output, will tend to reduce employment.[26] In addition, for some industries wage-employment changes may move in opposite directions as industries experience independent wage pushes that tend to reduce employment. Such seems to be the case in the short and long run for Kendrick's nonmanufacturing industries.

By comparing wage and employment changes for the extremes of the employment distribution, these offsetting factors might be eliminated. Brown and Browne used this device in finding a tendency for industries with the greatest employment growth to experience the greatest wage increase in a short-period,[27] but this tendency was not found for Kendrick's broad list of industries.

Arguments that differential wage changes might reflect varying wage pressures from the workers or that firms pay wages in response to differential willingness and ability to pay suggest the importance of institu-

---

[25] Reder, "Wage Differentials . . . ," pp. 288–289 presents a summary review of these findings.

[26] But Salter, *op. cit.*, p. 166, and Dunlop, *op. cit.*, p. 355, found almost negligible correlation between productivity and employment, suggesting that employment is not affected adversely by productivity gains.

[27] Brown and Browne, *op. cit.*, pp. 535–536. Lloyd Ulman, "Labor Mobility and the Industrial Wage Structure in the Postwar United States," *Quarterly Journal of Economics,* 1965, pp. 87–88, used the same procedure in finding a tendency for wages to rise more for the rapidly expanding than for the relatively declining industries in the immediate postwar period.

tional elements in the wage-setting process. The tendency toward a uniformity in wages for industries experiencing similar institutional wage pressures has long been recognized. To the extent that this tendency prevails, the operation of competitive forces is weakened, in that wages would be set for a group of industries somewhat independent of the effect of market forces and, presumably, independent of wages set elsewhere.

INSTITUTIONAL FORCES IN WAGE SETTING AND THE KEY GROUP. A recent study by Maher and one by Eckstein and Wilson reveal a group of industries having similar institutional background for wage setting, which have also experienced similar wage movements in the short run.[28] Eckstein and Wilson have called these industries a key group, although they do not find much evidence of transfer of wage movements in these industries from the group to other industrial sectors. Maher considers industries with similar institutional background—interdependence of input and output, geographical unity, with similar strong national unions representing the work force—as forming a wage pattern, again with little carry-over to other industries. These statistical studies, in effect, substantiate the earlier theoretical concepts of Ross' "orbit of coercive comparison"[29] in wage setting and Dunlop's "wage contour."[30]

Whether the pattern of similar wage movements over time for a group of institutionally related industries constitutes a denial of the competitive model has been questioned. Benewitz and Spiro, indeed, in criticizing Maher's conclusion to this effect, claim that the common wage experience of these industries, rather than contradict the competitive hypothesis, actually supports it.[31]

They argue that under competitive labor markets, wages tend to move together. (They assume, of course, competition in operation prior to the changes examined.) Further, they claim that in the short or inter-

---

[28] John E. Maher, "The Wage Pattern in the United States, 1946–1957," *Industrial and Labor Relations Review,* **15** (October 1961), pp. 3–20, and Otto Eckstein and Thomas A. Wilson, "The Determination of Money Wages in American Industry," *Quarterly Journal of Economics,* **76** (August 1962), pp. 379–414.

[29] Arthur M. Ross, *Trade Union Wage Policy,* University of California Press, Berkeley, 1948, *passim.*

[30] John T. Dunlop, "The Task of Contemporary Wage Theory," *The Theory of Wage Determination,* pp. 16–20. It is interesting to note that Dunlop's definition of a wage contour as a group of firms with similar product market, similar sources for their labor force, and common labor market organization is similar to Maher's institutional construct to which industries forming the pattern group belong.

[31] Maurice C. Benewitz and Alan Spiro, "The Wage Pattern in the United States, 1946–1957," *Industrial and Labor Relations Review,* **16** (October 1962), pp. 122–124.

mediate run there will be some divergence in wage changes, but that Maher has merely selected industries at the middle of the distribution of wage movements, so that his finding of similar wage movements for these industries conforms to expected behavior under competitive conditions.

There are two strong counterarguments to their position. In the first place, the industries in Maher's study, and also in Eckstein and Wilson's, share a common institutional background, but they do not employ the same type of labor. In effect, these studies test wage-pattern theory as this theory is described by Soffer:

"Wage-pattern theory was designed to explain the observed uniformity of wage changes among bargaining units which maintain wage relationships *in the face of non-uniform market changes.*"[32] That is, Maher found a similarity of wage changes for industries that do not employ workers of the same type, that is, workers not from the same labor market.

For the second counterargument to the Benewitz and Spiro criticism, the first point need not apply. Even if workers of the same type were hired,[33] the competitive model is not supported by a similar wage movement for the group of industries selected.

It is true that under competition, assuming competitive equilibrium at the time before changes occurred, similar wage changes would occur for a group of industries in the center of the distribution of wage changes.[34] But the important question is why these industries should be the ones with common institutional characteristics. Expressed differently, assuming a large group of industries hiring from a common labor market, Maher found a cluster of industries of similar institutional background that formed the central (uniform) group with respect to wage changes. Thus, for these industries (and it must be remembered that the assumption of a common labor market is posited here only to show that this factor alone would not support the Benewitz-Spiro position),

[32] Benson Soffer, "On Union Rivalries and the Minimum Differentiation of Wage Patterns," *Review of Economics and Statistics,* **41** (February 1959), p. 53. Italics not in original.

[33] Timothy W. McGuire and Leonard A. Rapping, "Industry Wage Change Dispersion and the 'Spillover' Hypothesis," *American Economic Review,* **56** (June 1966), p. 498, point out the difficulty in separating institutional elements that lead to wage uniformity from similar market or labor-supply factors, which may operate within a group of industries.

[34] Maher, "Reply [to Benewitz and Spiro]," *Industrial and Labor Relations Review,* **16** (October 1962), p. 129, notes that the pattern of wages found in a group of industries is tighter than the competitive model postulates, considering nonmonetary differences in jobs and heterogeneity within job classifications.

institutional nonmarket factors would account for their presence in the center of the wage-change distribution for the total group. Some group has to be in the middle of the distribution, and Maher presents institutional reasons for a particular group to form this center.

Industries in the pattern group do not employ workers from a common labor market. Even if there were some similarities in labor supply for the group and other industries, the finding of similar wage movements for the group is related to their institutional commonalities. Thus the phenomenon of the key or pattern group having similar wage movements in the short run must disappear in the long run if the competitive model is to be followed. Whether the influence of institutional factors establishes long-run uniformity in wage changes among a group of industries has yet to be tested.

SUMMARY

Testing the competitive model, which requires a tendency toward wage equalization within job classification in the long run, through examination of movements in industrial wages, leads to inconclusive results. Changes in the structure itself throw no light on the issue of the degree of competition in the labor market, since the industrial structure (if competitive) would have tended to narrow, under the influence of a contraction of occupational differentials, only if labor-market competition prevailed at the beginning of a period of study. Consequently, the failure of the structure to narrow does not necessarily argue against the operation of competitive forces.

When industrial wage movements are correlated with changes in other economic variables, the evidence is mixed, now in support of, now against, the competitive model, which requires that the influence of forces leading to wage differences among industries in the short run be eliminated in the long run. Long-run variations in physical productivity do not appear to be correlated with differential wage changes among industries but, in general, neither do the variables show a short-run relationship. Value productivity and wage changes, on balance, do move together in a discernible pattern in the short run. The long-run relationship, at least for two studies, is also positive, if not significantly so.

Stronger support for the competitive theory is found in productivity-price relationships over time. All existing studies show a significant negative correlation between productivity and price changes over time, indicating a tendency for wages to move uniformly among industries. But more direct testing of the competitive model requires that whatever small variation in wage changes occur be unrelated to other factors influencing labor demand in the short run.

The wage-employment relationship does not tend to confirm the competitive model. Some studies show a positive short-run relationship between wage and employment changes, while others find no significant correlation between them. But in one broad group of industries for which a long-run relationship is not found, neither is a short-run association apparent, while for a subgroup of these industries, for which there is a significant short-run association, this relationship persists over a long period, contrary to the competitive hypothesis.

Strong statistical support is found for the influence of institutional elements in leading to similar wage movements, among different types of workers, for a group of interrelated industries. If the influence of these elements continued into the long run, the competitive model, requiring a uniformity of wages for all workers of the *same* occupational category, would not be substantiated for these industries.

CHAPTER VI

Regional Wage Differences—the Southern Wage Differential

In a closed economy, with free internal movement of labor, under competition, workers of the same occupations, efficiency, and characteristics such as race, age, and sex which, to some extent, create noncompeting groups within the labor force, would tend to receive the same wage. Under these conditions, wage differences of a compensating nature may prevail. Preferences for particular job settings, because of nonwage benefits, satisfaction with present work associations, etc., explain why the trend toward equalization remains incomplete.

These forces, acting against wage equalization, may be considered as barriers to mobility, barriers that discourage workers from seeking the highest wage and prevent uniformity in wages for workers of the same occupation or for workers of the same characteristics. Apart from barriers created by preferences for a particular work setting and the ability and opportunity barriers discussed in Chapter IV, which prevent occupational wage differences from being exactly compensating, barriers to mobility between locations present a special source of wage differences.

The importance of these mobility barriers are reflected in the magnitude of the interregional difference in wages for the same type of labor, after correcting for other sources of wage differences not directly related to the workers themselves, such as community and firm size, and assuming that compensating wage differences are randomly distributed regionally.

The data indicate a persistent interregional wage difference, with lower rates for the South, within labor groups—whether classified by education, age, sex, or race.[1] Thus the evidence is consistent with the view that

---

[1] As in the last chapter, data limitations prevent a direct comparison of intraoccupational, interregional wage differences.

factor immobility prevents the wage equality among groups that would exist, were the nation a single labor market.

Another type of regional wage differential refers to the difference in wage levels attributable to interregional differences in labor mix, with the wage level in the South being lower than in the non-South because of the relative dominance of low-wage groups in the South's mix. Statistical series indicate a constancy in the overall Southern wage index, reflecting the combined influence of an upward movement in Southern relative wages for labor of the same type, offset by the relative growth in the low-wage labor force in the region.

This chapter discusses the statistical and conceptual problems involved in defining and measuring interregional wage differences. Then an explanation is offered for the relative stability in the low overall Southern wage differential. (Incomplete) factor mobility is presented as a cause of both the slow rise in the South's relative wage level within labor groups and the steady relative upswing of the region's labor mix.

DEFINING AND MEASURING REGIONAL WAGE DIFFERENCES

Before reasons for the presence and persistence of regional wage differences, specifically the low rate of Southern compared to Northern wages, can be explained, it is necessary to define what is meant by a regional wage level. This definition must be made in order to compare wages of one region with those of another or with the national level.

Most simply, and crudely, a regional wage level can be considered as the average hourly wage paid to all workers in a particular geographical area. Thus it would be calculated as the total area wage bill divided by the number of hours worked in the area. Of course, it would be impossible to find and calculate all wages and hours, so that a segment usually studied, for which data are available from the Census of Manutures, consists of the wages and hours of manufacturing production workers. The wage level for the South, W_s, would then become

$$W_s = \frac{\sum_{i=1}^{n} W_{i_s}}{E_s} \tag{1}$$

where W_{i_s} is the average hourly wage of Southern manufacturing production worker i. The wage of all workers is summed and divided by E_s, the total of manufacturing production workers in the South.

Since detailed wage data are available only on an annual basis, Formula

1, for purposes of calculation, takes the form

$$W_s = \frac{\sum\limits_{i=1}^{n} W_{i_s}}{\sum\limits_{i=1}^{n} H_{i_s}} = \frac{\sum\limits_{i=1}^{n} W_{i_s} H_{i_s}}{\sum\limits_{i=1}^{n} H_{i_s}} \tag{1a}$$

In Formula 1a, W_{i_s} is the annual wage of worker i and H_{i_s} is the number of hours he works in a year. In the absence of wage data for individual workers, because of the more detailed availability of annual wage data, the required wage level has been calculated on an industry basis where

$$W_s = \frac{\sum\limits_{i=1}^{n} X_{i_s}}{\sum\limits_{i=1}^{n} E_{i_s}} \tag{1b}[2]$$

In Formula 1b, X_{i_s} is the annual wage bill of industry i in the South, and E_{i_s} is the total production worker employment, as an annual average, of industry i in the region. Thus the wage level of the South, compared to the national average to derive an (unadjusted) index of Southern wage, is calculated by simply dividing W_s derived from Formula 1b by the value for the country as a whole, W_c, derived from the same formula.

In symbols

$$W_{L_s} = \frac{\dfrac{\sum\limits_{i=1}^{n} X_{i_s}}{\sum\limits_{i=1}^{n} E_{i_s}}}{\dfrac{\sum\limits_{i=1}^{n} X_{i_c}}{\sum\limits_{i=1}^{n} E_{i_c}}} = \frac{\sum\limits_{i=1}^{n} X_{i_s} \sum\limits_{i=1}^{n} E_{i_c}}{\sum\limits_{i=1}^{n} X_{i_c} \sum\limits_{i=1}^{n} E_{i_s}} \tag{2}$$

[2] Formula 1b was used for calculating regional wages by Victor Fuchs and Richard Perlman from Census of Manufactures data in their study, "Recent Trends in Southern Wage Differentials," *Review of Economics and Statistics,* **42** (August 1960), pp. 292–294.

In another study, Lowell E. Gallaway, "The North-South Wage Differential," *Review of Economics and Statistics,* **45** (August 1963), pp. 264–265 uses Formula 1a. The two studies attained almost identical values for the Southern wage level in 1954, relative to the national average in the former study and to the Northern states in the latter. Gallaway's method is conceptually superior in that the possibly distorting effect of interregional differences in hours per worker does not arise when hourly data are used. But Gallaway does not explain how he translated the annual data, found in the Census of Manufactures, into hourly values.

where W_{L_s} is the Southern wage index (i.e., when the fraction is multiplied by 100) with the national level as base, and the subscript C refers to national values. Alternatively, the South's wage index can be calculated with that of another region as base by simply substituting values for the other region for those of the country as a whole in Formula 2.

This value for the South's wage index, however, gives only a gross representation of regional wages. An important aspect of a regional wage difference refers to a comparison of regional differences in pay received for the same work. The gross index does not isolate wage differences, arising from regional differences in industry and occupational mix, from the differences that reflect unequal pay for the same type of work between the two regions. That is, Southern wages are lower than Northern wages because Southern workers receive lower wages for similar work, because Southern manufacturing is heavily weighted with low-wage industries and, possibly, because there is an interregional difference in labor mix within industries, with a tendency for the Southern firms of individual industries toward a poorer skill mix. The last two sources of wage difference introduce an element of incomparability into the measurement of regional wage differences. To correct for differences in industrial composition and to compare regional wage levels so that the only source of difference lies in pay differences for similar work, it is necessary to standardize wages for industrial and occupational mix. Standardization can be achieved by comparing Southern wages with, say, Northern wages if the regions had the same industrial mix by arbitrarily assigning to the South the North's regional mix.[3]

In symbols,

$$Ws_S = \frac{\sum\limits_{i=1}^{n} W_{iS}E_{i_N}}{\sum\limits_{i=1}^{n} E_{i_N}} \qquad (3)$$

where Ws_S is the standardized Southern wage. Then the standardized Southern wage index is found by dividing the South's standardized wage by the North's to yield

$$Ws_{S-N} = \frac{\sum\limits_{i=1}^{n} W_{iS}E_{i_N}}{\sum\limits_{i=1}^{n} W_{i_N}E_{i_N}} \qquad (4)$$

[3] The process of regional wage standardization was introduced by Frank Hanna, "Contribution of Manufacturing Wages to Regional Differences in Per Capita Income," *Review of Economics and Statistics*, **33** (February 1951), pp. 18–28.

where Ws_{S-N} is the Southern standardized wage, with the Northern industry-by-industry employment as weights. Of course, a different level would be reached if national employment weights were used for each industry.

Equation 4 corrects for differences in industry mix and permits a direct interregional comparison of wage differences for similar work.

For the South, with its preponderance of low-wage industries, standardization raises the Southern index toward the Northern or national level. There are at least four statistical shortcomings of this standardization technique, which makes its value as a guide to the measurement of the extent and variations in regional wage differences questionable.

First, regional wage differences may reflect interregional variations in industrial localities—urban or rural—differences in plant size, and degree of unionization.

Second, wage differences on an industrial basis may simply reflect different occupational mixes within industries between regions rather than different pay rates for the same work. This may be a serious source of error; the wide disparity in factor rates between regions may lead to different factor proportions in production.[4]

Third, standardization-by-industry mix assumes that the industry unit itself has a neutral effect on wages. Since each industry's contribution to the wage level, or wage index, is weighted by the size of its work force, to the extent that labor is specific to an industry and not interchangeable among industries, standardization gives undue weight to large industries The fact that the results would differ if unweighted industry average wages were used in calculating a region's standardized wage does not imply that an unweighted average is superior to the weighted, but rather suggests that the weighted method must be used cautiously if wages differ greatly for the same type of labor from industry to industry.[5]

---

[4] Frederick W. Bell, "The Relation of the Region, Industrial Mix and Production Functions to Metropolitan Wage Levels," *Review of Economics and Statistics,* **49** (August 1967, pp. 368–374, finds a strong tendency for factor substitution in production, with low-wage regions using relatively more labor and less capital than high-wage regions. Bell cites other recent studies which reach the same conclusion.

In an earlier study, Richard Lester, "Effectiveness of Factory Labor: South-North Comparisons," *Journal of Political Economy,* **54** (February 1946), pp. 60–75, found no evidence of significant differences between the North and South in factor proportions in producing the same goods.

[5] Martin Segal, "Regional Wage Differences in Manufacturing in the Postwar Period," *Review of Economics and Statistics,* **43** (May 1961), pp. 148–149, measures a regional index, with the Northeast as base, by finding the median ratio among

Finally, the most troublesome statistical difficulty associated with standardization concerns the problem of weights. In comparing standardized wages for different areas, which region's industrial mix should be used as weights? This problem is not solved by using the industry mix of a third area, say, the nation as a whole, which might not reflect the industry mix of either region.

If the North's industry mix is used as weights for both regions and if Southern wages are closer to Northern wages in those industries that are more important in the North, the Southern wage index would be higher than if Southern industry weights were used when Southern wages are relatively lower for those industries that are more important in the South. Thus the value of a region's wage index depends on the industry employment weights used.

If both regions had more or less the same industrial mix, then the problem of weights would not arise, nor would there be a need for the standardization process. But when regional wage differences are wide and not uniform among industries, this condition provides a background favorable for the presence of different industrial mixes. Furthermore, it is the presence of differential wages that is under analysis. As R. J. Wonnacott notes in his criticism of the standardization process, ". . . the success of the approach [of standardization] tends to be inversely related to the importance of the problem."[6]

Because of these shortcomings of standardization by industry mix, chiefly its inability to isolate all the elements that may account for differences in regional wages other than differences in pay for the same type of work, a better standardization procedure would eliminate more variables. Such an effort has been carefully made from Census data by Victor Fuchs.[7]

For all nonagricultural workers, Fuchs estimated Southern average hourly earnings at 80 percent of the non-South level in 1959. Standardizing for interregional difference in "labor quality," in this case for age,

---

193 industries of the area wage for each industry to that of the Northeast. This method of measurement yields a form of standardized wage, unweighted by employment differences among industries. It implicitly assumes a complete lack of interindustry interdependence in wage setting, in that each industry is treated equally despite varying importance among industries in a region's total employment.

[6] R. J. Wonnacott, "Wage Levels and Employment Structure in United States Regions: A Free Trade Precedent," *Journal of Political Economy*, **72** (August 1964), p. 415.

[7] Victor R. Fuchs, "Differentials in Hourly Earnings by Region and City Size, 1959," National Bureau of Economic Research, *Occasional Paper 101*, New York, 1967.

education, color, and sex, the Southern index is 93.[8] This means that if the South and non-South workers received the same pay, the Southern average wage level would have been only 93 percent of the non-South, because of differences in age, education, color, and sex, between the South and the rest of the country. The adjusted Southern index of 83[9] thus represents the ratio of Southern to non-South wages, with the effect of interregional differences in "labor quality"[10] taken into account; that is, the adjusted index measures interregional differences in pay for the same type of labor.

The addition of one further variable that affects wage levels—city size in which the work is performed—reduces the Southern wage differential substantially, raising the adjusted Southern index to 92.[11] This change reflects a strong tendency for wages to be higher, the greater the city size in which firms are located, and the tendency for Southern industry to be located in small communities.[12]

THE CONCEPT OF A REGIONAL WAGE INDEX. An important conceptual uncertainty associated with a comparison of regional wage levels concerns the very nature of a regional wage difference. Certainly it is important to measure and consider regional differences in pay for identical work, no matter how inadequately the process of standardization eliminates the impact of difference in worker quality on wage levels. But is it not also important to study why labor quality differs regionally, why industries that hire different grades of labor tend to locate in one region rather than in another? A great deal of the gross South-non-South wage difference can be explained by the lower-wage industry mix of the South. In fact, if Southern industries in 1954 had received the national average wage for each, the Southern wage level would have been some 12 percent below the national average, exactly the same deficit reflected by the region's standardized wage index.[13] This means that the lower Southern wage that year was equally determined by lower

---

[8] *Ibid.*, p. 8, Table 3. Fuchs' calculations use the South as base (100) with the non-South and other regions' comparable levels as relatives of this base.
[9] *Ibid.*, p. 9, Table 4.
[10] "Quality" is the word used by Fuchs to indicate differences in pay associated with a characteristic, not necessarily with efficiency difference.
[11] *Ibid.*, p. 20, Table 11.
[12] For an earlier study of the influence of city size on regional wage difference see Herbert Klarman, "A Statistical Study of Income Differences Among Communities," National Bureau of Economic Research, *Studies in Income and Wealth*, **6** (1943), pp. 206–226.
[13] Fuchs and Perlman, *op. cit.*, p. 293.

wages paid for similar work and by the presence of low-wage industries in the South.[14]

Expressing the problem differently, should a goal of Southern economic development be for equality of the region's standardized wages with those of the North or, less narrowly, of the country as a whole? It might be that the lower Southern wage for equal work might reflect underutilization of abundant unskilled labor there, so that a rise in Southern standardized wages would require a shift in production toward low-wage industries. The end result might then show a standardized Southern wage index closer to the Northern or national level with such a decline in the industry-mix Southern wage index that the unadjusted Southern wage index would fall below its previous level. Such an adjustment might not be considered a relative improvement in the economic condition of the region.

The above possible sequence suggests that perhaps the low standardized wage index for the South, Ws_{S-C}, and low Southern wage index because of difference in industry mix, W_{M_s}—the ratio of Southern to non-Southern wages resulting from differences in industry mix alone, assuming Southern and non-Southern wages in each industry were the same— are interdependent. Since Southern wages are relatively lowest for low-wage workers,[15] encouraging Southern industrial concentration in

---

[14] The frame of reference for the remainder of the chapter is the industry, rather than the labor force itself, because of the presence of intertemporal calculations of changes in Southern wage levels on this basis.

Fuchs, op. cit., Section 5, pp. 27–31, concludes that there is no significant effect of the regional location of an industry on its wage level, that wage differences among industries can be entirely explained by differences in labor quality, community size, degree of unionization and size of firm. This finding gives no role for differences in wages within industries because of a tendency for regional differences in pay for labor of the same type, if "type" includes the institutional elements of unionization, city size, and size of firm.

This conclusion is inconsistent with Fuchs' calculation of the presence of different pay regionally for labor of the same quality. Either this residual difference after standardization for worker quality and city size is entirely explained by degree of unionization and size of firm or these last two variables are imperfectly detailed in the regression equation because of date limitation, as Fuchs suggests. A theoretical, but highly unrealistic alternative, is that wages for workers of a given "type" are lower in the South than elsewhere, but that within industries, Southern firms employ a richer labor mix.

[15] Joseph Bloch, "Regional Wage Differentials: 1907–1946," *Monthly Labor Review*, **66** (April 1948), p. 375, finds Southern wages to be historically farther behind those of other regions for low-wage than for high-wage workers. The same results are found by Lloyd Saville, "Earnings of Skilled and Unskilled Workers in New England and the South," *Journal of Political Economy*, **63** (October 1954), pp. 400–402.

industries requiring these workers, the two values may move in opposite directions. But in any case, in offering reasons for lower Southern wages, both the condition of poorer industry mix and lower pay for similar work need explanation.

THEORIES OF REGIONAL WAGE DIFFERENCES— EXPLAINING THE LOW-WAGE POSITION OF THE SOUTH

An explanation for the low Southern wage index with regard to industry mix, W_{M_s}, can be given simply in terms of different regional factor endowment. With a relatively large supply of unskilled labor in the South, low-wage industries developed there and have been attracted to the region. In fact, the data included in studies of relative Southern wage movements indicate that, if anything, the tendency for Southern manufacturing to be weighted with low-wage industries has been increasing. For the period from 1925 to 1947, W_{M_s} did increase slightly from about 85 percent to 90 percent, but this movement might be attributable to wartime industrial development that was to some degree undertaken without consideration of economic factors. From 1947 to 1954, though, Southern wages, measured by applying national wages for the South's industrial mix, fell to about 88 percent of the national average.[16]

In other words, Southern industry grew relatively more rapidly in low-wage industries in the 1947–1954 period than it did in the past. This pattern of Southern industrial growth, which can be related to relative changes in employment, indirectly partially explains the sluggish growth in Southern standardized wages and in the more or less stagnant state of the gross or unadjusted Southern wage position.

EXCESS SUPPLY OF UNSKILLED LABOR AND FACTOR MOBILITY. These relationships can be explained in terms of factor endowments and factor immobility. Industries requiring much low-wage labor are attracted to the South not only because the South's labor-force mix is heavily weighted with low-wage workers, but also because labor costs tend to be relatively important for them. Thus, low-wage labor is cheaper in the South and, perhaps a more important feature, more available there so that expansion could occur without the wage increases that might

---

[16] Fuchs and Perlman, *op. cit.*, p. 293, Table 1. The values for the "South" presented here are an unweighted average of the South Atlantic and East South Central values presented in the table. The closeness of the values for the two regions minimizes the error in this rough calculation.

be required in the non-South. Consequently, although labor of all classes may be cheaper in the South, (manufacturing) employment would tend to grow relatively in the South for low-wage industries.

The data substantiate this argument. When regional employment growth is compared for the period 1947–1954, in terms of the industry mix in each region at the beginning of the period, the South was found to have grown more than any other region, even including the Pacific region noted for its industrial growth. This means that of all regions, the South had the greatest employment growth for "its" industries.

But the unadjusted growth in Southern manufacturing employment in the South only slightly exceeded that of the national average. The explanation for the relatively stable position of Southern total manufacturing employment changes at the same time that the growth in employment in "its" industries strongly outpaced the national growth in these industries stems from the fact that the South specializes in low-wage industries whose growth rate was much lower than that of high-wage industries. Thus, since the growth in Southern manufacturing employment did not much exceed the national average manufacturing employment expansion, the relative demand for Southern labor did not increase much. Furthermore, considering the relative stability of the Southern labor force for the period—population rising in step with the national growth from the balanced effect of greater natural growth and net emigration from the region—Southern wages were under but slight upward pressure. Accordingly, from these changes, the Southern standardized wage index rose slightly, the wage index by industry mix fell, and the overall, gross, relative wage level remained practically unchanged.

Continuation of these trends would tend to eliminate interregional differences in standardized wages, but would have no noticeable effect on the crude average, as the South continued to expand in low-wage industries. Thus, while differential factor endowment may account for the original differences in regional wages, factor mobility does not necessarily eliminate wage differences, measured by overall regional averages. Labor mobility alone, if perfect, would tend to equalize standardized wages. The movement of capital would hasten and strengthen the trend toward equalization.

At first view, then, it might appear that if labor mobility equalized regional wages for all classes of labor, there would also be a tendency toward a uniformity of industrial mix with a consequent interregional equalization of overall average wages. This would come about since, insofar as differential wages affected returns on capital, equal wages for all types of labor would tend to make the distribution of capital and industry randomly distributed throughout the nation.

But the above process assumes that mobility of labor takes place before mobility of capital. In reality, both factors move at the same time. The movement of capital Southward toward the low-wage industries, increasing the demand for Southern labor, reduces the need for outward movement of Southern low-wage labor to equalize wages for different types of labor. But more importantly, this movement of capital would tend to standardize wages before labor classes were distributed uniformly interregionally. Thus the equilibrium condition would be reached, from an original position of relatively lower-priced low-wage labor in the South, through outward movement of unskilled labor and inward movement of capital to use this labor, to a situation in which standardized wages would approach equality. But the relative supply of unskilled labor in the South would exceed that of the nation as a whole. Thus the role of capital movement would be one of equalizing standardized wages but, at the same time, perpetuating the relatively lower average wage of Southern labor.[17]

Once equalization of standardized wages is reached or approached, the incentive to further factor mobility is eliminated. To explain, then, why future economic expansion after this equality is achieved does not take place randomly throughout the nation, tending to equalize average area wages, it is necessary to postulate, assuming full employment,[18] that Southern industrial labor-force growth is relatively more heavily weighted with low-wage workers than any other region's. This assumption is supported by the relatively greater potential supply for industry from agriculture in the South, and perhaps also by interregional differences in educational and training facilities and opportunities.

What remains to be explained is why the differential against Southern wages for the same type of labor persists and why it arose in the first place. Furthermore, proposed remedies for the South's chronic low-wage status should be examined.

Persistence of the negative Southern standardized wage differential can be explained on the basis of incomplete adjustment to competitive conditions. Barriers to mobility of labor and capital, although certainly not so severe as those artificially imposed against international factor

---

[17] The usual text presentation views the mobility of labor and capital as equalizing (nonstandardized) wages interregionally. Expressed by Gordon Bloom and Herbert Northrup, *Economics of Labor Relations,* Richard D. Irwin, 1965, p. 301, "As new industry comes into the South and labor migrates out, the (North-South) differential should slowly tend to decline." As explained here, the standardized wage differences will tend to decline, but capital mobility acts to maintain the unadjusted wage difference.

[18] If there is an equal unemployment rate among worker groups, there would be a greater current available supply of unskilled than skilled workers in the region, a condition again serving as an attractive force for low-wage industries.

movement, prevent labor moving out of the South and capital into it to the degree necessary to offset the differential returns which induce these movements in the first place.

As for labor mobility, it is not sufficient explanation of its inability to equalize standardized wages by noting that the relatively great natural population growth of the South offsets the migration of labor to other regions. While, certainly, population growth counteracts the effect of outmigration on labor supply, the competitive model requires, then, simply greater mobility of the redundant labor force than if natural population increase were uniform nationally. Insofar as natural population growth adds to the labor supply and depresses wages, the incentive for labor to move out of the region is strengthened. Therefore, if mobility is insufficient to equalize interregional wages under this strong stimulus, it can be assumed that, in the absence of relatively greater Southern population growth, mobility would be incomplete under a weaker stimulus, even though less outward movement would be required to equalize wages.

Considering the barriers to mobility, an important question is whether or not the interregional wage pattern has reached an equilibrium position. With Southern standardized rates close to 90 percent of the Northern or national level, may not the remaining deficit merely reflect compensating differences? More specifically, apart from the social impediments to mobility—attachment to associations and customs, resistance to change—might not the existing wage differential reflect entirely the financial cost of long-range movement? These expenses include not only transportation costs but also the cost of job search in new areas and foregone earnings between jobs,[19] in the usual case in which movement to a new area involves giving up a present job to find or start another in a more attractive region.[20]

If the interregional wage difference reflects only compensating differences, associated with the costs of movement from low-to-high-wage areas, there would be no further net loss of labor, the Southern standardized wage index would become stable, and the index would fall

---

[19] George Stigler, "Information in the Labor Market," *Journal of Political Economy*, Supplement, **70** (October 1962), pp. 98–101, considers these costs as partial explanation of the wider dispersion of interregional wage rates than local labor market rates for the same type of labor.

[20] Robert L. Raimon, "Interstate Migration and Wage Theory," *Review of Economics and Statistics*, **44** (November 1962), p. 438, notes that more interstate job movement is voluntary, from one job to a better one, rather than involuntary, from job to unemployment to job, as characterizes many local labor market job changes. Raimon sees this difference as a major explanation for the high correlation between job mobility and wage-rate differences that characterizes interstate mobility, and the low correlation between the variables for local job changes.

in the future only under the influence of continued movement of capital and a reduction in the costs of interregional migration.

Labor would continue to flow out of the South as long as natural population growth there exceeded the national rate, or else the standardized index would fall below its current (equilibrium?) level under the pressure of excess labor supply. Labor tends to move in response to the attractive forces of higher wages and greater job opportunity. There is some question as to which of the two exerts greater influence. For interstate mobility, fortunately for the present discussion, the issue is unimportant, since the states receiving labor are those with both higher wages and greater job opportunity.[21]

Capital, directed mainly towards low-wage industries, would tend to flow into the area, raising the Southern standardized wage index, but probably not to the Northern or national level, because of barriers to mobility of capital. The latest data indicate that the Southern standardized wage index is drifting only slowly upward while relative Southern labor supply is remaining more or less constant, results that support the hypothesis that the current wage differences reflect only compensating costs of mobility for labor, if not yet for capital.

As for migration costs, these will tend to fall as more detailed information on job opportunities nationally reduces the cost of job search. Furthermore, as wage rates rise secularly faster than the costs of transportation, the equilibrium standardized index will tend toward equality nationally.[22]

As for explaining the origin of the lower Southern standardized wage index, the historically relatively greater supply of unskilled labor in the South can account for the initially lower Southern wages for this type of labor. The reasons for lower Southern wages for skilled labor are less obvious.

---

[21] Raimon, *op. cit.,* pp. 428–438, presents data to this effect. He does not, however, separate out the relative importance of each of the two elements on labor mobility.

[22] Stigler, *op. cit.,* p. 98, notes this trend in the relationship between costs of movement and wage rates. He considers this factor an important element in the gradual reduction of interstate standardized wage indexes. This leads him to the conclusion that "The comparison [of narrower interstate wage dispersion than in the past] timidly suggests that the difference in earnings increasingly represents differences in the quality of labor rather than in its compensation." Lester, "Effectiveness of Factory Labor: South-North Comparisons," concludes that there is little or no difference in labor efficiency interregionally. The argument here maintains that the remaining differences in interregional standardized wage indexes reflect not labor quality differences but incomplete elimination of migration costs, barriers to capital movements, and perhaps a residue of labor-market disequilibrium that might represent the intangible social costs attached to factor mobility.

One possible reason for lower skilled wages in the South, although the supply of these workers is relatively much less than that for other regions, relates to the development of production in industries that have a greater need for unskilled labor. Perhaps this direction of Southern industrial growth has made the supply of skilled labor, though small, still excessive.

Another reason lies in the tendency for wage structures in any setting, to be related to the wage level of the dominant groups. In this case, with Southern wages lower than those of other regions for lower-paid jobs, and with lower-ranked jobs dominating Southern industry, there would be some carry-over of the low-wage tendency to other jobs in a particular setting. Thus the relatively low wage for low-wage labor in the South constitutes an institutional drag on the wages of higher-paid workers.

In any case, the difference between high- and low-paid labor is much greater in the South than in other regions, or measured alternatively, the Southern rates for high-wage labor are much closer to those of other regions than the wages of Southern low-wage labor.[23] Apart from the fact that skilled labor is probably not so abundant relative to demand in the South as is unskilled labor, the transportation costs involved in migration would be of lesser importance to high-wage than low-wage workers. That is, measured in absolute values, the money difference in wages would be much greater for a high-wage than low-wage inter-regional difference of equal percentage magnitude. With transportation costs much the same for all workers, the costs would form a much lower percentage of a high-wage than a low-wage difference of equal relative size. Thus, insofar as transportation costs form an element in migration decisions, mobility would be a more complete equalizer of high-wage than low-wage regional percentage differentials.

As for improving the Southern average wage position, it has long been recognized that little hope can be held for achieving equality with other regions through the normal path of equalizing standardized wages through factor mobility, since low-wage industries thereby tend to develop in the region.[24] Perhaps high-wage industries could be lured Southward

---

[23] In his recent study, Fuchs, *op. cit.*, pp. 22–26, finds the Southern wage index, standardized for the other variables he includes, directly related to the level of education but still about 10 percent below the non-South level for the most educated groups.

[24] For example, Jesse W. Markham, "Some Comments on the North-South Differential, *Southern Economic Journal,* **16** (January 1950), pp. 279–283, bases the regional (unadjusted) differential on the type rather than on the amount of Southern investment.

by inducements such as discriminatory tax concessions or the provision of external economies. If such selective measures were successful, then a heavier burden would be placed on emigration of low-wage workers to equalize standardized wages for that group. Thus, while the industrial mix became richer in the South, raising W_{Ms}, the tendency might be for Ws_{S-C}, to fall, with an uncertain effect on W_{Ls}, the gross, unadjusted, Southern wage differential.

More positive steps to move Southern wages toward the national level would be in the direction of altering the composition of the Southern labor force, through advancements in training and education, at the same time that measures were taken to facilitate labor mobility.

The explanation of the origin and persistence of the low-wage status of Southern labor has been presented here in terms of differential factor endowment, and an incomplete equalization of even standardized wages because of barriers to factor mobility. Specifically, lower average Southern wages are considered a result of the initial large supply of unskilled labor, and the lower standardized Southern wage a reflection of costs of factor movement or of continuing disequilibrium.

This explanation of lower average Southern wages has been challenged as being "tautological" or an example of circular reasoning.[25] This criticism warrants attention.

GALLAWAY'S EXPLANATION OF THE REGIONAL WAGE DIFFERENTIAL. Certainly, as Gallaway views the "excess supply" of labor thesis, it would contain a definitional tautology. As he writes, "To define excess supply as existing when differentials exist and then to explain differentials by the presence of excess supply is certainly circular reasoning."[26]

But "excess supply" as presented here is not necessarily related to the presence of a (standardized) regional wage differential. The term refers to the initial presence of a greater supply of labor, especially unskilled low-wage labor in the South, than in other regions. This condition would tend to *cause* a wage differential to open up, until and unless sufficient mobility of labor and capital out of and into the region, respectively, erased or prevented the differential from occurring. In this sense a wage differential could persist even if the standardized differential were eliminated. The differential in question would be that of the crude average interregional wage levels or, alternatively, the regional wage index with respect to industrial mix.

Gallaway deals only with the standardized wage, and he cannot be

[25] Gallaway, "The North-South Wage Differential, p. 269.
[26] *Loc. cit.*

faulted for the choice of wage difference he wishes to measure and analyze. But when he then claims that the concept of excess supply "becomes ephemeral" unless it is related to other factors, he ignores the possibility of and importance of the regional difference in average wages. He is certainly correct that a larger supply of labor, in itself, would not necessarily lead to a relatively lower Southern standardized wage. What would be required as an explanatory element would be a large supply of labor relative to employment of capital on an industry-by-industry basis. In fact, he presents statistical evidence that shows just this relationship and further data indicating that the capital-labor ratio regional imbalance is growing slightly smaller. Thus he has a valid explanation for the origin of the standardized wage differential and its gradual narrowing, but stubborn persistence.

But labor supply was distributed regionally before industrialization and economic development. Therefore, a region would initially have a relatively lower capital-labor ratio in its early stage of development if it had a relatively large unskilled labor supply. Thus the low early capital-labor ratio in the South may not have resulted so much from the historical accident of early Southern development's being focused on agriculture, as Gallaway suggests,[27] but on the early presence of a relatively large unskilled labor supply there, which directed early investment into agriculture. Nevertheless, Gallaway does point out that for explaining the origin of interregional standardized wage differentials, an argument based on "excess labor supply" should explicitly state that the excess is relative to the early supply of capital.

This relationship, to repeat, is not needed for explaining the low average Southern wage, because of the low-wage mix of Southern industry. The "excess" or relatively large early supply of unskilled labor in the South directed investment toward industries using this labor. Thus, even if capital-labor ratios were equal for all industries, the average Southern wage would be below that of the national average.

SUMMARY

Average regional wage levels may differ because of differences in the quality or characteristics of the labor force or differences in pay for similar work. Statistical difficulties arise in measuring regional indexes for each of the three types of wage level: unadjusted average; index by characteristics of the labor force and employment—labor "quality,"

---

[27] Gallaway, *op. cit.*, p. 270.

community size, degree of unionization—or by industrial mix; and standardized wage index, which corrects for differences in labor characteristics or industrial mix.

Despite the uncertainty regarding the exact measurement of any Southern wage index, the values for the South are far enough below the national level, regardless of weighting method, so that it can be concluded that Southern average wages are relatively low both because the South has low-wage industries or a relatively large amount of workers who receive low pay, regardless of region, and lower than average pay received for the same type of labor. In fact, the data indicate importance of both elements in causing a relatively low Southern average wage level.

Thus, to explain the presence and persistence of lower Southern wages on average, it is necessary to explain the origin and continuation of the industry-mix and standardized wage differentials. The lower industry-mix wage arises because of the greater relative supply of types of labor—unskilled in general—that attracted capital to low-wage industries. The flow of this type of capital, in fact, tends to depress the skill-mix wage further.

On the other hand, the flow of capital Southward and labor out of the region are the forces that tend to equalize interregional standardized wages. Barriers to mobility of both factors may account for all the remaining difference in interregional standardized wages, but there is a possibility that even under existing barriers this movement has been incomplete. The same excess supply of labor that determined the origin of the industry-mix differential plays a role in the origin of the standardized wage differential but, in this case, "excess supply" is a term that implies a relatively lower capital-labor ratio in individual Southern industries.

Increased factor mobility will reduce the standardized wage differential but, with investment directed to low-wage industries, the industry-mix differential may widen. In fact, trends indicate the relative stagnation of the overall average Southern wage level, reflecting the counteraction of these two effects. Certainly, equal pay for similar work represents a type of equilibrium goal, but the average wage level can only increase in the South if the composition of Southern labor alters to match the national distribution, through advances in education and training. Steps to improve the skill-mix of Southern labor would make the barriers to interregional labor mobility an irrelevant factor in wage equalization and thus would serve to achieve the three goals of improving the "quality" of Southern labor and the industrial mix of the area, and raising Southern wages for comparable work to the national level, at the same time.

PART THREE

Unemployment

CHAPTER VII

Unemployment— The Classical and Keynesian View

The major difference between Keynesian and classical wage theory lies in their analysis of the effect of money wage changes on the level of employment and unemployment. Under the earlier theory, personified by pre-General-Theory Pigou, changes in money wages play an important part in changing the level of output, employment, and unemployment. For example, a sufficient reduction in money wages during slack periods could eliminate unemployment. According to the most simplified Keynesian version, money-wage changes would have no effect on the level of output and unemployment and, even after modifications, the theory considers wage reduction as an incomplete or, at best, slow-moving measure toward the restoration of full employment.[1]

Certainly depression wage policy seemed to adhere to Keynesian principles. Administrative decisions and legislative action in the mid-1930's, encouraging wage stability in the face of declining demand, almost anticipated Keynes. Today we have no depression wage policy. We have wage guidelines for stemming inflation but no handy policy formula for wage behavior during recessions.

In the absence of policy, the issue of the salutary effects of wage cuts during downswings would be entirely academic if wage practices themselves showed downward rigidity. Statistical evidence, though,

---

[1] How far Pigou came to accept the Keynesian framework, if not all its conclusions, is revealed in his preface to *Lapses from Full Employment*, Macmillan, New York, 1954:

"Professor Dennis Robertson . . . has warned me that the form of the book may suggest that I am in favor of attacking the problem of unemployment by manipulating wages rather than by manipulating demand. I wish, therefore, to say clearly that this is not so."

points to wage sensitivity to unemployment since the Great Depression.[2] Furthermore, even in institutionalized wage settings, unions have accepted wage cuts in slack periods.[3] Reder notes that this union wage behavior may not reflect an employment consciousness, or a belief that wage cuts will increase membership employment, but may simply indicate the weakened bargaining position of unions during bad times.[4]

Whatever the cause, however, as long as wage declines do occur, the effect of this wage behavior on employment and unemployment warrants study. The relevant issue is whether individual wage declines, if taken as a whole, serve to push the economy toward a full employment position, regardless of the motives behind the individual decision to permit or accept wage cuts.

In this chapter the similarities and differences between the classical and Keynesian view on the relationship between wage changes and employment and unemployment will be noted, and criticisms of the Keynesian position presented and appraised. The conclusion will be reached that the central Keynesian point that money-wage declines are a poor stimulant to a faltering economy remains intact. Keynesian theory, however, presents a weak a priori argument for the behavior of real wages during business expansion which, in fact, is invalidated by actual experience.

CLASSICAL AND KEYNESIAN INVOLUNTARY UNEMPLOYMENT— THE ROLE OF "MONEY ILLUSION"

To the classicist, the equilibrium real wage is determined by the interaction of labor demand and supply. The classical labor-demand schedule, in terms of real wages in accordance with marginal productivity theory, is simply the downward-sloping marginal physical productivity schedule. With a conventional upward-sloping labor-supply schedule, therefore, equilibrium is assumed to be at full employment. Any unemployment that arises would reflect the operation of market frictions and impediments which, when removed, would allow the restoration of full employment equilibrium.

If, on the other hand, labor-supply schedules were perfectly elastic

---

[2] Clarence D. Long, "The Illusion of Wage Rigidity: Long and Short Cycles in Wages and Labor," *Review of Economics and Statistics,* **42** (May 1960), pp. 140–151, presents the relevant data.

[3] George P. Shultz and Charles A. Myers, "Union Wage Decisions and Employment," *American Economic Review,* **40** (June 1950), pp. 362–380, indicate the extent of this tendency during the 1949 recession.

[4] Melvin Reder, "The Theory of Union Wage Policy," *Review of Economics and Statistics,* **34** (February 1952), pp. 42–43.

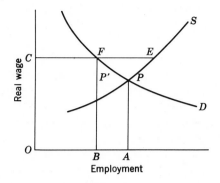

Fig. 7.1

Classical and Keynesian wage-employment relationships.

over part of their range, unemployment could be more or less permanent. But this unemployment would not be considered involuntary in that it resulted from the unwillingness of workers to accept a lower money (and real) wage that would permit the attainment of full employment.

Presenting these relationships graphically in Figure 7.1, full employment would be attained with labor supply meeting labor demand at P with real wage AP and employment OA. If labor supply were perfectly elastic over the range CE at real wage BF, with supply schedule $CFES$, then employment would fall to OB or CF, and unemployment FE would occur. But this unemployment would be voluntary in that it would be eliminated if the workers would allow their real wage to fall to AP.

Thus a working definition of classical involuntary unemployment would be as follows.

> Men are involuntarily unemployed if, being out of work, they would be willing to work for a real wage below the current level.

This definition has many similarities to the following much discussed Keynesian definition.

> Men are involuntarily unemployed if in the event of a small rise in prices of wage-goods relatively to the money wage, both the aggregate supply of labor willing to work for the current money-wage and the aggregate demand for it at that wage would be greater than the existing volume of employment.[5]

According to both definitions, voluntary unemployment would signify the unwillingness of workers to accept a reduction in their real wages.

[5] J. M. Keynes, *The General Theory of Employment, Interest, and Money*, Harcourt, Brace and Co., New York, 1936, p. 15.

More generally, according to both, whether unemployment were voluntary or involuntary would depend on the nature of the labor-supply schedule.

The central difference between the two concerns the different time dimension they employ. The classicist refers to current corrections to the unemployment problem; Keynes refers to the future. Thus the key words of the Keynesian definition are "in the event of."

To the classicist, the failure to accept a reduced real wage prevents the attainment of full employment now. To Keynes, this attitude would prevent the employment of these workers when aggregate demand rose. That is (with reference to Figure 7.1), to the classicist, full employment would be attained if employment were currently OB at real wage OC provided that the workers would let their real wages fall to P if their labor-supply schedule was SS. Thus, current unemployment would be temporary, resulting perhaps from the random establishment of too high a wage, OC, to clear the labor market. Of course, if labor supply were $CFES$, the workers would choose a higher real wage at the cost of unemployment.

To the Keynesian, however, the current real wage, OC, resulted from the state of aggregate demand. If future demand rose, requiring more workers at a lower real wage AP, unemployment would be eliminated, again if the workers allowed their real wage to fall. But with labor-supply schedule $CFES$, real wages would not be allowed to fall, the potential rise in aggregate demand would be thwarted, and unemployment FE would be permanent but voluntary.

Consider the problem of current unemployment. To be counted as unemployed in accordance with legal and statistical procedures, a worker must be willing to work but be unable to find a job at current wages. To be eligible for unemployment benefits, for example, he would not be expected to offer his services under the current rate for jobs that he could fill. Neither the classicist nor the Keynesian feels comfortable with this operational definition of involuntary unemployment. The classicist would claim that the question of availability and willingness to work at current wages does not put the unemployed worker to the correct test of whether his current unemployment is involuntary. He should be asked whether he would work at lower wages. If he answers in the affirmative, he should be considered involuntarily unemployed, receive benefits and, more importantly, draw comfort from the knowledge that his unfortunate position will be temporary, to be relieved when wages fall. A negative respondent has only himself to blame for continuation of his unemployment, and should not be eligible for benefits reserved for unlucky, temporary suffers from an economy in disequilibrium.

To the Keynesian, the question of the worker's availability at current wages is equally irrelevant. But the Keynesian attitude toward the worker would differ. Since both the volume of employment and the level of real wages are considered to be uniquely determined by the familiar elements of the Keynesian system, the worker would be powerless to alter his real wage.

If unemployed workers accepted lower money wages, with constant aggregate demand, competition would force prices down proportionately, leaving real wages unchanged. Consequently, whether unemployed workers would accept a lower money wage would not affect their real wages nor help them become currently employed. Thus in the *current* sense the workers would be considered involuntarily unemployed even if they would not work for less. In terms of Figure 7.1, unemployment *FE* is *currently* involuntary, and the workers may remain unemployed at current demand not because their supply schedule may be *CFES* but because aggregate demand has not risen to require real wages to fall to *AP* to attain full employment. If the legal and statistical services wish the current level of unemployment to be determined by labor-supply conditions, that is their business. A Keynesian might in all generosity consider the worker who refused to accept a lower real wage (if the economy advanced, thereby becoming involuntarily unemployed) eligible for unemployment benefits, since his *current* unemployment in no way depends on his negative attitude toward a reduction in real wages.[6]

In what sense then is a worker involuntarily unemployed if he will not accept a lower real wage when he has no control over his real wages? Keynes refers to the question of his willingness to accept the lower real wage that will be offered when aggregate demand and employment increase and there is a downward drift along the marginal productivity curve. Thus an unemployed worker is asked what his attitude would be today, and implicitly tomorrow, toward the reduction in real wages that will be necessary for his reemployment when aggregate demand rises.[7] If he refuses to accept a reduction in real wages, this would not affect his current position but his future one, and his refusal to accept

---

[6] Abba Lerner, a staunch Keynesian, notes, "If a man is not willing to accept a lower *real* wage, then he is *voluntarily* unemployed and Keynes does not worry about him at all." "The General Theory (1)," *The New Economics*, edited by Seymour Harris, Alfred A. Knopf, New York, 1948, p. 116 (italics in original). Lerner's statement is too strong. It would not be inconsistent for Keynes to worry about the worker's current plight of unemployment and still feel no sympathy for him if he prevents his reemployment, in response to an increase in aggregate demand, by his stubborn affection for his current real wage.

[7] If the word "today" were substituted for the final four words of the sentence, the question would be the classical one, not the Keynesian.

a lower real wage would not only prevent his reemployment but, in addition, lead to a labor bottleneck to economic expansion.

The growth in employment and output, consequent to a rise in aggregate demand, seems to depend on the willingness of the existing work force to accept real wage cuts as wages and prices rise with increasing demand, and marginal productivity falls with expanding output. Keynes calls this attitude "fortunate";[8] in reality it is unnecessary.[9]

Beset by a money illusion workers resist cuts in their real wage when this entails a reduction in their money wages, with prices falling less, but do not resist the same real wage cut when money wages rise less than prices. Leontieff calls this assumed behavior the fundamental postulate of the Keynesian system.[10] To Tobin on the other hand, money illusion means that "labor does attach importance to the money wage *per se*, and more labor will be supplied at the same real wage the higher the money wage."[11] This version does not quite fit the Keynesian system. To Keynes it is not enough for real wages to remain constant; they must actually fall if output and employment are to rise.

But Keynes never claimed that the supply of labor would increase when real wages fell, as prices advance faster than money wages. Referring to his definition of involuntary unemployment, the necessary condition is only that the supply of labor exceed the *existing volume of employment* when real wages fall as prices rise. Nothing is said about the relationship of labor supply after such a fall in real wages to the *existing supply* of labor. Keynes does not imply that workers will supply more labor because of a price-induced fall in real wages; he merely states that they will not withdraw their labor as a result of the fall.[12] In fact, some of the labor may be withdrawn without violating necessary Keynesian premises nor contradicting the conclusions reached.

Consider the conventional labor demand and supply schedules in Fig-

[8] *General Theory*, pp. 9 and 14.
[9] Much of this explanation of the unimportance of money illusion in permitting an expansion in output and employment can be found in Richard Perlman, "A Reformulation of Keynesian Wage Theory," *Southern Economic Journal,* **26** (January 1960), pp. 229–233.

Using a different approach, Edgar O. Edwards, "Classical and Keynesian Employment Theories: A Reconciliation," *Quarterly Journal of Economics,* **73** (August 1959), pp. 407–428, reaches the same conclusion that money illusion is not a necessary condition for the attainment of full employment.

[10] Wassily Leontieff, "The Fundamental Assumption of Mr. Keynes' Monetary Theory of Unemployment," *Quarterly Journal of Economics,* **51** (November 1936), p. 195.
[11] James Tobin, "Money Wage Rates and Employment," *The New Economics,* p. 580.
[12] *General Theory*, pp. 9 and 14.

ure 7.1. *BF* is the current level of real wages with employment at *OB*, both determined by the level of total demand. *FE* represents the limiting volume of Keynesian involuntary unemployment at real wage *BF*, since a slightly smaller labor surplus would be willing to work for the smallest decline in real wages. The volume of involuntary unemployment shrinks with the drop in the real wage[13] until it is eliminated at real wage *AP* and employment *OA*. With supply schedule *SS*, output could not expand beyond this point where there would be no involuntary, or even voluntary, unemployment.

If the labor supply schedule had been *CFES*, unemployment would have been voluntary in the Keynesian sense. Employment would not expand beyond *OB,* and output could not rise in response to a growth in aggregate demand. Nevertheless, it would not be inconsistent for *FE* labor to be considered *involuntarily* unemployed in the *current* sense, since these workers could not receive a lower real wage even if they wanted to, given the state of aggregate demand that determined the level of real wages at *OC* and employment at *OB*, respectively.[14]

As employment rises and the real wage falls, point *P* at full employment is reached. There is nothing of money illusion in this adjustment. The labor supply declines with the reduction in real wages. More importantly, the Keynesian condition for involuntary unemployment is followed; both the demand for and supply of labor are greater than the previous levels, before aggregate demand rose.

REAL WAGES AND ECONOMIC EXPANSION

Expansion and Money Illusion

Money illusion was found to be an unnecessary condition for permitting economic expansion because even under a conventional forward-sloping labor supply curve enough surplus labor beyond a depressed level of employment would be available to make an increase in aggregate demand effective in expanding output. In this section, it will be argued

---

[13] Edwards, *op. cit.,* p. 422, notes that while Keynes carefully defines the concept of involuntary unemployment, he never explains how to measure it.

[14] The difference between the Keynesian view of involuntary unemployment as related to business expansion with the concept in its current sense is no more clearly revealed than in Lerner, *op. cit.,* p. 116. There Lerner wrote first, "If a man is not willing to accept a lower *real* wage, then he is voluntarily unemployed . . . ." (See above, p. 231, n. 6.) But at the bottom of the page he writes: "This, [an attempt by workers to lower real wages by reducing their money wages] however, only brings about a proportionate fall in prices so that they are in fact not able to vary their real wages. That is why their unemployment is *involuntary* even if they refuse to accept a lower money wage." (Italics in original.)

that money illusion is not needed, for the additional reason that there is no theoretical basis for real wages to tend to fall as output expands. Furthermore, the data do not show this relationship. This argument is not made to inflict further blows on the corpse of money illusion but to explain the invalidity of Keynes' view on the relationship between real wages and economic expansion, while not questioning the major Keynesian contribution that wage declines do not lead to short-run recovery.

In accordance with his view that real wages would fall when aggregate demand increased, Keynes speculated that the data would show that real wages fell when money wages rose with output and employment.[15] Statistical studies by Dunlop, Tarshis, and Ruggles refuted this hypothesis, finding that real and money wages tended to move upward together during the prosperity phase of the cycle.[16]

R. A. Gordon claims that these studies contain time-series analysis and are therefore dynamic in character while the Keynesian presentation is essentially static. These studies do not distinguish between movements along a demand schedule and shifts in the schedule. In Gordon's words, "Ordinary time series data do not reveal static schedules."[17] The studies, however, were not questioning the validity of the negatively-sloped, real-wage, labor-demand curve. Instead, they tested the Keynesian hypothesis that money wages and real wages move in opposite directions or that real wages and output move inversely.

Keynes' contention regarding the relative movements of real and money wages inappropriately applies static analysis to a dynamic situa-

---

[15] Keynes, *General Theory,* p. 10.

[16] John T. Dunlop, "The Movement of Real and Money Wage Rates," *Economic Journal,* **48** (September 1938), pp. 413–434; Lorie Tarshis, "Changes in Real and Money Wages," *ibid.,* **49** (March 1939), pp. 150–154, and Richard Ruggles, "The Relative Movements of Real and Money Wage Rates," *Quarterly Journal of Economics,* **55** (November 1940), pp. 130–149.

But, consistent with the Keynesian hypothesis, Tarshis found a negative relationship between real wages and employment for the depression years, which he studied. It should be noted, however, that Keynes' view of the divergent movement between real and money wages was based on the assumption that output and employment would be expanding, with rising money wages. Furthermore, for boom periods, Dunlop in his study of English data over a long span found that real wages did tend to fall as money wages continued to rise.

In a more recent study over a longer period, Clarence D. Long found that in the 99-year interval, 1860–1958, real and money wages moved together about three-fourths of the years. "The Illusion of Wage Rigidity: Long and Short Cycles in Wages and Labor," pp. 140–151.

[17] Robert A. Gordon, "Discussion of Keynesian Economics," *American Economic Review,* Papers and Proceedings, **38** (May 1948), p. 355.

tion. For the Keynesian hypothesis to apply, all the other variables except output and employment would have to be unaffected by an increase in aggregate demand, for "a given state of organization, equipment, and technique" to remain constant during the expansion. Certainly, static schedules cannot serve as the basis for forecasts of wage behavior as the economy changes. Both theory and evidence refute this view.

Demands for labor and other factors are interdependent. Lerner's contention that capitalists would rather get something for their property than let it lie idle[18] implies that capital will be fully utilized during bad times. But plants do shut down when firms fail to cover their variable costs.

The need to cover variable costs only explains why output can increase during the upturn without a reduction in real wages in plants that have shut down during depression, because the upturn will be met with a reemployment of both capital and labor with no necessary decline in labor productivity. Idling of machines will also take place, however, in many firms that continue to operate at a reduced level during a slump.

While equipment costs are, for the most part, sunk fixed costs, if capital is not a perfect substitute for labor, with labor alone being idled at first, the marginal product of capital would eventually reach zero. Then capital, whose use entails some variable costs, would also be idled.

If the use of capital did not add to variable costs, then it might be argued that the firm would be indifferent to using all available capital even if some units added nothing to output. There are two answers to this argument.

First, the firm may idle some of its machines even if it cost nothing to use them merely because it thought it did. To some firms, it must always seem irrational to employ factors that yield no return, although they may cost nothing to use.

Stronger than this psychological rebuttal, the assumption of zero-variable costs for capital can be questioned. Machines wear out from use. Thus, if there is a cost of employing capital having zero marginal productivity, it will not be used.

But the real issue here is not whether capital, having zero-marginal productivity, will be used. It is whether the employment of labor will reduce labor's marginal productivity, leading to a reduction in real wages under competitive conditions. Adding labor to this unproductive capital would not decrease labor's marginal product. That this superfluous capital contributed nothing to output means that it needed more of the other

[18] Abba P. Lerner, "The Relation of Wage Policies and Price Policies," *American Economic Review*, **29** (March 1939), p. 163.

factors to become productive. Adding labor to this capital would thus have the same effect on labor's marginal product as adding labor to idle capital. The presence of zero-marginal-productivity capital whether idle or employed serves to keep capital from becoming a bottleneck to output expansion, or to keep labor's marginal productivity from falling with increased employment.

The assumption that machines and equipment are not idled in depression is needed to explain why, in the early stages of the upturn, additional units of labor would work with more or less the same volume of capital as before the revival. Under these conditions, labor's marginal product would diminish with increased employment, and a static labor-demand schedule would apply to the dynamic situation. But relatively full employment of capital would only be maintained during mild recessions. Certainly, Keynes deals with much more serious slumps. Business revival from depression is accompanied by reemployment of both men and machines, not just the former. Furthermore, growth in new plant and equipment adds to the increase in labor productivity. Usually an expansion in capital production accompanies reemployment of old capital during the upturn. Therefore, the Keynesian argument of fixed capital in the short run is doubly invalid.

In any case, without introducing the supporting factor of increased supply of capital for, in truth, the labor supply is also expandable, indications are that productivity increases with expanding plant utilization. As Mills has observed, "The economy as a whole seems to operate more effectively during periods of rising employment, advancing output, and increasing use of productive capacity."[19] More pointedly, Hultgren has found that productivity tends to increase in the early stages of revival and decline in the early stages of recession,[20] a movement with exactly opposite influences on real wages under competitive conditions to those Keynes assumed.

Thus, in the return to full employment, the demand curve for labor may shift to the right, as it may shift to the left in the downturns. If labor is the bottleneck in output expansion, the resultant growth in

[19] Frederick Mills, "The Role of Productivity in Economic Growth," *American Economic Review,* Papers and Proceedings, **42** (May 1952), p. 547.
[20] Thor Hultgren, *Changes in Labor Cost During Cycles in Production and Business,* Occasional Paper No. 74, National Bureau of Economic Research, New York, 1960, pp. 22–28.
George W. Wilson, "The Relationship between Output and Employment," *Review of Economics and Statistics,* **42** (February 1960), pp. 37–43, shows that the strong relationship between productivity and output contradicts the facile assumption made by Keynes and other theorists that an increase in output is necessarily synonymous with an increase in employment.

productivity would serve as the force for an increase in real wages during recovery.

In an interesting case, immediately following World War II, conditions were ideal for a capital bottleneck when civilian production expanded. Workers were freed from war industries and, together with the discharged military forces, formed a large labor pool for civilian production. At the same time, it was difficult to reconvert capital to civilian goods. This was not a period of change from recession to recovery, but it served as an example of conditions necessary for a reduction in productivity and real wages. Money wages did rise less than prices during that period. Following Keynesian analysis, Hansen was able to claim that full employment would not have been achieved in 1946, had labor been unwilling to accept a reduction in its real wage.[21]

Although Keynes was mistaken in arguing that real wages would fall during recovery, this error does not disturb the validity of his primary conclusion. That real wages tend to rise in recovery periods does not affect the reaction of the economy to a money-wage fall during bad times.

In fact, in response to the statistical studies of Dunlop and Tarshis, which contradicted his supposition that real and money wages moved in opposite directions, Keynes, in admitting that his General-Theory statement on wage movements needed correction, noted that the statistical findings sharpened rather than dulled the distinction between his and classical wage and unemployment theory. He writes:

> That I was an easy victim of the traditional conclusion [that real wages fell when money wages rose during recovery] because it fitted my theory is the opposite of the truth. For my own theory this conclusion was inconvenient, since it had a tendency to offset the influence of the main forces which I was discussing and made it necessary for me to introduce qualifications [money illusion], which I need not have troubled with if I could have adopted the contrary generalization founded by Foxwell, Mr. Dunlop and Mr. Tarshis.[22]

[21] Alvin Hansen, "Cost Functions and Full Employment," *American Economic Review*, **37** (September 1947), pp. 562–563.

[22] J. M. Keynes, "Relative Movements of Real Wages and Output," *Economic Journal*, **49** (March 1939), p. 40.

Among other reasons for his earlier error, Keynes notes that his assumption that firms were operating at increasing (marginal) costs during the upswing does not hold when allowance is made for reemployment of capital, as well as labor, when the economy recovers (*loc. cit.*, p. 44). Thus, Keynes here drops the assumption of fixed employment of capital.

At the peak, Keynes still argues that firms will be operating at increasing portions of their cost curves, and he refers to Dunlop's calculation of opposite movements of real and money wages during boom periods to support this view. But the

Keynes goes on to point out that the classicists relied on the fall in real wages that followed expansionist policies as the causal element in stimulating recovery in output and employment, while he considered this fall only as an element permitting the expansion. If, in truth, real wages do not decline with expansion, the classical explanation "must, of course, fall to the ground."[23] The effect on his own theory is the helpful one of making the contrivance of money illusion unnecessary.

Keynesian wage theory is weak in both aspects of its reliance on money illusion in the upturn. First, money illusion would be unnecessary for employment to expand if real wages fell under pressure of rising aggregate demand and, further, they do not tend to fall as the economy strengthens. Nevertheless, Keynesian wage theory still explains the futility of wage cuts to eliminate depression.

Pat:nkin's Modifications

Keynes not only contends that real wages fall as output expands, but also that real wages rise as output contracts. Neither position is supported by the data. Patinkin offers reasons for the latter view not to hold and, from his theory, the invalidity of the former can be inferred.

According to the downward-sloping classical labor-demand curve, based on the premise of declining marginal productivity, which Keynes accepts, a decline in employment leads to a rise in real wages. While Keynes claims that when output falls, the real wage at which the reduced volume of employment will work lies off the labor-supply curve, as noted in Figure 7.1, he places the real wage, *BF*, on the labor-demand curve. According to Patinkin, the tentative equilibrium[24] real wage lies off the demand curve as well, at *BP'*, making the relationship between the full-employment and underemployment real wage indeterminate, even if all nonlabor factors are fixed.

Consider a decline in aggregate demand with no immediate reaction on prices and wages. Firms will reduce output and employment as inventories pile up. Employment would lie to the left of the intersection of the labor supply and demand curve at the same real wage. According

---

data are not conclusive. Jaroslav Vanek, "The Labor Market, Technology, and Stability in the Keynesian Model," *Kyklos,* **16** (1963), p. 116, notes that full employment may be reached before capacity. With labor the bottleneck, maximum production may be reached before marginal labor cost increases. Thus, in accordance with the Keynesian competitive assumption that real wages equal labor's marginal physical product, full employment may be reached before real wages would fall.

[23] Keynes, *loc. cit.,* p. 40.

[24] Equilibrium is only tentative because, to Patinkin, continued downward price and wage pressure generates increased output through the cash-balance effect. The process may alter real wages.

to Keynes, competition would force the real wage directly upward to the labor-demand curve. With the same capital employed, the marginal product of the reduced work force would increase and would exceed the real wage. But to Patinkin, since the firm would not be able to sell the additional output, the marginal product of labor at that employment is indeterminate.[25]

A Keynesian might then counter that the issue is not whether employment will expand but whether competition would drive up real wages to remove the profits earned on the last workers, not additional ones. Although Patinkin does not address himself to this problem, it could be argued that while the value of the marginal product of the former workers does lie below their wage, there is no competitive real-wage push. Profits have been lowered, if not eliminated, as the reduced sales must cover the same fixed costs, under the Keynesian assumption of labor as the only variable factor.[26]

The power of Patinkin's analysis lies in its applicability to a realistic dynamic economy as well as to the stilted Keynesian condition, as explained above. If, instead of using the same volume of capital as under full employment conditions, the employment of capital is reduced *pari passu* with that of labor, the profit position of the remaining producers will be maintained, but the marginal productivity of labor would also remain unchanged as the reduction in labor was matched by a fall in employment of capital. In effect, the assumption of factor variability simply translates the Patinkin analysis into that of the adjusted Keynesian, presented above.

Patinkin's modifications do not postulate constancy of the real wage. That is, in Figure 7.1, P' need not be at the same height as P. Under the Keynesian assumption of fixity of nonlabor factors, the real wage would rise or fall when output and employment fell from the full employment level, depending on the strength and direction of the profit push on wages when employment is reduced, to the point where the resulting output can all be sold.[27] The real wage, however, must be lower than

[25] Don Patinkin, *Money, Interest and Prices,* 2nd ed., Harper & Row, New York, 1965, pp. 322–323.

[26] Albert Rees, "Wage Determination and Involuntary Unemployment," *Journal of Political Economy,* **59** (April 1951), pp. 143–153, maintains that the presence of involuntary unemployment weakens competition for labor, permitting a wage to be set below the value of labor's marginal product. The argument here notes that weakness in the product market also softens upward pressure on wages.

[27] Lerner shows his complete acceptance of Patinkin's modification by moving from his earlier position that labor would not lower its real wage by accepting money-wage reductions to one of conceding that real wages might change, with no effect on employment. He writes, "What is relevant is not the inability of labor to reduce the real wage but the inability to bring about an increase in demand

the rise represented by a movement along the static labor-demand curve because whatever profit pressures pushed real wages above the full-employment level would be dissipated before the real wage, determined from the old demand curve at the reduced level of employment, was reached.

Under the assumption of factor variability in the Patinkin model, duplicating the adjusted Keynesian, real wages would fall or rise from their full-employment level, depending on whether labor productivity increased or decreased with a decline in output. In any case, the new real wage would fall below the level predicted by Keynes, based on movement along a labor-demand curve, all other factors being fixed.

In summary, Patinkin's modifications lead to three changes in the Keynesian model.

1. The relationship of the underemployment real wage to the full-employment wage is indeterminate. Allowing for variability of all factors assures this result, but indeterminacy results even if labor is considered the only variable factor.

2. Given a positively sloped aggregate labor-supply curve, the current level of tentative equilibrium unemployment is lower than under the Keynesian conditions of fixed nonlabor factors. This result follows from the fact that the real wage reached falls below that determined by movement along the demand curve.

3. The takeoff point for the cash-balances effect, to be discussed below, lies at a lower real wage than Keynes would place it. But still the real wage arrived at does not result in an equilibrium position. The labor surplus exerts downward money-wage pressure. The wage decline would act to push product prices down. But prices would be under an independent downward force besides that transferred from the labor market, for while output matched sales at the tentative equilibrium point of employment (and real wages), accumulated inventories would establish a condition of excess supply, if not of output.[28]

MONEY ILLUSION AND UNDEREMPLOYMENT DISEQUILIBRIUM

If money illusion is an unnecessary *deus ex machina* for explaining output and employment growth in response to an expansion in aggregate

---

which increases employment whether this would lower the real wage or *raise* it."
Abba Lerner, "On Generalizing the General Theory," *American Economic Review,* **50** (March 1960), p. 137. (Italics in original.)

[28] Patinkin, *op. cit.,* p. 319.

demand, it is also suspect as a necessary artificial postulate for the assumption of underemployment equilibrium. That is, if it is not necessary for workers to accept real wage cuts when money wages rise as a condition for growth in employment and output, is it necessary that they refuse money wage cuts as a (futile) remedy for unemployment in order to satisfy the Keynesian conditions of *underemployment equilibrium?*

If wages did fall and, in accordance with Keynesian theory, prices fell proportionately leaving real wages unchanged, this process of wages and prices chasing each other downward could scarcely be considered descriptive of an equilibrium situation. The economy could be more accurately described as in a state of continuing underemployment disequilibrium.[29]

More damaging to the Keynesian theory is the possibility that reductions in money wages and prices will, in themselves, generate an increase in real spending and in output and employment. If this were the case, then, in the absence of money illusion that created worker resistance to downward wage movements, wage cuts would, in effect, lead to increased employment. But wage cuts are the classical prescription for unemployment, not the Keynesian.

Three major attacks have been made against the Keynesian position that, even if wages and prices fell, unemployment would not decline as a consequence. These are the so-called Keynes and Pigou (real-balance) effects and the factor-substitution effect. The first two grant that a reduction in wages will not lead to a fall in real wages. Instead, they tacitly accept the Keynesian conclusion that employment can only increase through a rise in aggregate demand and, therefore, describe influences that will tend to increase the major components of demand, investment and consumption. They differ in that, while the Keynes effect would lead to only a partial restoration of a decline in employment, the Pigou effect could, in principle, eliminate involuntary unemployment.

The possibility of factor substitution, on the other hand, constitutes a frontal attack on the Keynesian position. If wage reductions lead to a substitution of labor for other factors, then the effect on employment would not only be direct and rapid but would also fit the classical premise that a money wage fall would lead to a decline in real wages. This follows, since substitution of labor for other factors would take place if the price of these factors did not fall as much as wages, thus keeping the decline in (competitive) prices from matching the wage fall. In

---

[29] Allan Cartter, *Theory of Wages and Employment,* Richard D. Irwin, Inc., Homewood, Illinois, 1959, p. 141, uses this term.

this neoclassical view, employment increases without output expansion. A strong factor-substitution effect could weaken the central Keynesian conclusion that wage cuts are an ineffective and incomplete means for returning to a full employment condition.

The three effects will be studied in turn, and the conclusion reached that only the Pigou effect contains the theoretical, if not practical, elements for invalidating the central Keynesian conclusion, that employment does not rise as a result of a decline in money wages or, more generally, that the advance of employment is unaffected by changes in money wages.

Keynes Effect

According to the Keynes effect, the reduction in prices consequent to a drop in money wages would reduce the transactions demand for money, lower interest rates, and induce investment. This effect faces two limiting influences.

First, the "liquidity trap" concept suggests that the need for some liquid cash limits the effect of price reduction in depressing the transactions demand for money. In theory, however, as prices approached the limit of zero, the need for lower cash balances to satisfy liquidity preferences would also fall toward zero.

Second, and more important, if, as is probably the case in deep depression, investment demand were interest inelastic, even if the interest rate fell to zero because of the reduced transaction demand for money, the resultant rise in investment might not be large enough to match intended savings at full-employment income. Because of interest inelasticity of investment demand alone then, the Keynes effect would be unlikely to lead to a full employment situation.

Pigou Effect

While the Keynes effect probably but slightly modifies the Keynesian contention of underemployment disequilibrium, the Pigou effect, in theory at least, would suffice to restore full employment as wages and prices fell. At first view, the Pigou effect, which refers to the stimulation of consumption from an increase in the real value of liquid assets, appears very weak. Net liquid assets that increase in value when prices fall are cash out of banks, instruments of government debt, and that portion of demand deposits that does not arise from private borrowing (roughly equal to bank reserves). Furthermore, the bulk of these liquid assets is held by high income groups, likely to have relatively low-consumption propensities.

Granted that the Pigou effect from a single price decline may be weak, in theory a continual reduction in prices can eliminate all savings. If the real value of even the limited liquid assets that count approaches infinity as the price level approaches zero, total savings would tend to fall toward zero, too, and income would be pushed up to its full employment level where the wage and price declines would be arrested.[30]

Even the negative influence of expectations would not offset the growing desire to reduce savings as prices fell. A continuous fall in prices might induce a desire to save for further reductions, but this incentive to save reaches a maximum influence while the Pigou effect continually strengthens as prices fall.

As Haberler expresses this difference,

> There may be a rational incentive for indefinite continuation of hoarding— viz., the expectation of a continued fall in prices. But, in all circumstances, it remains true that the incentive to dishoard must *grow continuously* with the growth of hoards in terms of money and goods.[31]

Thus because of the cumulative nature of the Pigou effect, underemployment equilibrium cannot exist under conditions of downward wage and price flexibility. But how practical or possible to implement is a policy that permits or encourages wages and prices to fall toward zero? While the theoretical possibility of reestablishing full employment through the Pigou effect exists, the time it would take and the disruption it would cause would make it an impractical policy instrument. Wage and price stabilizing measures would probably be instituted before the full effects were felt.

If it seems illogical to argue that a move to keep wages and prices from falling supports the Keynesian position, since the very point of the classical argument is that the failure of wages to fall prevents the attainment of full employment, the Pigou effect reveals the difference in the two theories to be one of degree rather than kind. Under the classical position, a fall in wages would lead to quick and certain stimu-

---

[30] Pigou, himself, emphasizes the cumulative nature of the effect on an individual's consumption of a rise, "in terms of real income, of his existing possessions. As this increases, the amount that he desires to save out of any assigned real income diminishes and ultimately vanishes." A. C. Pigou, "The Classical Stationary State," *Economic Journal,* **53** (December 1943), pp. 349–350.

It might not be necessary for savings to dwindle to zero for full employment to be reached, but what is important in the present case is that, as long as savings are falling, or the consumption function rising, as a result of falling prices, underemployment equilibrium cannot exist.

[31] Gottfried Haberler, *Prosperity and Depression,* 3rd ed., United Nations, Lake Success, 1956, p. 390, n. 1. (Italics not in the original.) In this passage, Haberler was describing the relative effects of expectations and increases in hoards in general—not just through the Pigou effect.

lation of output and employment, so that the question of whether to arrest a precipitous wage and price decline would not arise. But the required wage-and-price decline, to bring about the same stimulation under the Pigou effect, would be greater and continue a longer time. The question of whether these massive adjustments would be permitted then arises. If the Keynesian analysis is short-run, any antidepression policy or formula must get results quickly, if its effects are to be worked out without modification, or be abandoned altogether.

Writing soon after the appearance of the *General Theory*, Champernowne argues that even if nothing is done to stop the wage decline, the monetary authorities would take steps to halt the price decline. He writes:

> . . . if labor is so disorganized by unemployment that the competition of the unemployed continually lowers money wages, a situation must eventually arise in which the monetary authority takes action to check any resultant fall in price, and so make effective the attempts of the unemp'oyed to accept a lower real wage.[32]

If such action were taken, the monetary authority would, in effect, be seeking to lower real wages and increase the degree of monopoly—in the Lerner sense.[33] This form of price-support program would not describe "monetary management by the Trade Unions, aimed at full employment, instead of the banking system,[34] as Keynes admitted the monetary effects of a wage reduction, but trade union or labor market practices inducing monetary measures.

But Champernowne's prescription assumes away the working of competitive forces. As real wages fall because of a price freeze, pressure among employers would raise wages to a level that stabilized real wages at the previous higher level. According to Keynesian analysis, efforts to strengthen the economy through price-supporting measures confuse cause and effect by attacking the symptom of underemployment rather than its cause. The economy is not weak because real wages are high, but real wages are high because the economy is weak. Similarly, trying to force real wages down will not strengthen the economy, but raising demand will lower real wages.

But any outside move to stabilize wages and/or prices would not strictly follow the rules of the Pigou effect game. All that can be said against it, and that should be sufficient to expose its ineffectiveness

---

[32] D. G. Champernowne, "Unemployment, Basic and Monetary: The Classical Analysis and the Keynesian," *Review of Economic Studies*, **3** (1935–1936), p. 201.

[33] Abba Lerner, "The Concept of Monopoly and the Measurement of Monopoly Power," *Review of Economic Studies*, **1** (1933–1934), p. 169, defines the degree of monopoly power as the ratio of price less marginal cost to price.

[34] *General Theory*, p. 267.

as an important antidepression measure, is that it takes too long to work and its side effects are intolerable.

Even as strong a critic of the weaknesses of Keynesian monetary theory as Patinkin concludes simply at one point, ". . . I feel that it is impractical to depend upon the Pigou effect as a means of policy."[35] Again, in maintaining that the elimination of unemployment, even in a world of freely declining wages and prices, might not take place "within a socially acceptable period of time," Patinkin notes that the Pigou effect (and Keynes effect), even under competition, depend on individual decisions to consume (and invest), which "respond only 'stickily' to market changes in interest and prices. They are the rigidities of sovereign consumers' (and investors') unwillingness to modify their expenditure habits on short notice."[36]

Factor Substitution

Even abandoning the assumption of money illusion that keeps workers from accepting lower money wages in proportion to price declines, neither the Keynes nor the Pigou effect seriously damages the Keynesian theory of short-run underemployment disequilibrium. But the possibility of factor substitution with wage declines poses a serious threat to the theory that unemployment would persist, without recourse to the concept of money illusion, with a fall in money wages. If a fall in money wages led to a rise in employment through substitution of labor for other factors, then the validity of the theory of short-run underemployment disequilibrium would depend on the extent to which employment would move toward the full-employment level without a rise in output.

According to Tobin,[37] one of the more serious shortcomings of the Keynesian analysis is its implicit assumption that labor is the only variable factor. If there were other variable factors, the conclusion that a reduction in money wages could not directly increase employment would not hold. Even if a reduction in wages would not lead to a restoration of full employment along the path of increased output, could not the same goal be reached by the substitution of labor for other factors to produce the same output? This issue might not interest the monetary theorist, since this adjustment path implies a drop in real wages, as money wages fall more than other factor returns and, consequently,

---

[35] Patinkin "Price Flexibility and Full Employment," *American Economic Review*, **38** (September 1948), p. 558.

[36] Patinkin, *Money, Interest and Prices*, pp. 342–343.

Whether strictly competitive conditions permit slow reactions has been questioned in this context by John G. Cross and John Williamson, "Patinkin on Unemployment Disequilibrium," *Journal of Political Economy*, **70** (February 1962), pp. 76–77, n. 4.

[37] James Tobin, "Money Wage Rates and Employment," p. 578.

less then prices, but it certainly exposes a possible flaw in the Keynesian analysis.

Given other variable factors, Tobin notes that a wage decline would not lead to factor substitution only if all other factors were fully employed with completely flexible prices, that is, with perfectly inelastic supply schedules. Under these artificial conditions, if wages fell, the incentive to substitute labor for other factors would be eliminated by a proportional fall in return to the other variable factors to keep them fully employed.

Relaxing these unrealistic conditions, a wage decline would result in some labor substitution. But if the depression were relatively severe, it is unlikely that this substitution of labor for other variable factors would be sufficient to restore full employment. The concept of a "complementarity trap" can be introduced here. Even if wages fell to zero, substitution would halt when further substitution of labor for other factors could not increase output. In the absence of a "complementarity trap," it might appear that the distinction between classical and Keynesian wage theory would only interest the pedant, since what would it matter if full employment were reached through output expansion or factor substitution, as long as it was reached?

But the presence of factors with a degree of fixity, because of sunk costs, prevents the easy restoration of full employment, even assuming substitutability between labor and these factors. Consider the effect of variation in employment of capital.[38]

Considering the effect of wage reductions on producing units differentially affected by the downturn, it can be explained that the total effect of factor substitution provides but a slow and incomplete adjustment toward the restoration of full employment. First, we shall examine the firm uneffected by the cycle; then the firm slightly affected to the extent that it does not idle any capital; third, the firm that just decides to use all of its capital; and finally, the firm that is so depressed that it idles some machines.[39] The usual assumptions of perfect competition in factor markets, of homogeneous efficiency within factors, and of divisible units apply.[40]

[38] The following analysis could apply to the relationship between untrained and trained labor, having some sunk costs, as well as between "labor" and "capital." This aspect of training was discussed in Chapter V.

[39] Note that the assumption of fully utilized capital, which describes the first three cases, precludes substitution of capital for labor if wages increase. We are of course concerned here only with the possibility of substituting labor for capital because of wage declines.

[40] Much of the following analysis can be found in Thomas F. Dernburg and Duncan

THE UNAFFECTED FIRM. This firm has undergone no change in its employment of labor and capital because of the depression. It employs an amount of capital and labor such that the ratios of their prices equals the ratio of their marginal products. The immediate effect of a wage decline on factor substitution is zero. Since capital costs are sunk, it pays to employ the same capital as before. (This assumes negligible variable costs for capital.)

In the long run, when capital becomes variable through the process of depreciation and obsolescence, the firm no longer will be indifferent to the choice of producing the same output by replacing machines or hiring more labor. It will now hire more labor from the ranks of the unemployed and will continue to do so until factor-price ratios are once again brought into equality with marginal-product ratios. The process of substitution will be greater the greater the wage decline. For firms of this type, therefore, the substitution effect is important. But, on the other hand, if the recession is severe, few firms would not suffer a fall in production.

THE SLIGHTLY AFFECTED FIRM. The immediate effect of a decline in demand would be to maintain employment of all fixed capital but to lay off workers. But as machines depreciate and become obsolete, labor would be rehired first (instead of machines being replaced), *even without a wage decline*, because the ratio of the marginal product of capital to that of labor would have fallen below the ratio of the price of capital to that of labor. The additional increase in the use of labor without a wage decline does not indicate a movement toward full employment. It merely corrects the excessive impact on employment that occurred during the brief (instantaneous?) period when capital was fixed. Thus the increase in employment following a wage decline would occur only after a longer time than for the unaffected firm, for which the very first worn-out or obsolete machine would have been replaced by new workers. For the slightly affected firm, then, the employment effect of a wage decline would not be felt until some time after capital became replaceable.

THE FIRM JUST USING ALL OF ITS CAPITAL. This case differs from the previous one only in degree. For the slightly affected firm, it is implied that, although all capital were used, its marginal product was greater

---

M. McDougall, *Macro-Economics*, McGraw-Hill, New York, 1963, pp. 160–162. Their emphasis differs, however, in that they merely try to demonstrate that some capital will be idled during depressions, not that substitution of cheapened labor for capital is therefore made difficult.

than zero, so that had more capital been available, it too would have been utilized, assuming, of course, negligible variable costs for capital.

Now, in this case, all capital is used but the marginal product is zero, so that had any more capital been available, it would have been idled. Again (as in the previous case), in the short run, capital would be replaced by labor without a wage change. With the marginal product of capital at zero, replacement of capital by labor would occur at any positive price for capital. Therefore, it would take longer than for the slightly affected firm for additional workers to be hired because of a wage cut.

THE SEVERELY AFFECTED FIRM. With the firm so badly affected that it idles machines, the possibility of increasing employment through wage reductions becomes remote. The immediate effect of the sharp output decline is to lay off workers and those machines that are at the point of zero-marginal productivity. Consequently, when capital becomes variable through depreciation and obsolescence, the worn-out machines will be replaced by idle ones in the firm's stock, since the variable cost of capital is slight.[41] Wage declines would have no effect during this period. Only after all the excess capital had been used would firms in this category follow the adjustment path of firms of the preceding type.

Thus a long time must elapse before a wage cut for a severely affected firm would be reflected in additional employment. The fact that labor productivity tends to rise during the early stages of recovery suggests the unemployment of idled machinery,[42] with many firms having been severely affected by the depression. Consequently, it can be concluded that substitution of cheapened labor for factors with a fixed-cost element offers little promise as a major measure for the restoration of full employment from a depressionary state.

Expressed less strongly, the larger the wage cut, the greater the employment effect, once substitution of labor for other variable factors with or without a degree of fixity begins. Thus, full employment could be approached through this effect, although not reached if the depression were severe enough,[43] without invalidating the central Keynesian point

---

[41] It is really not necessary to assume that the excessive machines were idled. If they were all used, for some irrational reason, even though some of them contributed nothing to output, the employment of machinery would simply become less redundant as depreciation and obsolescence set in.

[42] The present analysis deals only with replacement of capital, but it is based on the presence of surplus capital. Labor productivity could not rise if bottlenecks in capital occurred during early recovery.

[43] The substitution of cheapened labor for capital faces a complementarity trap, too.

that wage cuts do not serve as a ready device for the quick restoration of full employment.

The above analysis points out that the length of time that must elapse before a wage reduction results in additional employment through factor substitution during a slump is a function of the severity of the depression. The more severe the depression and the more firms that belong to the severely affected class,[44] the longer the period before substitution of labor for factors with a fixed-cost elements begins. For these firms, capital is a variable factor long before it becomes a variable cost. The Keynesian short-run period, during which effects on employment of wage cuts are worked out, can be very long indeed.

The factor-substitution effect belongs with the Pigou effect, theoretical means by which labor can be reemployed, although but of little practical importance as ways to achieve full employment because of the time they take and the disruption they cause.[45]

In the Pigou effect, the economy is subject to the problems associated with steadily falling wages and prices. For operation of the factor-substitution effect, labor must not only divest itself of money illusion, with respect to wage declines, but it must actually also accept a lower real wage for the benefits of added employment.

SUMMARY

The most important contribution of Keynesian wage theory is its conclusion that a reduction in money wages will not serve as an effective short-run depression cure. This somewhat attenuated conclusion retreats a good distance from the simplified Keynesian conclusion, not even held by Keynes himself, that a reduction in money wages could not increase the level of employment. But the Keynesian argument, or that part of it still intact, holds that recovery could much better be achieved through monetary and fiscal measures and that, more importantly, any recovery instituted by wage reductions would be incomplete and/or too slowly operating to serve as a significant contributor to restoration of full employment.

[44] Wage reductions would lead to product substitution as the price of labor-intensive goods fell more than other prices. Thus, firms producing these goods would enjoy relative prosperity and would more likely fall into the unaffected and slightly affected groups.

[45] They differ in that, in theory, full employment can be achieved through the Pigou effect. The cash-balance path has no "liquidity trap," interest inelasticity barriers, or "complementarity trap." Thus, one could argue equally as effectively that the substitution effect parallels the Keynes effect more closely than the Pigou effect.

In his *General-Theory* view that real wages would rise in the downturn and fall during recovery, Keynes misapplied static schedules to a dynamic condition. Thus, money illusion becomes an unnecessary contrived mechanism to explain reaction to a situation that probably seldom arises. In fact, this view puts him, at least superficially, too close to the classical position. As Patinkin observed, "It might be noted that this inverse relation (between real wages and output) characterizes the Keynesian theory of employment no less than the classical."[46] But to clarify the vague term "characterizes," it should be emphasized that the inverse relationship represents a causal sequence in the classical system from a decline in real wages to an expansion in output, while, in the earlier Keynesian system, it is the rise in output that induces the decline in real wages.[47] Keynes, himself, later welcomed the findings of parallel money and real wage movements as support to his own theory and contradiction of the classical.

Only if the supply of other factors were fixed could the static demand schedule apply to the behavior of labor demand during cyclical change. More realistically, the tentative equilibrium point at which wage reductions would lead to the Keynes and Pigou effects and substitution of cheapened labor for other factors would lie off both the labor demand and supply curves, not just the supply curve, as Keynes implied.

Money illusion, representing the unwillingness of workers to suffer a real wage decline by taking wage cuts during depression, could justify a theory of underemployment equilibrium. But holding to this unrealistic view of worker behavior makes the Keynesian vulnerable to the charge that his theory requires rigid money wages as the cause of continued unemployment, placing him in the classical camp. The Keynesian can live with the corrections that would ensue from abandonment of this assumption of money illusion. Underemployment disequilibrium would result, but the central Keynesian view could still be held that the beneficial effects of wage reduction, through the Keynes effect, the Pigou effect, and the factor-substitution effect, would lead to only partial and/or slow movement along the path toward full employment.

---

[46] Patinkin, *Money, Interest and Prices,* p. 324, n. 10.

[47] As E. J. Mishan, "The Demand for Labor in a Classical and Keynesian Framework," *Journal of Political Economy,* **72** (December 1964), p. 611, succinctly expresses it, quantity demanded is usually considered as a function of price but, for the Keynesian demand curve, the price established (real wage) is a function of the quantity demanded.

In short, the dependent and independent variables of the classical system are reversed by Keynesian theory.

CHAPTER VIII

Unemployment—
Inadequate Demand
and the Structural
Hypothesis

Interest in structural unemployment arose in the late 1950's when the unemployment rate seemed to lose its resiliency. Deviating from the postwar pattern of recession and recovery in which the rate would rise above and then fall substantially below 5 percent, after reaching its recession high in 1958, the rate did not fall below the 5 percent level for seven years.

During this period a running debate developed between two schools of thought on the causes of the high unemployment plateau that developed. One school, the inadequate demand proponents, chief among whom has been the Council of Economic Advisers, argued that the cause of the high unemployment rate was the incomplete nature of the post-1958 recovery. According to this school, the main need was for greater income generation.

The structuralists, on the other hand, claimed either that unemployment could have been substantially reduced at the current level of national income by adapting the unemployed to the job openings, or that increased spending would reduce unemployment only at the cost of substantial inflation as bottlenecks appeared. Thus, to them, structural elements were at the root of the failure to approach full employment. Although the long-awaited movement of the rate below 5 and even 4 percent following the tax cut of 1964 seemed to substantiate the inadequate demand position, the debate still continues.

Before sensible discussion of the issues can be undertaken and conclusions reached, it is necessary to formulate a precise definition of structural unemployment. Much of the confusion in evaluating the impact of structural aspects has resulted from illogical or loose definitions of the term, made mainly by detractors of structuralism. After defining the term, some of the misdirected blows against structural unemployment as a significant contributor to overall unemployment will be noted. The relationship between unemployment in general and structural unemployment in particular to job vacancies is studied throughout.

DEFINITIONS AND CONCEPTS OF STRUCTURAL UNEMPLOYMENT

FUNDAMENTALS. For structural unemployment to have any significance it must constitute a component of overall unemployment. That is, total unemployment must fall if structural unemployment were reduced. Defined most simply, a worker is *structurally unemployed*

> if he is unemployed and a job opening (vacancy) exists that he is not qualified to fill.[1]

Given the above definition, the total level of structural unemployment is

> the number of vacancies minus the number of unemployed workers qualified to fill them, provided that the total number of unemployed exceeds the total number of vacancies.

But if there are more vacancies than unemployed, then the volume of structural unemployment becomes

> the total number of unemployed minus the unemployed who can fill the vacancies.

When vacancies exist and qualified unemployed workers can fill some of these vacancies, these unemployed are considered *frictionally unemployed*. Thus the total of frictional unemployment can be measured as a residual, if structural unemployment is calculated, as

> the sum of job vacancies minus the structurally unemployed—those unqualified to fill the vacancies—when total unemployment exceeds total vacancies.

But when the number of vacancies is greater than the volume of unemployment, frictional unemployment can be measured indirectly as

> total unemployment minus the unemployed unqualified to fill existing vacancies—the structurally unemployed.

[1] At this preliminary stage, the issue whether the vacancy and the unemployed worker must be in the same labor market will be deferred.

Finally, cyclical, or inadequate demand unemployment, can only occur when the volume of unemployment is greater than the number of vacancies. Under these conditions, cyclical unemployment is simply

> the total number of unemployed minus the total number of vacancies.

Expressed algebraically, when $U > V$,

$$U = U_s + U_f + U_c$$
$$V = U_s + U_f$$
$$U_c = U - V$$

When $V > U$,

$$U_c = 0$$
$$U = U_s + U_f$$

These expressions explain that little can be learned about the volume of structural unemployment at a particular time from either vacancy or unemployment data themselves. They do not permit disentangling structural from strictly frictional unemployment. This difficulty can be resolved to some extent by a microeconomic approach. Occupation-by-occupation enumeration[2] allows an estimation of the degree to which total job vacancies are matched by the structurally and frictionally unemployed. Overall, it is quite possible for some unemployment to be structural even though the volume of unemployment exceeds the number of vacancies, provided that for some occupational classifications vacancies exceed unemployment.

If $U_i > V_i$ for occupation i, then all the vacancies are matched by frictionally unemployed workers, and the excess of unemployed to job openings measures the contribution of the occupation to overall cyclical unemployment and/or to structural unemployment. If the excess is to contribute to structural unemployment, there must be occupations for which $V_j > U_j$. These relationships depend on the assumption that all workers attached to an occupational classification are qualified to fill openings for that particular job. (This assumption will require modification when the effects of discrimination are examined.)

Thus, assuming labor surpluses for some occupations, a necessary and sufficient condition for an occupation to contribute to structural unem-

---

[2] In this context, "occupation" stands for a job requiring particular skills and demanding specific responsibilities. On the weakness of the current data, which serve as the source of this information, see James Scoville, "The Development and Relevance of U. S. Occupational Data," *Industrial and Labor Relations Review,* **19** (October 1965), pp. 70–79.

ployment is that the number of job openings exceed the volume of unemployed workers attached to the job. The maximum contribution of such an occupation to structural unemployment is measured by this excess. This value is a maximum because it must be matched by an excess of unemployment over vacancies in other occupations for the full value to be counted. Oddly enough, the key to the measurement of structural unemployment lies in the sectors in which labor is in short supply and not in a count of unemployed workers themselves.[3]

For structural unemployment to exist, then, there must be some occupations for which the number of vacancies exceeds the number employed. These occupations may be called *Structurally Overemployed Counterparts* (SOC). Thus, to calculate the total volume of structural unemployment, the problem of separating structural from frictional unemployment can be avoided by measuring the excess of vacancies over unemployment in the SOC.

Algebraically,

$$U_s = \sum_{i=1}^{n} (V_i - U_i) \tag{1}$$

for all SOC, provided that the resulting value is less than $\sum_{i=1}^{n} (U_i - V_i)$ for the other occupations in which the volume of unemployment exceeds the number of job vacancies.

If $\sum_{i=1}^{n} (V_i - U_i)$ in the SOC exceeds $\sum_{i=1}^{n} (U_i - V_i)$ for the labor surplus occupations, then the volume of structural unemployment becomes simply $\sum_{i=1}^{n} (U_i - V_i)$ for all non-SOC, that is, for all occupations in which $U_i > V_i$.

Combining macro and microeconomic relationships, if there is some cyclical unemployment, so that $U > V$, since $V = U_f + U_s$, (1) can be rewritten in the form

$$V - U_f = \sum_{i=1}^{n} (V_i - U_i)$$

[3] Richard Lipsey, "Structural and Deficient-Demand Unemployment Reconsidered," *Employment Policy and the Labor Market,* edited by Arthur M. Ross, University of California Press, Berkeley, 1965, p. 222, maintains that nothing can be learned about the nature and extent of structural unemployment by a study of the unemployed themselves.

for all SOC. Since all unemployment in SOC is frictional, there is no need to measure frictional unemployment to calculate structural unemployment.

On the other hand, if the total volume of vacancies exceeds the volume of unemployment, so that there is no cyclical unemployment, since

$$U = U_s + U_f \quad \text{and} \quad U_s = \sum_{i=1}^{n} (U_i - V_i)$$

for all non-SOC, then

$$U - U_f = \sum_{i=1}^{n} (U_i - V_i)$$

for all non-SOC.

Again, the microeconomic approach permits indirect count of the structurally unemployed while avoiding the difficulty of differentiating between the structurally and frictionally unemployed imposed by the macroeconomic left-hand side of the above equality. Since, in the non-SOC, all job vacancies are offset by frictionally unemployed workers and all the remaining (structurally) unemployed would be paired off with vacancies in the SOC, which they are unqualified to fill, the excess of unemployed over vacancies in the non-SOC comprise the structurally unemployed.

With the primary requirement for structural unemployment the presence of tight job markets in some (occupational) sectors, it becomes evident that structural unemployment is more a product of good times than bad. When the overall unemployment level is high, certainly interoccupational variations in unemployment rates exist, but there is only slight probability that many occupations fall in the SOC category, jobs for which the number of vacancies exceeds the number of unemployed. On the other hand, when times are good and the overall unemployment rate low, the chances that labor shortages exist for particular occupations are great; structural unemployment probably forms a significant part of the total level of joblessness.

Structural imbalance, defined as differential unemployment rates among occupations, can be looked upon both as a cause of unemployment and as a factor hindering reemployment during business recoveries.[4] Considering the nature of structural unemployment and national concern over the difficulties in reducing the unemployment rate, in particular

---

[4] Arthur Ross, Introduction to *Employment Policy and the Labor Market*, p. 13, makes this distinction.

without causing inflation, the second aspect has become a more important area of controversy. When the overall rate exceeds, say, 5 percent, the important question is not whether structural unemployment contributes greatly to this rate. It probably doesn't, since recessions are bad times for structural unemployment. The crucial question becomes whether the rate can be reduced much below this level without causing inflation. The relationship between the reduction of structural unemployment and inflation will be treated later in this Chapter and in Chapter IX, but at this point the confusion between structural imbalance and structural unemployment should be resolved.

Structural imbalance is not a sufficient condition for structural unemployment and, under some circumstances, is not even a necessary condition. For example, if unemployment rates were uniform among occupations, structural unemployment might still exist because of interoccupational differences in levels of frictional unemployment. If rates were uniformly high in all occupations, then it could be assumed that all unemployment was nonstructural; unemployment would exceed vacancies for all jobs. But if the uniform rate were low, there might be some jobs for which frictional elements were of minimal importance, so that even a low rate for them would exceed the number of vacancies. Only if frictional rates were uniform among occupations would structural imbalance be a necessary condition for structural unemployment. Then if all rates were above the frictional level, no job classification would represent an SOC, while if all rates fell below the frictional level, all jobs would be classified as SOC, but there would be no unemployed available to fill the openings that existed.

Thus, assuming uniform frictional levels, the necessary and sufficient conditions for structural employment are that both labor surplus occupations and SOC occur at the same time. Many of the discussions of structuralism based on the presence, absence, or change in structural imbalance overlook these requirements. Confusion regarding the difference between structural imbalance and structural unemployment has led to many irrelevancies and errors in statements, tests, and policy recommendations concerning the presence, intensity, and trends in structural unemployment.

For example, the Council of Economic Advisers argues that ". . . since structural maladjustments tend to flourish in slack markets, a vigorous expansion in demand helps cut structural problems down to size."[5] Now, structural imbalance does tend to become more severe during recessions

[5] *Annual Report of the Council of Economic Advisers,* Appendix A, Washington, 1964, p. 168.

as increased unemployment falls most heavily on those groups that characteristically suffer from relatively high unemployment rates. But "structural problems," insofar as they contribute to structural unemployment, are a product of good times, not slack markets. When times are bad, all segments of the labor force tend to experience high unemployment, although at different rates. SOC are scarce or nonexistent, and total unemployment would not fall from labor force shifts from groups with high rates to those with lower levels of joblessness, where unemployment rates were still above their frictional level.

As a numerical example, assume an economy with two occupations of equal memberships, one of which has an unemployment rate of 7 percent, the other 3 percent. Assume further that at the 3 percent rate, the number of unemployed exceeds the number of vacancies, that is, that all unemployment for the job is either cyclical or frictional. Then labor mobility from the high to the low unemployment occupation would have no effect on the overall rate. The shift might correct structural imbalance, establish a uniform rate of 5 percent for both jobs, and equalize the probability of unemployment for all workers, but would leave the overall rate unchanged. In this case, structural imbalance existed but not structural unemployment.

That there are an excessive number of square pegs, which cannot fit round holes, contributes nothing to a given level of total unemployment as long as there is also a surplus, no matter how small, of round pegs. Structural unemployment is in a sense a threshold concept, not a continuous element in rising unemployment. When the unemployment rate rises above the frictional level for a particular overemployed classification, the contribution of this former SOC to structural unemployment does not grow smaller—it disappears. It grows smaller only as the unemployment rate rises toward its frictional level.

The Council's statement regarding the prevalence of structural unemployment in bad times probably reflects the widening in group unemployment rates during recessions, noted above. The rate for groups with characteristically heavy unemployment—blue-collar workers, older and younger workers, Negroes, the uneducated and unskilled—tends to rise faster than the rate for groups that show labor shortages during good times. But divergence in rates contributes nothing to structural unemployment when the sectors with lower rates themselves have labor surpluses.

Thus, studies of the tendency toward differential rates to narrow or widen throw no light on the questions of the extent or direction of structural unemployment. That the rate for disadvantaged groups approaches the overall average does not necessarily reflect a lessening of structural unemployment.[6]

It is surprising that the Council should argue that structural unemployment is a product of bad times, or that *"These high specific rates* [for disadvantaged groups] are the essence of the problem of structural unemployment,"[7] considering the closeness of its observation that the high unemployment at the time was due partly to the fact that "the characteristics of our available workers do not fully match the characteristics employers are seeking in filling the jobs that are available . . ."[8] to the definition of structural unemployment presented in this chapter. Of the characteristics noted by the Council—location, skill, education, training, race, sex, and age—examination of the geographic, racial, and educational aspects of structural unemployment will serve to clarify the concept further. These considerations will affect the definitions and relationships presented above. Before examining these factors, the relationship of structural to total unemployment will be studied further.

STRUCTURAL UNEMPLOYMENT AS A COMPONENT OF TOTAL UNEMPLOYMENT. In the first sentences of this section it was implied that structural unemployment was an additive component to total unemployment and not merely a substitute for, say, cyclical unemployment, so that a reduction in structural unemployment would result in an equal decline in total unemployment. Musgrave questions this view, arguing that a

---

[6] Robert A. Gordon, "Has Structural Unemployment Worsened?" *Industrial Relations,* **3** May 1964), pp. 53–77, measures the relative changes in unemployment rates of these groups as a guide to the changing importance of structural unemployment.

Similarly, that long-term unemployment tends to fall on particular groups (see the studies of Barbara Berman, "Alternative Measures of Structural Unemployment," *Employment Policy and the Labor Market,* pp. 256–268, and Norman Simler, "Long-Term Unemployment, The Structural Hypothesis and Public Policy," *American Economic Review,* **54** (December 1964), pp. 985–1001) only points out further evidence of structural imbalance, not necessarily structural unemployment. But this imbalance does suggest that some groups will be more susceptible to structural unemployment than others when it arises.

[7] 1964 Annual Report, p. 173. (Italics in original.)

[8] *Ibid.,* p. 166. Charles C. Killingsworth, "Automation, Jobs, and Manpower," *Nation's Manpower Revolution,* U. S. Senate, Subcommittee on Employment and Manpower of the Committee on Labor and Public Welfare, Hearings, 88th Congress, 1st Session, Washington, 1963, p. 1494, uses almost the same wording to define what he calls "labor market imbalance," which in his usage is synonymous with structural unemployment as posited here, not with differential sector unemployment rates.

program to reduce structural unemployment would only entail employment diversion rather than employment creation, and that total employment would only increase through a rise in aggregate demand.[9]

Although Musgrave does not elaborate on his position, the claim of employment diversion implies that if surplus workers in occupational groups A are trained to fill the vacancies in B, output using B workers, whose number now includes the recently trained, would rise and output of A workers would fall. Neglecting difference in demand and in production functions between the two-product groups, employment (and unemployment) would remain constant as a fresh supply of unemployment among A workers arose because of a fall in demand for their services as output produced by A workers fell.

But the very presence of SOC, the labor-shortage component of structural unemployment, indicates an excess of aggregate demand over aggregate spending.[10] The shortage of B workers might have reflected a switch in demand toward B-worker goods or a change in relative wages in favor of A workers, not related to a shift in labor demand. The resultant shortage of B workers might have been alleviated somewhat by accommodating movements in relative wages and product demand toward A-worker goods.[11] But that this adjustment was incomplete is measured by the degree of excessive vacancies for B workers.

[9] Richard A. Musgrave, "Demand Versus Structural Unemployment," *Unemployment in a Prosperous Economy,* edited by William G. Bowen and Frederick H. Harbison, Princeton University Industrial Relations Section, 1965, pp. 95–96.

[10] Musgrave was criticized for equating the two. Discussion of Papers on the Aggregate-Demand Approach," *ibid.,* pp. 102. If demand and spending were equal, then Musgrave's formulation would apply, but then there would not be any structural unemployment.

[11] The shortage might have also been eased somewhat by a substitution of weaker workers in the production process. In fact, David M. Blank and George J. Stigler, *The Demand and Supply of Scientific Personnel,* National Bureau of Economic Research, New York, 1957, p. 24 consider that "a shortage exists when . . . activities which once were performed by (say) engineers must now be performed by a class of workers who are less well trained . . . ." In the omitted parts of their definition of a shortage, Blank and Stigler note that this substitution occurs after a relative rise in the wages of the skilled workers in short supply, an element related to the inflationary aspects of reducing structural employment, to be discussed below.

But to the extent that shortages are eased by using less qualified workers, structural unemployment is reduced because vacancies are filled, even if unsatisfactorily. Note that the Labor Department's definition of a vacancy for its Job Vacancy Survey Program states that, for a vacancy to exist, the job must be unoccupied. *Job Vacancy Statistics,* Joint Economic Committee Hearings, 89th Congress (May 1966), pp. 105 and 108.

If the adjustment had been complete, B jobs would not have constituted an SOC, and all unemployment not frictional would have been cyclical. Accordingly, with the adjustment incomplete, a shift, through training of A workers into the B group, would serve as a substitute for an accommodating shift of wages and product demand, and allow for a net increase in output and employment. If this shift of workers continued to the point where B-worker fields no longer constituted SOC, and a surplus of unemployment over vacancies still prevailed in the A-worker fields, remaining nonfrictional unemployment would be cyclical. But what is important to the present discussion, this volume of unemployment would be below the level previous to the shift of newly trained workers, by the number who found jobs in B-worker fields.

The structural component of unemployment has been overlooked before. Lord Beveridge's definition of full employment as an excess of vacant jobs over unemployed workers is a case in point.[12] If all individual occupations showed an excess of vacancies over unemployment, all unemployment would be frictional,[13] and the economy might be considered one of "full employment."[14] But on an overall basis, a total surplus of vacancies over unemployment merely indicates that demand is adequate to establish full employment. Some sectors might have a surplus of unemployment over vacancies, indicating the presence of structural unemployment. Referring to Beveridge's definition, would unemployment be just as full in an economy in which there were 14 million vacancies and 13 million unemployed as in one in which there were 4 million vacancies and 3 million unemployed?

[12] William H. Beveridge, *Full Employment in a Force Society*, Norton, New York, 1945, p. 18.

[13] As Jacob Mincer, "Comment on Papers in Part I, ['Measuring the Current Demand for Labor']," *The Measurement and Interpretation of Job Vacancies*, National Bureau of Economic Research, New York, 1966, p. 126, differentiates between frictional and structural unemployment, all unemployment is frictional if vacancies are more or less equal to unemployment on an occupation-by-occupation or a region-by-region basis, while unemployment is structural when vacancies exceed unemployment and unemployment exceeds vacancies in some regions and/or occupations. It is argued here, however, that unemployment would still be only frictional if vacancies *exceeded* unemployment for all regions and occupations.

[14] Thus, Albert Rees' definition of frictional unemployment, as that which includes "all unemployment, not excepting seasonal, that exists in the presence of 'adequate' total demand for commodities and labor in the economy," "The Meaning and Measurement of Full Employment," *The Measurement and Behavior of Unemployment*, National Bureau of Economic Research, New York, 1957, p. 13, fits the analysis of the chapter if he subsumes structural unemployment into the frictional component. Otherwise, like Beveridge's definition, it denies the possibility of structural unemployment.

LOCATION, RACE, EDUCATION, AND
STRUCTURAL UNEMPLOYMENT

Although the three characteristics to be related to structural unemployment in this section may seem to be unrelated to each other, there is a connecting thread running through them. Each contains an element that may lead to structural unemployment even though workers may fit the technical requirements demanded by job openings. Obstacles may impede unemployed workers with the skills required for vacancies from moving to them. Negroes and uneducated workers with skills to fill vacancies may not be permitted to fill vacancies because of racial prejudice or preference for educated personnel practiced by employers.

Of course, many workers in labor surplus areas are technically unqualified to fill the vacancies in job-shortage regions, and many Negroes and uneducated workers do not have the skills required by vacancies. But these workers will not be considered in the present discussion, which is about the effect on the analysis of structural problems specifically related to location and discrimination, whether preference or prejudice.

Location and Structural Unemployment

There is some question over whether joblessness related to geographical immobility should be considered a component of structural unemployment or of frictional unemployment.

The arguments for considering it structural seem convincing. Even if a worker has the capabilities to fill a job opening, of what service is it to him or the economy if the vacancy is inaccessible? In the same sense, is a worker not unqualified to fill a job if he is miles away from it?

Our definitions, though, may also be considered as looking at structural unemployment from the employer's viewpoint. The central question would then become whether the employer would hire the worker for an opening if he were available. Given this approach, regional imbalance then would operate as a source of frictional unemployment, not structural.

This question represents much more than semantic quibbling. To settle the issue, an inflation test should be introduced. In addition to the functional definition of structural unemployment, presented above, that provides the basis for measuring the phenomenon, a condition that should be stipulated is that unemployment can be structural only if its short-run elimination, through demand expansion, creates inflationary pressures. Otherwise the problem of matching worker to vacancy should be considered a frictional one.

Much of the regional imbalance in unemployment that leads to a surplus of qualified workers in some areas matched by a deficit in others could be corrected without causing inflationary pressures. Improved information regarding job opportunities and development of a national labor exchange are low-cost methods for reducing this imbalance. A program of government resettlement subsidies would also help solve the problem at relatively low cost.

That all regional imbalance is not to be excluded from the structural category would be evidenced by the failure of the entire imbalance due to immobility to be eliminated by the above and similar low-cost measures. Some workers resist relocation to the point that only inflationary measures, which increased demand for them in their present location, or raised wages more in labor-deficit areas, thus attracting them there,[15] could eliminate regional structural unemployment.

For example, if an electrician in an area with a surplus of electricians would not move to an electrician-deficit area unless the interregional wage differential for the occupation widened, which might occur from a general increase in demand that raised wages more in the labor-deficit area, the price stability test would be failed, and he would be considered structurally unemployed. Thus the functional definition needs modification. Assume an overall balance between vacancies for and unemployment of electricians. The occupation would not constitute an SOC nationally, but if some of the vacancies that existed could only be filled by a relative rise in wages in labor-deficit areas, then this occupation would contribute to structural unemployment.[16]

Although $U_E = V_E$, not all unemployed electricians would fill the vacancies at current wages. To adjust for this, U_E should be reduced by a mobility factor, with mU_E equal to the number of electricians who would fill openings, in a short time,[17] at current wages in labor-shortage areas. The term m could be enlarged by measures to facilitate mobility. Thus, $1 - m$ represents the proportion of unemployed workers who would

[15] As was noted in Chapter VI, mobility might be induced even if wages rose by an equal percentage in both areas, if transportation and search costs rose less than wages.

[16] A rise in particular wages would undoubtedly reduce frictional unemployment for an occupation, too. But here we are concerned only with the special impediment to full employment of regional immobility. Obviously, the delineation between frictional and structural elements is not finely drawn in this case. One clear difference, however, is that regional immobility would create an artificial shortage for particular jobs in one area that would lead to the appearance of true structural unemployment, in that other unemployed workers in the area could not fill these jobs. This situation does not arise from local frictional unemployment.

[17] The implication here is that whatever adjustment will result from mobility has not yet taken place, after regional unemployment imbalance arises.

fill openings only at higher current wages in labor-shortage areas. Thus the amended expression for an SOC becomes,

if $V_i > mU_i$, then i is an SOC'.

It is evident that the correction of the earlier functional definition to include regional immobility will tend to be required the greater the resistance to mobility and the smaller the positive difference between U_i and V_i.[18] Certainly, if unemployment greatly exceeds vacancies for a job, then the reluctance of some workers to move to areas where openings existed would not contribute to overall unemployment if there were enough other workers willing to move to fill all these vacancies.

The complication of regional immobility makes the calculation of structural unemployment more difficult. Vacancies and unemployment for individual jobs must be counted on a labor-market basis. While on a simple macroeconomic basis each occupation is an SOC' if $V_i > mU_i$, this term obscures a great deal of difficulty in calculation. The vacancies are clear enough and $V_i = \sum_{l=1}^{n} V_{i_l}$ where the subscript l refers to individual labor markets.

For the unemployed workers though, when $V_{i_l} > U_{i_l}$, all the unemployed workers should be counted, since there is no questions of immobility *from* these areas. For them, m has a value of 1. For the other, labor-surplus areas, resistance to mobility will vary from region to region, so that m is a weighted average of m_l for labor-surplus areas, weighted by the volume of unemployment in the area.

$$\text{Hence,} \qquad m_i = \frac{\sum_{l=1}^{n} m_{i_l} U_{i_l}}{U_i}$$

with, of course, m_{i_l} for markets with labor shortage equal to l.

$$\text{Then} \qquad m_i U_i = \sum_{l=1}^{n} m_{i_l} U_{i_l}$$

$$\text{and if} \qquad V_i > \sum_{l=1}^{n} m_{i_l} U_{i_l}$$

the occupation is an SOC'.

Notice the difficulties this modification causes in the calculation of structural unemployment. An accurate estimate would require knowledge of the different values for m for different regions, to say nothing of

---

[18] Obviously, if $V_i > U_i$, the occupation is an SOC in any case. But interregional immobility would add to its contribution to structural unemployment.

mobility differences among occupations. Furthermore, m is not a constant but a parameter, depending on the stage of the cycle, as workers tend to become more mobile with expansion of job opportunities elsewhere. Surplus workers in one region will be likely to move to another as the shortage for their qualifications becomes tighter in these areas. Thus, this regional component to structural unemployment tends to grow less important as the economy expands.

Superficial statistical evidence does not indicate that regional unemployment differences have been a serious contributor to structural unemployment. Denison's studies show a marked narrowing in interregional differences in unemployment rates between 1950 and 1960, years of similar overall unemployment rates. Those states that deviated the most, both above and below the national average in 1950, moved closer to the average in 1960, and the standard deviation rate for all states shrank by one-third.[19]

It is impossible to estimate the importance of structural unemployment by examination of unemployment itself, without considering vacancies. But assuming a level of 2 percent for frictional unemployment, a value that could not be considered low for illustrative purposes, it could therefore be concluded that any state with a rate above 2 percent experienced only cyclical and frictional unemployment with fewer vacancies than unemployed. Under these assumptions, the narrowing of the interstate difference between the census years had a negligible influence on structural unemployment, which was practically nonexistent on an interstate basis, in either year. More precisely, using the 2 percent criterion for frictional unemployment, except for Iowa, there was no state where vacancies exceeded unemployment in either year.

Thus the data show that while there was a reduction in regional imbalance in unemployment between 1950 and 1960, this did not lead to a reduction in structural unemployment, which was negligible in both years. Admittedly, the relatively high national unemployment rate of about 5 percent in both years makes them questionable choices for testing the strength of regional structural unemployment.

Denison's more detailed metropolitan study yields results parallel to his interstate findings. On a city-wide basis the unemployment differential narrowed between the census years but, for both years, only one locality, Cedar Rapids, Iowa, for 1960 had an unemployment rate under 2 percent.[20]

[19] Edward F. Denison, *The Incidence of Unemployment by States and Regions* (mimeographed), Committee for Economic Development, New York, 1962, pp. 6, 7, 10, and Table 3.

[20] *Idem., The Dispersion of Unemployment Among Standard Metropolitan Areas, 1950 and 1960* (mimeographed), Committee for Economic Development New York, 1962, p. 4.

Data for 150 major labor areas from 1958 through 1964, a period when the annual national rate exceeded 5 percent, show no area rate below 2 percent, except again, Cedar Rapids in 1963 and 1964.[21] Thus, neglecting the effect of differences in industrial and occupational unemployment rates for the moment, the only net improvement in the unemployment record that could have resulted from interarea movement of workers would have been from a migration into Cedar Rapids from other metropolitan areas. It would be belaboring a point to question that community's absorptive power before it too would have become a labor surplus area.

Of course, interarea data, whether by state or city, do not tell whether or not within each area SOC for particular occupations exist—except that if the area rate is below the frictional level or, expressed differently, if area vacancies exceed unemployment, some occupations must have labor shortages. Data are needed on an occupational basis, area by area.

The closest to such figures, skimpy though they are, appear in a Bureau of Labor Statistics comparison of unemployment in 1959 between areas of favorable labor-market conditions with an average unemployment rate of 4.9 percent—compared to the national average of 5.5 percent—and depressed areas with an average rate of 6.3 percent. Little difference appeared in the occupational distribution of unemployment between the two groups.[22] There was a suggestion of structural elements in unemployment *within* both areas for professional and technical workers, in that the unemployment rate for both groups was below 2 percent in each. Thus, unemployment in both the favorable labor markets and in depressed areas was probably partially attributable to the inability of unemployed workers in other occupational classifications within each area type to qualify for professional and technical openings.[23]

Between the two groups, however, the big difference in unemployment patterns was in the much higher rate in the depressed areas for operatives

[21] *Report on Manpower Requirements, Resources, Utilization, and Training,* U.S. Department of Labor (March 1965), pp. 243–245.

Otto Eckstein, "Aggregate Demand and the Current Unemployment Problem," *Unemployment and the American Economy,* edited by Arthur Ross, Wiley, New York, 1964, pp. 119–121, also presents data to show the narrowing in the differential among the 150 areas, but maintains that this trend indicates a reduction in structural elements in unemployment.

[22] *The Structure of Unemployment in Areas of Substantial Labor Surplus,* Bureau of Labor Statistics, Study Paper No. 23 for the Joint Economic Committee (January 1960), pp. 6–11.

[23] Seymour L. Wolfbein, "The First Year of the Manpower Act," *Unemployment and the American Economy,* p. 63, observed that there were enough job vacancies, even in the areas of high, persistent unemployment that qualify for Area Redevelopment Act training funds, for which to train all the workers that limited funds permitted.

and laborers, workers for whom the rates were highest in both areas. How much progress in reducing total unemployment would have been achieved by a transfer of laborers from depressed areas where the unemployment rate was 14.1 percent to high employment areas where their rate was 10.9 percent? Consequently, in 1959, although there were regional differences in unemployment rates, evidence of structural imbalance, there was no evidence of regional structural unemployment.

Prejudice and Preference—Racial and Educational Structural Unemployment

RACIAL ELEMENTS IN STRUCTURAL UNEMPLOYMENT. Much of what has been said above about the need to change the definitions and procedures for estimating the extent of structural unemployment because of interregional mobility applies to the complications that arise because of prejudices toward and preferences for particular groups. Consider first the effects of racial prejudice on structural unemployment.[24]

Despite the pressures of laws and, in some areas, of public opinion, many employers discriminate against Negro job seekers. Thus, for any job classification, it is not certain that, merely because the number of unemployed exceeds the volume of vacancies, the occupation does not constitute an SOC. If Negroes are attached to the job and are discriminated against in employment, then it is quite possible that a large part of their unemployment could not be considered frictional. They would be willing and able to fill the openings but would not be hired by discriminating employers who, satisfying their "taste for discrimination,"[25] prefer the uneconomic condition of unfilled openings rather than hire qualified Negroes.

Thus, unemployment could exceed vacancies for a job, but the number of "qualified" unemployed, in the employer's warped understanding of the word, would fall short of the number of vacancies. To show the adjustment for racial discrimination symbolically, if $U_i > V_i$, occupation i is not an SOC. But if $nU_i < V_i$, it is an SOC". In this case, n is a value less than 1, equal to $(1 - p)$, where p represents the discrimination coefficient, or the fraction of total unemployed who are excluded Negroes, who would be able to fill vacancies were they not discriminated against. As was the case for regional structural elements, the need for

---

[24] The analysis would apply to prejudices associated with age and sex as well.

[25] Gary Becker, *The Economics of Discrimination,* University of Chicago Press, Chicago, 1957, Chapter II, introduces this term to describe the willingness to pay "to associate with some persons instead of others." In this case the employer is paying for confining his work force to white workers in the form of artificial labor bottlenecks.

adjustment for the factor of racial prejudice only tends to arise when U_i is not very much greater than V_i. Otherwise, conditions would be such that discrimination, in itself, did not contribute to unemployment. With many more job seekers than openings, prejudice would allocate Negroes to the unemployed group, but the removal of prejudice would not reduce the volume of unemployment. The likelihood that, when $U_i > V_i$, the occupation will not become an SOC" because of prejudice is greater the more U_i exceeds V_i, the smaller the proportion of Negroes attached to the occupation, and the less the degree of employment prejudice.

Again, as was the case for regional immobility, the problem of measuring the contribution of racial prejudice to unemployment is complicated by the existence of differential degrees of prejudice by occupation and region. But the actual application of unemployment prejudice is a function of the tightness of the particular labor market. When labor is in general short supply, employers find satisfaction of their tastes for discrimination very costly.

The cost of not hiring technically qualified Negroes in this case is a curtailment of output. Thus the actual incidence of structural unemployment in tight labor markets caused by racial prejudice must be slight. In fact, a study by Gilman shows that the differential unemployment rate for the highest labor classifications, professional and managers, for whites and nonwhites is very slight.[26] Gilman attributes this result to the ability to practice wage discrimination instead of only employment discrimination against these highly trained workers. The alternative hypothesis suggested here, in the absence of relevant wage data, is that little racial discrimination is actually practiced in these occupational classifications because of their relatively general short supply, in comparison to less skilled occupations.

Unfortunately, existing data do not permit a detailed evaluation of the extent of racial structural unemployment. What is needed is occupational unemployment data by race. Then racial discrimination would be a factor in unemployment for a particular occupation, only if the white unemployment rate were below the frictional level and the Negro rate were above it.

A Bureau of Labor Statistics examination of occupational data in 1962 gives little support for the view that racial discrimination is an important contributor to overall unemployment, even if it is to Negro

---

[26] Harry Gilman, "Economic Discrimination and Unemployment," *American Economic Review*, **4** (December 1965), pp. 1087–1090. The same finding appears in Jacob Mincer, "On the Job Training: Costs, Returns and Some Implications," *Journal of Political Economy*, Supplement, **70** (October 1962), p. 71.

unemployment. For the occupational classifications listed in the study, no white occupational group had an unemployment rate below 3 percent,[27] a rate probably above the frictional level for any classification.

For example, the unemployment rate for white clerical and sales workers was 3.8 percent, compared to the nonwhite rate of 7.7 percent. Thus, relaxation of prejudicial employment policies that would have led toward an equalization of the two rates, as qualified workers were no longer selected on the basis of race, would not have reduced the overall rate for clerks, assuming a frictional unemployment level of 2 percent. It would, of course, have made unemployment among them an industrial accident, resulting from slack times rather than a predictable consequence of prejudice; elimination of prejudice has other virtues besides a possible reduction of structural unemployment.

Whatever racial structural unemployment might exist in good times, like all forms of structuralism, tends to disappear in bad times. Paradoxically, during periods of greater employment prejudice—bad times—the effect of prejudice on the overall level of unemployment may be less than in periods when employment prejudice is more weakly applied— good times. The year 1962, with a national unemployment rate as high as 5.6 percent, was a bad year for structural unemployment of any form.

As was the case for structural unemployment due to labor immobility, much of racial imbalance in unemployment is frictional, in the sense that it could be eliminated at relatively low cost. Closer application of existing laws, passage of stronger new ones, a change in attitude, responding to the pressure of public opinion, could all reduce racial unemployment imbalance. The residual of effective employment prejudice that remained, resulting in vacancies in the presence of technically qualified unemployed workers who wanted to fill them, would represent racial structural unemployment.

STRUCTURAL UNEMPLOYMENT AND EDUCATIONAL PREFERENCE. Much that has been discussed about the complications introduced by racial discrimination into the estimation of structural unemployment applies to what might be called educational structural unemployment. Educational preference reflects a favorable attitude toward job applicants who have had more education than others, equally capable of performing the job.[28]

---

[27] Matthew A. Kessler, "Economic Status of Non-White Workers, 1955–62," *Monthly Labor Review*, **86** (July 1963), p. 783.
[28] The terminology reflects the emphasis given. One could say that there is preference for whites and prejudice against the uneducated. But in the discussions of race,

Educational considerations, however, differ from the racial element in structural unemployment in two important respects. First, in response to educational bias, one possible adjustment is to meet the terms of the discriminating employer; the uneducated worker can undergo the expense and effort of an education.[29]

Second, simple formulas for estimating the effect of educational preference cannot be devised because the effects cut across occupational lines. One job's surplus workers may be able to fill another job's vacancies, given a reduction in educational preference.

The presence of educational preference has undoubtedly unnecessarily aggravated structural bottlenecks. Killingsworth, in his frequently cited defense of the structural position, uses the differential rate between college graduates and the lesser educated as a basis for his stress on the significance of structural unemployment.[30] But his study implies that the different rates reflect only differences in technical qualifications for available jobs and that expansion in the number educated is required to widen the bottleneck. To the extent, though, that preference, rather than technical competence, plays a part in hiring decisions, the same effect could be achieved by adoption of a less bureaucratic personnel policy that judged applicants by technical qualifications, rather than by uncompromising observance of a formal educational criterion.

This is not to deny that there is a real shortage of highly educated workers that could be alleviated by greater educational attainment of the work force. But it is claimed here that the volume of structural unemployment is exaggerated by not considering that some of the structural imbalance is artificial, based on preference for educated (or trained, or experienced) workers, for specific jobs that surplus uneducated (or untrained, or inexperienced) workers could fill.

In keeping with the framework of this chapter, then, some so-called structural unemployment resulting from educational bottlenecks is really frictional. A change in employment practices toward a more objective appraisal of an applicant's ability to do the job would allow surplus

---

the emphasis is usually on the unfavored group and, in the treatment of education, on the group most wanted by firms.

William G. Bowen, *Economic Aspects of Education,* Princeton University Industrial Relations Section, 1964, p. 18, uses the apt phrase "conspicuous production" to refer to the practice by employers of hiring only college graduates for jobs which do not require college training.

[29] Thus the relationship of prejudice against older and younger workers, and against women, none of whom can attain favored characteristics, to structural unemployment, parallels the racial case, not the educational one.

[30] Killingsworth, *op. cit.,* pp. 1476–1482.

workers in lower-ranked jobs to fill openings in higher-rated jobs without accompanying inflationary pressures.

A reduction in this frictional element of educational preference would, on average, reduce the financial benefits of education. Studies of the returns to education implicitly assume either that preference plays no part in employment decisions or that no change will occur in the intensity of educational preference.

With elimination of the frictional component of preference, the residual, or hard-core, preference that remained, comprising the structural element in preference, would be less than before the changed attitude. Then, in estimating the financial returns to education, future differences in the income stream of educated and uneducated workers would tend to fall, reducing the internal rate of return on education. The income differences in the future would grow smaller as the wage differential between educated and lesser-educated fell, while the movement of surplus workers from lower-rated jobs to higher-rated ones reduced the labor surplus in the former and eased the tightness in the labor market of the latter. Thus the demand for education would tend to fall.

VACANCIES, STRUCTURAL UNEMPLOYMENT, AND THE INFLATION TEST

The principal conditions for structural unemployment are the presence of excess demand for labor in some and excess supply of labor in other sectors of the economy. More specifically, unsatisfied labor demand, measured by an excess of vacancies over unemployment and modified by immobility and prejudicial considerations, must exist for some job classifications and a labor surplus, measured by an excess of modified unemployment over vacancies for others. In effect, then, the question is one of comparing excess demand and supply, with vacancies serving as a guide to the extent of excess demand and unemployment of supply. Statistics on unemployment have long been available, but any estimate of the extent and changes in structural unemployment becomes meaningless until accurate and detailed vacancy data become available.

VACANCIES. The problem of calculating vacancies adds to the statistical difficulties imposed on the relevant unemployment values by immobility and prejudicial elements. As for measuring vacancies themselves, one difficulty in their compilation is that all vacancies are not reported. An English study of structural unemployment points out the parallel between the withdrawal from, or the failure to enter into, the labor force of workers in slack periods, who feel that search for work would be futile, and the reluctance of a firm to list a job opening in a tight labor market because of its pessimistic view that it would not be filled.[31]

Another parallel problem of measurement between unemployment and vacancies relates to occupational classifications. Unemployment is assigned to the last employed occupation of the worker, even though he may be looking for work in another field. Similarly, a vacancy refers to a particular job opening and, therefore, not necessarily to an occupation for which labor demand has increased.

For example, if a firm practices promotions from within and if a job opportunity arises for a skilled job, the actual opening, or vacancy, would appear at the unskilled level. This practice tends to concentrate vacancies in a few lower-skilled jobs and thus misrepresents the direction of actual labor demand,[32] just as classification of the unemployed by previous employed occupation may misrepresent the fields of excess labor supply.

No matter what obstacles impede their accurate calculation, a measurement of vacancies is essential for estimating structural unemployment. In the absence of vacancy data, only a guess can be made as to the extent of labor surplus for jobs with high unemployment by roughly estimating the degree to which unemployment is frictional and subtracting this component from total unemployment. Accurate vacancy data would eliminate this guesswork.

But without vacancy data, estimates of demand, essential for calculating labor deficits in tight labor markets cannot even begin to be made. Many erroneous conclusions can be made by ignoring the importance of vacancies in the estimate of demand.

For example, Killingsworth in his persuasive defense of the structural position equates employment with labor demand.[33] This omission of the contribution of vacancies to demand is particularly serious in his analysis of educational structural imbalance. With the employment rate for college graduates so low during the period he studied, he neglected excess demand for educated workers that might have been present and would have been reflected in unfilled vacancies. Thus, he did not present his case for structuralism in fullest strength.

[31] J. C. R. Dow and L. A. Dicks-Mireaux, "The Excess Demand for Labour: A Study of Conditions in Great Britain, 1946–1956," *Oxford Economic Papers,* **10** (February 1958), pp. 4–7.

[32] This point is made by John T. Dunlop, "Job Vacancy Measures and Economic Analysis," *The Measurement and Interpretation of Job Vacancies,* pp. 32–37. Dunlop cautions against the indiscriminate use of vacancy data as a guide to areas of labor shortage in the planning of vocational training programs.

[33] Killingsworth, *op. cit.,* pp. 1476–1477.

Related to structural inbalance by educational levels, the Council viewed the rise in the college graduate unemployment rate from 0.6 percent to 1.4 percent from 1957 to 1962 as an indication of a reduction in structural unemployment over the period.[34] Perhaps this conclusion is correct. But a rate of 1.4 percent might still have been well below the frictional level for college graduates. Thus the higher rate might have had no more significance than a reflection of greater difficulty in cutting into the frictional core of a tight labor market; there might have been many more vacancies in 1962 and, therefore, greater educational structural unemployment than in 1957.

A further hasty conclusion, omitting the importance of vacancies and equating employment with labor demand, arises in the usual explanation for the fact that unemployment changes for skilled workers are less volatile than those of the unskilled. In bad times, unemployment rises faster and further for those on the lower rungs of the skill ladder, with a reverse path of reemployment as recovery sets in. An important reason offered for this pattern is the desire of employers to retain their professional and technical staffs during downturns both to assure later returns on the investment in training made in them and to maintain a reserve against shortages in labor of this type that characteristically occur during prosperous periods.[35] But sometimes this argument is used to explain too much. In 1954 and 1958, for example, two recession years in which overall employment declined substantially, employment of professional and technical workers actually rose. No one has seriously argued that employers actually add to their professional and technical staff during downturns to hedge against possible future shortages.

Certainly the wish to retain key personnel plays an important role in the relative stable employment experience of these workers. But an additional, if not alternative, explanation for this stability relates to the difference between employment and labor demand. A simple explanation for the failure of highly rated workers to gain in employment during upturns as much as others follows from the concept of unsatisfied labor demand. Higher-rated workers might not have been available to the extent that employers wanted to hire them. A high vacancy figure for workers during this period would have indicated unsatisfied demand. The growth in their employment during slack times would then have resulted from the steady expansion in supply of these workers, who though wanted

---

[34] 1964 Council Report, p. 180.

[35] This point is made by Walter Heller, "The Administration's Fiscal Policy," *Unemployment and the American Economy,* pp. 97–100 and appears in the 1964 Council Report, pp. 175–176. The effect of investment in training on stabilizing demand for skilled labor was discussed in Chapter IV.

less urgently than in prosperous periods, would have been employed to the extent of their supply, with fewer vacancies present.

The availability of vacancy data will permit a test over future cycles of the importance of the alternative hypotheses for explaining the relative cyclical stability of the work force elite.

Static and Dynamic Structural Unemployment and Inflation. In a static sense, that is, at a point in time, structural unemployment is a characteristic of good, not bad, times. Thus, when Heller argues the Council's position that the unemployment increase in the late 1950's could not have been attributable to structural factors because the number of vacancies—indicated roughly by the National Industrial Conference Board's Help-Wanted Index—declined with the rise in unemployment,[36] he is attacking a straw man. By the very nature of the concept, structural unemployment tends to decline as overall unemployment rises, and no economist has seriously claimed that rising unemployment was caused by structural elements.[37]

What structuralists do claim is that as full employment is approached when the economy strengthens, structural unemployment appears, and reduction in this structural element is associated with inflation. This is the dynamic element in structural unemployment. Furthermore, those

---

[36] Walter Heller, *op. cit.*, pp. 103–104. See also Simler, *op. cit.*, pp. 986–987, for the same argument. Similarly, Walter Galenson, *A Primer on Employment and Wages,* Random House, New York, 1966, p. 4, states that a test of the rival theories would involve a comparison of vacancy rates when unemployment rose or fell, with evidence of structural unemployment suggested by a parallel movement of unemployment and vacancies. Even the "Gordon Committee" Report, which was so influential in leading to Labor Department Job Vacancy Surveys, implies the same test. In detailing uses of job vacancy data, the Report argues that "High or rising unemployment accompanied by mounting job vacancies suggests the need for emphasis in private or public programs upon training, retraining, or relocation of the unemployed." *Measuring Employment and Unemployment,* President's Committee to Appraise Employment and Unemployment Statistics, Washington, 1962, p. 199.

In effect, the argument of this chapter holds that the relationship between unemployment rates and vacancies, when structural unemployment was a factor, would be inverse. As Eleanor G. Gilpatrick, *Structural Unemployment and Aggregate Demand,* Johns Hopkins Press, Baltimore, 1966, p. 11, points out, asking for an increase in unemployment to be matched by an increase in vacancies is asking for an increase in frictional not structural, unemployment.

[37] Lipsey, *op. cit.*, p. 243, stresses that Killingsworth, *op. cit.*, an outspoken structuralist, only argues that the structural problems that impede the path to full employment as the economy strengthens appear earlier and resist solution more stubbornly than in the past, not that structural elements cause the unemployment rate to rise.

who argue that dynamic structural unemployment is becoming a more serious deterrent to attainment of full employment claim that structural unemployment tends to arise at higher overall unemployment rates, as the rate moves downward, than in the past, and that efforts to reduce unemployment through expanding aggregate demand will be associated with stronger inflationary pressures.

Thus, the late 1950's and early 1960's would be a poor time to test for the importance of structural elements in unemployment. With the overall rate relatively high during the period, there was little opportunity for effective structural imbalance to arise, effective in causing structural unemployment in the sense that particular occupational classifications had labor shortages, with vacancies greater than the unemployment level.[38]

Furthermore, in its more important dynamic aspect, testing for structural unemployment by relating declines in unemployment to price increases would have yielded meaningless results. The unemployment rate never fell sufficiently for the inflationary trend associated with structural unemployment to arise. Thus, a conclusion that structural elements had diminished after 1961 because the unemployment rate fell from a 6.7 percent level that year to 5.7 percent the next, without an accompanying price increase,[39] puts the dynamic structuralist position to an unfair test. The overall unemployment rate was probably much too high for any latent structural difficulties to appear, even at the lower 1962 level.

Before questioning the ability to test for dynamic structural unemployment, the relationship between structural unemployment and inflation needs explanation. Structural unemployment arises either because of shifts in product demand or changes in productive methods, which alter the demand for specific types of labor or for workers from different regions. If relative wages fail to adjust to the shift in labor demand, surplus and deficits in labor supply occur.

Unemployment results for some workers because they do not accept a wage low enough to be used as a substitute, either in production or operating through the product market for those workers in short supply.[40]

---

[38] Through statistical analysis, strongly questioned by Lipsey, *op. cit.*, the study, *Higher Unemployment Rates, 1957–60: Structural Transformation or Inadequate Demand,* Senate Subcommittee on Economic Statistics of the Joint Economic Committee, Washington, 1961, concludes that structural elements were an unimportant cause of high unemployment in the period, a conclusion that could have been reached on a priori grounds alone.

[39] Heller, "The Administration's Fiscal Policy," pp. 102–103, makes this argument.

[40] Vladimir Stoikov, "Increasing Structural Unemployment Reexamined," *Industrial and Labor Relations Review,* **19** (April 1966), p. 376, writes, "In fact it is difficult to conceive of increasing [or even stable] structural unemployment in a world of perfectly flexible wages."

This would explain structural unemployment on both an occupational and discriminatory basis. The wages of lower-skilled workers would be above the level that would encourage firms to use them in place of unavailable skilled workers. The wages of qualified uneducated workers would not be low enough to induce firms to hire them as substitutes for scarce educated workers. The wages of Negro workers would not be low enough to have them substituted for unavailable whites—the cost of indulging a "taste for discrimination" would be below the tolerable level.[41] On a regional basis, wages in the labor deficit areas would not be sufficiently high, relative to wages in the labor surplus areas, to induce labor migration toward job openings.

Besides the failure of specific wages to respond to relative changes in labor demand, relative wage movements may in themselves indicate structural unemployment. If union wages are raised not in response to an increase in demand for the affected workers.[42] or if minimum or unskilled wages are raised, again, not in response to increased demand,[43] sectoral surpluses and deficits may arise in the labor market.[44]

Whatever the source of structural unemployment, whether a shift in product demand or production method, which alters the demand for labor occupationally or regionally and which is not matched by adjustment in relative wages to clear labor markets, the suppression of structural unemployment through a rise in aggregate demand will be inflation-

---

[41] Gilman, *op. cit.*, p. 1093, argues that the smaller racial unemployment differential in the South than in the non-South is partly attributable to the weaker pressure in the South for racial wage equality. Of course, it is not suggested by Gilman nor in the argument here that lower wages for Negroes are to be advocated as a substitute policy for ending employment discrimination as a means to eliminate racial structural unemployment.

[42] Lowell E. Gallaway, "Labor Mobility, Resource Allocation, and Structural Unemployment," *American Economic Review,* **52** (September 1962), p. 714, notes that differential wage gains for the unionized sector could have been a source of substantial structural unemployment if the labor market had not operated smoothly enough through an increase in supply of nonunion labor.

[43] George H. Hildebrand and George E. Delehanty, "Wage Levels and Differentials," *Prosperity and Unemployment,* edited by Robert A. Gordon and Margaret S. Gordon, Wiley, New York, 1966, pp. 269–272, argue that the failure of the skill differential to widen, in response to a relative increase in supply of the unskilled, was a source of chronic unemployment of the unskilled in the post-War era.

[44] Eleanor Gilpatrick, *op. cit.*, pp. 12–13, criticizes the argument that relative wages that do not match relative labor demand is a source of structural unemployment. She points out that there have been high unemployment rates among unorganized and uncovered workers as well as for unionized and covered (by minimum wage laws) workers. Even confining the comparison to periods of low overall unemployment, when unemployment above the frictional level is structural and not just cyclical, this condition does not deny that failure of relative wages to adjust to changing demand within the labor force can lead to structural unemployment.

ary. Moreover, inflation associated with removing structural unemployment through increasing aggregate demand will be greater than if the same volume of unemployment were cyclical rather than structural. This follows, since a greater increase in total demand is required for wiping out a given amount of structural than cyclical unemployment.

The following very simplified example explains the relationship. Assume a frictional "full employment" unemployment rate of 2 percent. Assume further a two-sector economy of equal labor force. If the unemployment rate were 3 percent in both sectors, that is, entirely cyclical above the frictional level, then a given uniform increase in aggregate demand could push unemployment down to its 2 percent ("full-employment") frictional level in both sectors.

On the other hand, if the above frictional unemployment level were entirely structural with the rate 4 percent in one sector and 2 percent in the other, the same increase in aggregate demand would not eradicate above-frictional unemployment in the former and would lead mainly to an expansion of vacancies in the latter. (There might be a slight reduction in frictional unemployment). Further expansion in total demand, with accompanying inflationary pressure, would be required to reduce unemployment to the frictional 2 percent level in both sectors. The end result would find full employment, with excessive vacancies in one sector, and higher prices than if unemployment had been originally uniform in the two sectors.[45]

Thus a decrease in unemployment along the path of expanded demand, with structural elements swamped, can only be achieved at the cost of higher prices.[46] On the other hand, if structural elements are not

---

[45] This simplified analysis assumes a linear relationship between reduction in unemployment and inflation. If the relationship were nonlinear, it could be argued that the combination of a reduction in unemployment from 4 percent to 3 percent in one sector with an increase in vacancies by an equal percentage in the other sector—assuming no inroads were made in the frictional base there—would be more inflationary than a demand-induced reduction in unemployment from 3 percent to 2 percent in both sectors. If this were the case, then the inflationary effect of complete elimination of structural unemployment through demand expansion would be even stronger. See Chapter IX for a discussion of nonlinearity in the inflation-unemployment level relationship.

[46] Thus the definition of frictional unemployment appearing in a Labor Department study, which subsumes structural among frictional elements, ". . . as that level of joblessness that could not be reduced significantly in the short run by increased aggregate spending," *The Extent and Nature of Frictional Unemployment*, Bureau of Labor Statistics, Study Paper No. 6, Joint Economic Committee (November 1959), p. 2, would only be accurate if the words "without raising prices" were added to it.

Robert M. Solow, "A Policy for Full Employment," *Industrial Relations*, **2** (October 1962), pp. 3–4, seems to overstate the inflationary aspects of swamping

suppressed but eliminated, through removal of racial and educational preference and prejudice, reduction of barriers to mobility and, most of all, by training and retraining for scarce skills, employment can be increased without an increase in demand and without inflation.

It would seem then, that a superficially good test of the presence or absence of structural elements would study periods of unemployment reduction, concluding their presence if prices rose when unemployment fell. Apart from the limited practical importance of such a test for policy, in that it would only indicate whether structural elements had been present after action were taken to increase demand, it suffers from the fatal flaw of not being conclusive. This follows, since even if no structural elements were present and all unemployment beyond the frictional level were cyclical, an increase in aggregate demand and reduction in unemployment might lead to inflation. Thus, without detailed vacancy data, it would be impossible to tell whether a decline in unemployment that resulted in inflation, say the post-1964 taxcut expansion and price rise, reflected the presence of structural elements or merely followed the usual pattern of cyclical upturn and inflation.[47]

In an interesting study of the problems associated with the analysis of the unemployment-vacancy relationship, Myron Joseph claims that an excess of unemployment over vacancies might not indicate an insufficiency of demand "if by insufficient demand we mean that an increase in demand will reduce unemployment without increasing prices."[48] This limitation on the concept of insufficient demand is much too restrictive. By any reasonable criterion, demand could be inadequate even if a reduction in unemployment led to price increases. The presence of inadequate demand should be judged on whether a reduction in unemployment required the creation of new jobs (openings).

Certainly from a policy point of view, Joseph's extreme position has some validity. If insufficiency of demand were judged by whether it were worth the cost of reducing unemployment, that is, the possible consequent price increase, then there might be some who would maintain that at a given level of unemployment, steps should not be taken to

---

structural unemployment through increasing aggregate demand when he claims that structuralists argue that structural elements have raised the "full employment" rate of unemployment, which he defines as the level of unemployment at which increases in demand will result primarily in money wage increases rather than in employment expansion.

[47] The relationship between unemployment (reductions) in general and price changes (increases) will be discussed in Chapter IX.

[48] Myron Joseph, "Job Vacancy Measurement," *Journal of Human Resources,* Vol. 1 (Fall 1966), p. 67.

reduce the level through expanding demand if the process led to any price increase at all. Thus, in the policy sense, insufficiency of demand would be a relative concept, depending on the degree of inflation that would be associated with expansion. Joseph accepts this view in his earlier statement, "The meaning of 'insufficient demand' will depend on the weight given to different policy objectives, and the estimated costs of alternative policies. So that demand could be considered insufficient even though an increase would raise prices as unemployment declined."[49]

If it is impossible to recognize the presence of structural unemployment from an analytical point of view without accurate detailed vacancy data, the need for vacancy statistics is even more acute for policy purposes. Vacancies could be matched against unemployment on a microeconomic occupation-by-occupation basis to discover whether structural elements were present at any time. Of course, policy recommendations would differ depending on the presence and intensity of structural unemployment. If the vacancy-unemployment relationships, discussed earlier in this chapter, indicated the absence of structural elements, then to reduce unemployment would require demand expansion. It is true that inflation might still accompany expansion in this case, but it could not be attributable to structural difficulties. If the suppression of structural elements, when present, represents an additive source to inflationary pressure, then it could be concluded that the inflation that resulted from expansion without these elements would be less severe than with them. Consequently, counteracting fiscal and monetary measures, designed to ease this pressure, could be more weakly applied. Steps to alleviate structural elements when they were not present would not only be logically inappropriate but would also do nothing to reduce the unemployment level. Of course, elimination of geographical and discriminatory structural imbalance is desirable for its own sake.

On the other hand, if vacancy-unemployment data indicated the presence of structural elements, demand expansion would suppress those elements, but only at the cost of higher prices, with inflation being more severe for a given reduction in unemployment than if these elements had not been present. Noninflationary reduction of unemployment would be effected through steps to reduce or eliminate the structural elements. Reduction of the geographical and discriminatory barriers, if contributors to structural unemployment, could lower overall unemployment in a relatively short time. The probably more important source of structural

[49] *Idem,* "Current Surveys on Measuring Job Vacancies," Proceedings of the Business and Economic Statistics Section of the American Statistical Association (1965), p. 308.

unemployment—jobless workers being technically unqualified for existing vacancies at current relative wages—would take longer to eliminate or reduce. The process of training and educating for existing and foreseeable vacancies takes time. Perhaps policy makers might wish to expand demand, even in the presence of structural unemployment, in order to reduce unemployment more quickly and substantially than the removal or reduction of structural elements would allow. But the presence of vacancy data that told them these elements were present would warn them that such a policy runs the risk of substantial inflationary pressure.

SUMMARY

The presence of structural unemployment requires a surplus of workers in some job categories and a deficit in others. This latter condition makes the phenomenon a characteristic of good rather than bad times, for only then would there tend to be substantial labor-deficit pockets. Similarly, if extreme boom conditions prevailed, the little unemployment that remained would not be substantially structural either, because most unemployment would be frictional as almost every occupational classification felt a labor shortage.

The chief element in structural unemployment is the inability of unemployed workers to qualify technically for job openings. Barriers to mobility of qualified unemployed workers, as well as racial prejudice and educational preferences, form additional sources of structural unemployment.

These elements, if present, can all be suppressed by an expansion of demand, and total unemployment reduced. But the process necessarily involves the creation of inflationary pressures as labor and product demand are directed toward surplus labor, while shortages in the existing labor deficit sectors become more severe. On the other hand, elimination or reduction of structural elements can always lead to a reduction in unemployment without the inflation related to demand expansion and new job creation.

Since inflation results from demand expansion in any case, it is impossible to tell, without prior knowledge of unemployment-vacancy relationships, whether the inflation associated with a reduction in unemployment depended on the suppression of structural elements or on cyclical factors alone. In the future, detailed vacancy data would not only provide the answer to this question but would also serve as a policy guide for steps to reduce unemployment. As long as unemployment beyond the frictional level contains no structural elements, demand expansion and the creation of new jobs are required to reduce unemployment. This does not mean that structural problems could not be forecasted with the strengthening of the economy and steps taken to minimize their impact. But in this case antistructural measures alone—mainly expanded training programs—would have no initial impact. On the other hand, the presence of structural elements informs the policy makers that demand expansion, without alleviation of structural bottlenecks, would necessarily stir up inflationary forces.

Policy makers operate in the dark without data on unemployment-vacancy relationships. Improved unemployment data are needed, too, mainly series by occupation and race and education together, but the greatest need now for judging the importance of structural elements at any time is reliable, detailed vacancy information.

PART FOUR

Wages, Prices, and Productivity

CHAPTER IX

Demand Pull, Cost Push, and the Phillips Curve

While demand-pull and cost-push adherents disagree on the fundamental cause of inflation, both consider inflation as a consequence of a .strong economy. Demand-pull elements are obviously directly associated with high levels of output, and costs are pushed up more forcefully by workers and/or sellers of output when the risk of unemployment or reduced sales following this practice is slight.

The study of inflation has recently shifted from an analysis of the relative strength of demand-pull or cost-push elements to the relationship of prices to the level of unemployment, implied in the Phillips curve. In its simplest form, the curve relates wage changes to the level of unemployment, with the former an indicator of price changes. As such, the curve relates changes in costs (wages) to changes in prices, but takes no position as to whether costs rise directly with the state of the economy because of demand-pull or cost-push factors.

But the wage-unemployment relationship does suggest that a reduction in unemployment must be traded against a rise in wages (and prices). As Phelps has expressed it, this new concept of cost inflation means *"that kind of inflation which can be stopped only by a reduction of the employment rate* through lower aggregate demand and which thus raises a cruel dilemma for fiscal and monetary policy."[1] If the 18th and 19th centuries had their iron law of wages, the 20th century has its Phillips curve to demonstrate that economics is indeed the dismal science.

Economists are continuing to pursue the elusive question of the basic cause of inflation, whether demand-pull or cost-push, because the issue still has great relevance for policy decisions. A reduction in aggre-

[1] Edmund S. Phelps, "Money-Wage Dynamics and Labor-Market Equilibrium," University of Pennsylvania Discussion Paper No. 70, 1967, p. 4. (Italics in original.)

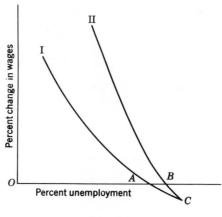

Fig. 9.1

gate demand can reduce either type of inflationary pressure. From the demand-pull side, this reduction could weaken the tendency of purchasers to bid up the prices of goods and labor services. Similarly, from the cost-push side, a slackening of demand would inhibit monopolistic sellers[2] of goods and factors from raising their prices as the cost of potential loss of sales increased.

Since a downward shift in aggregate demand will tend to depress wages in any case, the presence of cost-push elements implies a steeper Phillips curve than in their absence. This follows, since the weakening of wage pressure that accompanies a slackening of demand-pull forces as unemployment rises is reinforced by the reduction in cost-push pressure.

In Figure 9.1, Phillips curve I describes the situation in which cost-push forces do not operate. Wages would be stable at unemployment level OA. For Phillips curve II there are cost-push forces. Wages would fail to increase only for an unemployment level above OB. It is assumed that cost-push, though weaker than at lower unemployment rates, would still be felt at unemployment OB, so that the tendency for wages to fall, from demand conditions alone, would just be offset by this cost-push

---

[2] Cost-push depends on the presence of imperfect markets or else, in the short run, any upward movement of wages and/or prices, not in response to a prior increase in demand, would lead to total unemployment and/or loss of sales for the groups involved. This quality of cost-push, of emanating from suppliers' autonomous wage-price increases, has led Lerner to the apt term of "sellers' inflation" as a substitute expression for cost-push inflation. See Abba P. Lerner, "Inflationary Depression and the Regulation of Administered Prices," Compendium of Papers to the Joint Economic Committee, 85th Congress, 1958, p. 258.

pressure. At C the two curves would meet as cost-push elements in II disappeared under the influence of high unemployment rates.

But reduction in aggregate demand through monetary or fiscal policy carries the danger of starting a larger downward movement in the economy. If cost-push factors contribute to a current inflation, then they will be subject to removal or, at least, attenuation of their influence by direct pressure against wages and prices, such as the Wage-Price Guideposts. In other words, for reducing cost-push inflation there is not only a possible trade-off between lower prices and higher unemployment but also one between wage and price controls or guidelines and unemployment.[3] If regulation and/or government exhortation are considered socially costless, then surely the latter trade-off would be preferred. But if, as is likely, there is resistance to even informal regulation of, say, the guidepost type, then policy makers, in the case of cost-push inflation, could adopt measures leading to different combinations of three interrelated variables—inflation, the level of the economy (unemployment), and wage-price regulation.

The difficulties in assigning demand-pull or cost-push factors as the prime causal factors in inflation will be noted in the first section. Basically, uncertainties arise because of identification problems. Three examples of these problems will be discussed, namely, the wage-productivity relationship, the wage-price relationship, and the demand shift theory of inflation. The second section deals with the Phillips curve and with the inflation-unemployment trade-off. Specifically, discussion will center on the difficulties in interpreting the Phillips wage-unemployment relationship and in explanations of the general shape of the curve. The conclusion is reached that forces are at work in the United States that lead to the troublesome tendency for the curve to shift to the right, at least for low levels of unemployment. Because of the close relationship of the inflation causation issue and the Phillips curve, some aspects of both subjects will appear in both sections.

DEMAND-PULL OR COST-PUSH—IDENTIFICATION PROBLEMS

THE WAGE-PRODUCTIVITY TEST. When wages rise faster than productivity,[4] prices tend to rise. But that this sequence implies nothing

---

[3] Of course, direct wage and price controls could check or reduce any type of inflation. But in alleviating demand-pull inflation, such measures would have the added, perhaps prohibitive, cost of disrupting product and labor markets and misallocating resources. This difference between cost-push and demand-pull inflation will be explained in the first section of this chapter and in the following chapter.

[4] Strictly speaking, the reference is to marginal productivity, but statistical studies and policy formulas use the more easily measured average concept.

about causation has been recognized.[5] In fact, the closeness of the relationship among the three variables reflects nothing more than the constancy of relative shares.

If cost-push elements operated, and workers, probably operating through unions, succeeded in gaining wage increases, not based on an increase in product demand, above the growth in productivity, firms would tend to raise prices, reduce output, and lay off workers in the affected sectors. But if government policy was established to prevent widespread unemployment, the test of whether cost-push forces led to rising prices would apparently depend on whether full employment were maintained through fiscal and monetary policy.

It is next to impossible to test for the tie between stimulating fiscal and monetary measures and the threat of unemployment as a result of cost-push inflation. In fact, Gallaway claims that inflationary fiscal measures of the 1950's were independent of attempts to offset actual and potential unemployment possibly induced by cost-push forces. This led him to attribute the inflation of the period to these measures themselves rather than to cost-push factors.[6]

The unemployment test suffers from two additional shortcomings other than the inability to associate the timing of fiscal and monetary action with incipient unemployment. First, if the inflation is general, through most sectors of the economy, or if factor supply adjustment to changing demand conditions created by differential price rises is quick enough, a noticeable increase in unemployment might not take place. This would be especially likely if the economy fit the Keynesian rather than the classical model.

Second, even if unemployment arose, there would be no assurance that the accompanying inflation were produced by cost-push rather than demand-pull factors. In Phillips curve relationships, it will be seen that wages may rise as unemployment increases, without any particular indication as to whether the inflationary pressure comes from an independent increase in costs or from excess demand. If unemployment rose to high levels, the critical height at which demand-pull could no longer be considered operative being uncertain, and prices still increased,[7] cost-push forces could be assumed to be active, but the economy does not seem to behave in this manner; high rates of unemployment are not accompanied by price increases.

---

[5] For example, see Paul A. Samuelson and Robert M. Solow, "Analytical Aspects of Anti-Inflation Policy," *American Economic Review,* Papers and Proceedings, **50** (May 1960), pp. 182–183.

[6] Lowell E. Gallaway, "The Wage-Push Inflation Thesis, 1950–1957," *American Economic Review,* **48** (December 1958), pp. 967–972.

[7] The issue of the level of unemployment at which demand cannot be considered excessive is discussed in the next section.

If the unemployment test is inadequate for assigning causes of inflation, so too is the factor-share test. If wages outrun productivity gains and the labor share of national income rises, it might be hastily concluded that wage-push initiated the consequent price increase. But wages might have risen faster than productivity simply because increased demand was translated into money-return gains in the labor market before the product market.

Similarly, although prices rise more than wages, reducing labor's share of national income, this does not necessarily signify that the price rise resulted from the operation of demand-pull forces. Perhaps wage-push was not responsible for the price increase. But prices might have risen because of other types of cost-push, such as a profit-push.

The failure of productivity-wage relationships to indicate the nature of inflationary pressure is reflected in the obvious identification problem inherent in the more direct wage-price relative movement. It has long been recognized that upward movements in wages and prices, whether uniform or at different rates, offer no information on whether the price rises pull-up wages or wage increases push-up prices.

WAGE-PRICE RELATIONSHIP. Studies of the Phillips curve relationship have noted that the association between wage changes and unemployment levels varies with movements in the price level. At any given level of unemployment, there is a tendency for the wage increases to be greater, the greater the rise in the price level.

Phillips curve analysts, though, usually carefully point out that this correlation implies nothing about causation. For example, in his study of the wage-unemployment level correlation for the United States in which he finds only a loose relationship over a long period, Bhatia finds a significant relationship between recent earnings changes and cost-of-living movement. He clearly notes, however, that "from the present study alone it is not possible to determine whether changes in prices are the causal variable, or whether prices rise because the unions are able to extract large wage concessions independently of price changes."[8]

Note that Bhatia assigns to unions the exclusive role of the monopolistic element required for the exertion of a wage push. Much the same assumption is implied in Garbarino's study of changes in the overall wage level in the preunion period.[9]

[8] Rattan J. Bhatia, "Unemployment and the Rate of Change of Money Earnings in the United States, 1900–1958," *Economica*, **28** (August 1961), p. 296.

[9] Joseph W. Garbarino, "Unionism and the General Wage Level," *American Economic Review*, **40** (December 1950), pp. 893–896.

In this early analysis of the wage change-unemployment level relationship, which antedates the more formal establishment of the Phillips curve by almost a decade, Garbarino notes that for the period 1899–1929 wages did not rise significantly, above 3 percent annually, except in subperiods during which the price level rose substantially. This leads him to the conclusion that for nonunion labor markets wages will not rise enough to induce inflation, that is, faster than productivity growth, unless at the same time the price level is increasing substantially. He writes, "It seems that the statement that full employment is likely *to lead to* 'undue' wage increases under non-union market conditions would be more accurate if 'price inflation' were substituted for 'full employment'."[10]

Here is a clear instance of an assumption of the nature of the underlying cause of inflation, in this case of demand-pull elements. Garbarino's findings would be just as consistent with a conclusion that read "undue" wage increases (above the 3 percent level) are likely to lead to "price inflation." With this conclusion, we would, of course, be assuming a wage-push model, but there can be no indication from the data, which show that when wages rise above 3 percent (the critical level for price changes, the approximate average annual productivity growth), prices rise, whether prices are pulling up wages or wages pushing up prices.[11]

Thus, when Garbarino concludes that unionism would introduce a new element in the unemployment level-wage change relationship if wages rose at all when unemployment exceeded 8 percent or wages rose by more than 3 percent, with the unemployment at or below the 5 percent level, he writes of unionism "generating" the wage increase.[12] In truth, different wage change-unemployment level relationships in union periods, after the 1930's, from the preunion era would merely indicate an association and not necessarily a process of causation running from union wage-push to price increases.[13]

---

[10] *Ibid.*, p. 895. (Italics not in original.)

[11] The former adjustment would necessarily be the only possible one if it were assumed that unions alone can make labor markets noncompetitive.

[12] *Ibid.*, p. 896.

[13] It is interesting to note that Samuelson and Solow conclude that, in the postwar (unionized) period, wages would be stable at an unemployment rate of 8 percent and would rise 2 to 3 percent per year with a 5 or 6 percent unemployment rate. These critical values duplicate Garbarino's findings for the nonunion period.

There is conflicting evidence on whether the aggregate wage-change-unemployment level relationship has changed, in the direction of higher-wage increases associated with a given level of unemployment, in the more recent (unionized) period than in earlier periods. See Robert R. France, "Wages, Unemployment, and Prices in the United States, 1890–1932, 1947–1957," *Industrial and Labor Relations Review,* **15** (January 1962), pp. 171–190, and Kenneth M. McCaffree, "A Further

SCHULTZE'S DEMAND-SHIFT INFLATION HYPOTHESIS.[14] One of the most intriguing explanations of the "creeping inflation" of 1955–1957, when the consumer price index increased at an annual average of 2.6 percent while the unemployment rate averaged 4.3 percent was offered by Schultze. In Schultze's theory, price rise occurs, with aggregate demand unchanged, as a result of differential shifts in sectoral demand. Prices and wages rise in sectors experiencing growth in demand, and overall prices rise, too, because sectors losing demand in paying competitive factor prices fail to experience price declines.

Thus, at first view, Schultze's hypothesis appears to follow the cost-push syndrome. Inflation is derived from differential changes in demand, but the proximate cause is the failure of wages and prices to fall in the sectors losing demand. This resistance to wage cuts for these sectors is an expression of cost-push, no less than would be a rise in wages in sectors where demand was constant.[15] It will be argued here that, even in this tight hypothesis, there is a classification problem and that, even though tests have presented data not inconsistent with the hypothesis, there is still the possibility that inflation associated with sectoral changes in demand may be classified as demand-pull in nature.

Selden's well-known study of the "creeping inflation" supports the Schultze hypothesis even though Selden claimed that his findings denied the importance of cost-push elements in the period.[16] In 1955 and 1956,

---

Consideration of Wages, Unemployment, and Prices in the United States, 1948–1958," *ibid.*, **17** (October 1963), pp. 60–74.

Both conclude that the only change in the unionized period has been a tendency for wages not to fall as much as in the past during periods of high unemployment.

If unions tend to put a floor on wage reductions, this practice contains an inflationary element for, if demand shifts away from goods produced by union workers, the market mechanism can only operate through price increases in the sector gaining demand. This is the crux of the demand-shift hypothesis, discussed next.

In a study of English data, A. G. Hines, "Trade Unions and Wage Inflation in the United Kingdom 1893–1961," *Review of Economic Studies,* **31** (October 1964), pp. 221–252, finds degree of unionization more closely related to wage changes than was the level of unemployment for the period studied.

[14] Charles L. Schultze, *Recent Inflation in the United States,* Study Paper No. 1, *Study of Employment Growth and Price Levels,* Joint Economic Committee, Washington, 1959, especially pp. 73–77.

[15] As Ackley expresses it, " 'Cost' forces do not originate the inflation, but they generalize it from its original locus." Gardner Ackley, *Macroeconomic Theory,* Macmillan, New York, 1961, p. 446.

[16] Richard T. Selden, "Cost-Push Versus Demand-Pull Inflation, 1955–57," *Journal of Political Economy,* **47** (February 1959), pp. 1–20.

when admittedly the economy was strong, Selden found that, by far, the largest part of the rise in the Wholesale Price Index resulted from price increases in industries experiencing strong demand (output gains). But this is just what the Schultze hypothesis would expect. It is not the rise in prices of the expanding industries that causes inflation, but the fact that the industries which contracted did not have price declines.

In another study, which supports the Schultze hypothesis, Bowen and Masters found that in the post-Schultze period, from mid-1957 to early 1963, prices were more or less stable, while intersectoral demand was more or less uniform.[17] This pattern provides indirect support to the Schultze hypothesis in that, with about the same unemployment rate over both periods, the one characterized by dispersed sectoral demand was the one during which prices increased.

Although tests of the Schultze demand-shift hypothesis have been neither numerous nor conclusive, they do support the view that inflation has been associated with shift in sectoral demand. Nevertheless, it will now be argued that the inflation associated with demand shift may be of the demand-pull rather than the cost-push type.

As a first attack on the cost-push position, Hancock in commenting on the Bowen-Masters study points out that differential changes in demand and prices among industries are characteristic of inflationary periods, especially in the early stages.[18] Thus, Hancock suggests that the line of causation may run from inflation to sectoral differences in demand and price, rather than vice versa. If this were the case, then the underlying basis of inflation, whether cost-push or demand-pull, would still be in doubt, since the price rise would not be attributable to the demand shift.

For the period 1954–1957, there is no evidence of a significant increase in overall demand. But inasmuch as demand-pull inflation operates at positive unemployment rates, it is possible that with an unemployment rate averaging below 5 percent for the period, the accompanying inflation was of the simple demand-pull type. But operating against this position

---

[17] William G. Bowen and S. H. Masters, "Shifts in the Composition of Demand and the Inflation Problem," *American Economic Review,* **54** (December 1964), pp. 975–984.
[18] Keith Hancock, "Shifts in Demand and the Inflation Problem: Comment," *American Economic Review,* **56** (June 1966), pp. 518–519. That the Bowen-Masters period is longer than the Schultze period leads Hancock to argue that the longer time period can partially account for the sectoral uniformity in demand from 1957–1963. Furthermore, Hancock correctly questions the validity of sales data, used by Bowen and Masters, as a proxy for demand and price changes. But these are empirical questions not related to the theoretical problem at issue here.

is the fact that, in the prior period, the unemployment rate was slightly lower with stable prices.

More damaging to the assumption that the demand shift hypothesis implies a cost-push inflation, is the possibility that demand shift, in itself, leads to inflation because of nonlinearity in the wage-unemployment relationship. With the shift in demand, if the wage-unemployment relationship were nonlinear on a sectoral basis, wages and prices would rise more in the sector gaining demand than they would fall in the sector losing demand. It remains only to state at this point[19] that nonlinearity is based on the tendency for wage pressures, whether from the demanders or suppliers of labor, to be greater upward when demand is excessive than the downward pressure when demand falls short of available supply, in order to claim that an inflation based on demand shift may be demand-pull rather than cost-push in character.

Thus, while the "creeping inflation" of the mid-1950's may have been *caused by* demand-shift among economic sectors, as Schultze hypothesized, there is still uncertainty whether demand-shift inflation reflects the operation of cost-push or demand-pull forces.

THE PHILLIPS CURVE

A. Characteristics of the Curve

Although it is only a decade since the first Phillips curve was drawn,[20] interest in the subject has expanded and the literature proliferated to the point where books in the field contain extensive summaries of past studies.[21] Professional interest stems from the important policy problem that the curve treats.

While a country may have full employment as a policy goal, a close long-term negative relationship between wage changes and the level of unemployment suggests that attainment or movement toward this goal must be accompanied by higher prices. Phillips' original work may have been intended simply as a statistical study of the price (wage)-economic level (unemployment) relationship, but its results, and those of other

[19] The issue of nonlinearity in the Phillips curve will be detailed in the next section.

[20] A. W. Phillips, "The Relation Between Unemployment and the Rate of Change of Money Wage Rates in the United Kingdom, 1861–1957," *Economica*, **25** (November 1958), pp. 283–299.

[21] For examples, George L. Perry, *Unemployment, Money Wage Rates, and Inflation*, M. I. T. Press, Cambridge, Mass., 1966, Chapter 1, and Ronald G. Bodkin, *The Wage-Price-Productivity Nexus*, University of Pennsylvania Press, Philadelphia, 1966, Chapter 1 and *passim*.

analyses, have been used as an indicator of the inflation-unemployment reduction "trade-off"—the extent of inflation resulting from a strengthening of the economy to a given low overall unemployment rate.

COST-PUSH, DEMAND-PULL, OR NEUTRAL ASPECTS OF THE CURVE. On the surface, it appears that the statistical relationship in itself yields no insights into the nature of inflation that accompanies low unemployment rates. Wages and, presumably, prices could rise higher with lower unemployment rates either because firms, spurred by rising product demand, bid against each other for scarce labor, or because workers bid up their offer prices as the risk of becoming unemployed by doing so declines.

It is interesting to note that the earliest formulators of the Phillips curve, Phillips and Lipsey, were less inclined than their followers to avoid suggesting the form of the inflation. In fact, Lipsey offers three strong reasons for the formulation of a model describing the relationship, which have relevance for any quantitative pattern; the model allows for easy interpretation of the relationship; it establishes the conditions under which the relationship is expected to remain unchanged and can explain deviation from the pattern; and it will yield testable predictions on the effect of other variables on the relationship.[22]

On the very first page of his study, Phillips implies that rising wages at low levels of unemployment result from demand-pull forces. He writes,

> When the demand for labour is high and there are very few unemployed we should expect employers to bid wage rates up quite rapidly, each firm and each industry being continually tempted to offer a little above the prevailing rates to attract the most suitable labour from other firms and industries.[23]

Then he explains the nonlinearity of the unemployment-level-wage-rate change curve on the reluctance of workers "to offer their services at less than the prevailing rates when the demand for labour is low and unemployment is high so that wage rates fall only very slowly."[24] Here, clearly, Phillips suggests that cost-push forces prevent wages from falling during weak periods in the economy, accounting for a chronic inflationary bias.

---

[22] Richard G. Lipsey, "The Relation Between Unemployment and the Rate of Change of Money Wage Rates in the United Kingdom, 1862–1957: A Further Analysis," *Economica,* **27** (February 1960), p. 12.

[23] Phillips, *op. cit.,* p. 283.

[24] *Loc. cit.* It should be noted, however, that Phillips finds a high degree of nonlinearity in the wage-change-unemployment relationship at low levels of unemployment, too.

At this point it will merely be mentioned that Lipsey's model, which relates wage changes to the degree of excess demand or supply in the labor market, is essentially demand-pull in nature. This model will receive fuller treatment in the second part of this section.

OTHER VARIABLES RELATING TO WAGES—PRICES AND PROFITS. Analysts after Phillips, who have noted that the two-variable system often yields but a loose fit, have entered variables additional to the unemployment level into their wage-estimation equation. Of these other variables, the three most prevalent have been the rate of change of unemployment, profit rate levels, or changes—either current or immediately prior to the wage change, and changes in prices—most often with the Consumer Price Index as the price measure. The last two interrelated variables form the subject of the present discussion. The first will be treated below.

It has already been emphasized that wage and price relationships in themselves indicate nothing about causation. Profits were offered as a possible independent influence on wages by Kaldor, who suggested that wage changes are determined by labor's bargaining strength. When an industry was prosperous (profitable), unions would be "eager" to press for higher wages, and firms would show a "willingness" and "ability" to meet these demands.[25] Kaldor links profit rate increases to the growth in productivity associated with rising investment and production. If wages respond to profit-rate increases from this source, though, there is no question of inflationary causes from wage increases since, in competitive markets, prices would not tend to rise because of the wage increase. By getting higher wages, workers would be merely retaining their share of output, increased by the productivity gain. Phillips curve analysts are aware of the offset of productivity growth to the price increasing effects of wage increases. They usually not only specify the level of unemployment at which wages will start to rise but, in addition, the level of wages, equal to the former level plus average annual-productivity growth at which wage increases lead to price increases.

But profits may also rise in association with price increases, either because of an expansion in product demand or an independent profit-push, as product sellers strive for a higher share of current output. Thus the relationship of wage to profit change, when prices are increasing, does not indicate whether the inflationary process results from demand-pull or cost-push forces. For the latter case, if workers secured higher wages to match or approach the profit gains, the wage increase would

---

[25] Nicholas Kaldor, "Economic Growth and the Problem of Inflation," *Economica*, **26** (November 1959), p. 293.

not be related to a wage-push inflation, but would be the reflection of a profit-push price increase.[26]

Studies of wage-profit relationships yield little support to Kaldor's hypothesis that wages are related to profit levels, when profits are considered as independent elements in wage determination, unrelated to other variables. Lipsey and Steuer, in testing Kaldor's hypothesis for English data, found that profits, in general, were not significantly related to wage changes and were certainly a weaker indicator than the unemployment level of wage changes.[27] Bodkin derived similar results for American data.[28]

Studies that show a close correlation between profits and wages do not include price changes as an explanatory variable.[29] This means that a great deal of the association between profits and wages could more suitably be attributed to the price increases resulting from increased demand for products or from profit-push.[30] When price changes entered into the wage estimation equation as an explanatory variable, the association between wages and profits can be attributed to their mutual dependence on productivity growth, but they can and do move together then without affecting prices.[31]

---

[26] It could be argued that although the initial price rise resulted from profit-push, wage-push continues the inflation, as sellers raise their prices again to try again to get a larger share of income, an attempt that was temporarily thwarted by the wage increase. This sequence is suggested by Gardner Ackley, "A Third Approach to the Analysis and Control of Inflation," *The Relationship of Prices to Economic Stability and Growth,* Joint Economic Committee, Washington, 1958, pp. 619–636. In any case, though, the inflation is of the cost-push type.

[27] Richard G. Lipsey and M. D. Steuer, "The Relation Between Profits and Wage Rates," *Economica,* **28** (May 1961), pp. 137–159.

[28] Bodkin, *op. cit.,* pp. 128–140.

[29] Bodkin, *op. cit.,* pp. 138–139, notes this omission in the close tie between wages and profits found by Harold M. Levinson, *Postwar Movements of Prices and Wages in Manufacturing Industries,* Study Paper No. 21, Joint Economic Committee, Congress of the United States, Washington, 1960, pp. 3–4, Eckstein and Wilson, *op. cit.,* for industries in the "key group," and Rattan J. Bhatia, "Profits and the Rate of Change in Money Earnings in the United States, 1935–1959," *Economica,* **29** (August 1962), pp. 255–262.

[30] If prices rise because of profit-push, should not then the rise in profits be considered the factor explaining the consequent wage rise? But this is not the issue here. The relevant question is whether, considering only profits and prices, profits move with wages, prices being held constant, or do prices move with wages, profits being held constant? The latter shows a closer fit, although in the case of profit-push the price changes would not enter the price-wage relationship, since profits would be rising. But similarly, the profit-wage relationship would not be affected since profit-push would only occur through the price increase.

[31] Perry, *op. cit.,* pp. 89–92, relates changes in profits positively to changes in product prices and productivity in his wage-estimation equation.

A CLOSER LOOK AT THE PHILLIPS CURVE. The Phillips curve relates wage changes as the dependent variable to the unemployment level, the independent or explanatory variable. In effect, though, wage changes for inflation models stand as a proxy for price changes. In fact, crude formulations of the influence of wage changes on price changes relate the two series directly, with price increases appearing only after the wage level has risen by an amount greater than the productivity gain. Then for small changes, the percentage change in price is assumed to approximate the percentage change in wages minus the percentage-productivity growth.

As productivity increases over time, the price rise associated with a given wage increase declines. But in tight labor markets, the wage increase associated with a low level of unemployment would understate the effect of low unemployment levels on prices. This follows since, when labor is scarce, firms have as an alternative to wage increases, a lowering of hiring standards.[32] This practice would not affect wage levels but

---

[32] Melvin Reder, "Wage Structure and Structural Unemployment," p. 310, notes a functional relationship between the number hired, the vacancy period, the wage rate, and worker quality. Raising the wage rate or reducing worker quality can increase the number hired and/or shorten the vacancy period, desired goals when rising product demand increases labor demand. William G. Bowen, *The Wage Price Issue,* Princeton University Press, Princeton, 1960, p. 96, introduces increased recruiting expenses as a further variable, but this is also a cost-increasing element that may substitute for wage increases. Allan Cartter, *Theory of Wages and Employment,* pp. 62–64 points out that in monopsonistic labor markets, the employer may choose to lower hiring standards because the marginal labor cost to him would be less than if he increased wages, the increase applying to his existing work force as well as to new hires.

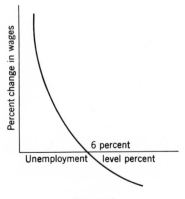

Fig. 9.2

would raise labor costs, for a given output, and would consequently raise prices.

The Phillips curve, itself, is drawn to fit a scatter diagram of wage-change and unemployment levels for a series of years. Such a curve is drawn in Figure 9.2..

Points lie off the curve because of random disturbances associated with any statistical relationship. In addition, different combinations of demand-pull and cost-push forces, which are additive insofar as their influences as wages are concerned, can lead to differing wage changes at the same level of unemployment. Furthermore, differing rates of change in unemployment, a factor to be treated below, may affect wage changes associated with a given *level* of unemployment.

Four characteristics of the curve noted here serve as the basis of the analysis of part B.

1. The curve is nonlinear, especially for extreme values of unemployment.

2. The curve indicates a constant (annual) wage change at any given level of unemployment. This means that the forces inducing wage changes at any given level of unemployment are constant over time.

3. To the left of the X-intercept, wages would tend to rise even if labor markets loosened and the rate of unemployment increased.

4. Although the 6 percent level of unemployment for the X-intercept is, of course, arbitrarily chosen, every Phillips curve drawn indicates that wages rise at unemployment rates clearly above what can be assumed to be the frictional level.

B. Lipsey's Inflation Model, Structural Unemployment, and the Expandable Labor Force

Lipsey's Sectoral Excess Demand Inflation Theory.[33] Lipsey's explanation of inflation at the aggregate level is based on a nonlinear relationship between wages and unemployment rates below frictional values at the sectoral level. Related to this description are one assumption and one condition. The assumption is that changes in the wage level are linearly related to the rate of excess labor demand, measured by the difference between labor demand and supply as a percentage of supply.[34]

---

[33] The analysis presented here is derived from Lipsey, *op. cit.*, pp. 12–23, unless otherwise specified.

[34] Lipsey implies the usual assumption that price changes move directly with wage changes.

The condition is that wages will not tend to rise unless part of total unemployment is structural in nature.

The first link in Lipsey's excess demand inflation theory leads toward explanation of the role of the above assumption and condition in his theory. Wages rise in any sector only when demand for labor exceeds supply. The two are equal at the frictional level of unemployment, so that the "little Phillips curve" for individual sectors crosses the unemployment-level axis at the sectoral frictional unemployment rate.

At levels of unemployment above the frictional rate, excess supply of labor—unemployment over vacancies—increases linearly with unemployment by an amount equal to the increase in unemployment, since vacancies remain unchanged. Thus, with changes in the wage level related linearly to the rate of excess demand, in this case a negative rate, the sectoral Phillips curve is linear in the range of wage declines for unemployment rates above the frictional level.

At unemployment rates below the frictional level, though, excess demand for labor will increase by more than a given reduction in unemployment. That is, to reduce unemployment to zero by cutting into the frictional base requires an increase in labor demand such that the number of vacancies will increase over the previous level.[35] Thus, wages, which are assumed to move linearly with excess demand, will rise by a greater percentage than the reduction in the unemployment level.

Combining these two patterns, the percentage change in wages in the aggregate will be greater for any given level of unemployment than the wage increase associated with a sectoral unemployment rate at that level, *provided that the unemployment rate is below the frictional level in some sectors.*

To explain this conclusion and its condition, assume first an aggregate unemployment rate of 6 percent in a three-sector economy of equal labor force in each, with unemployment rates of 4 percent, 6 percent, and 8 percent, all above the frictional level. Since the unemployment rate is on the linear part of the "little Phillips curve" for each sector, the wage level change (decrease) associated with the 6 percent aggregate unemployment level would be identical with the wage change estimated for the 6 percent unemployment level.

But if the sectoral rates were 1 percent, 6 percent, and 11 percent, then the wage change at the aggregate unemployment level would exceed that for the 6 percent unemployment sector. In fact, the wage increase

---

[35] The analysis is not affected other than to make the sectoral Phillips curve vertical at the frictional level of unemployment in the extreme case treated in the previous chapter, for which the frictional level cannot be reduced.

in the 1 percent unemployment sector may balance out the declines in the other two, so that a constant wage level is associated with an aggregate unemployment level of 6 percent.

The above analysis explains why wages will tend to rise at overall unemployment rates above the frictional level. This rise will occur even if much of the unemployment is cyclical, above frictional levels for many sectors, provided that there is some structural unemployment, manifested by an excess of vacancies over unemployment—that these are Structurally Overemployed Counterparts, in the terminology of the last chapter. This does not mean, though, that the presence of a small amount of structural unemployment assures average wage increases. Wage declines in sectors of high unemployment will outweigh the increases that occur in the few sectors of excess labor demand. In short, there may be some structural unemployment at unemployment rates higher than the X-intercept rate on the aggregate Phillips curve. This would make the aggregate Phillips curve nonlinear over a range of wage declines and unemployment rates up to that level of unemployment at which structural unemployment disappeared, that is, when there were no longer any SOCs.

Because of nonlinearity in the sectoral Phillips curve for low levels of unemployment, the wage change associated with any (low) aggregate level of unemployment would be higher the more divergent the sectoral levels. In a simple extension of this conclusion, Lipsey claims that the apparent tie between the rate *of change* of unemployment and percentage wage changes stems from the fact that sectoral divergence in unemployment rates becomes more pronounced when the economy is strengthening and unemployment falling than when the economy is weakening and unemployment rising. In advancing this theory, Lipsey rejects the more widely accepted explanation of the tie between the rates of change in unemployment and percentage wage changes, which is based on the effect of expectations on wage levels. According to this theory, when unemployment is falling to a certain level, employers and, perhaps, worker wage-push bid up wages in anticipation of still tighter labor markets; when unemployment is rising to this level, pessimistic expectations of still further declines in labor demand weaken upward wage pressure.[36]

---

[36] Lipsey claims that a change in expectations will not only affect wages but, in addition, the level of unemployment, as employers react to their expectations by both raising wages and hiring more workers when expectations are optimistic, with opposite practices when expectations are pessimistic with unemployment rising. Thus to Lipsey, changing expectations would only lead to movements along the wage change-unemployment level Phillips curve.

Lipsey's view has been criticized on the grounds that in reaction to changing

In any case, the inflation associated with Lipsey's excess demand model would be mainly the demand-pull type. It could be argued that cost-push forces might operate, too, bidding up wages in individual sectors when unemployment is below the frictional level, but it is a weak form of cost-push that confines itself to situations in which the risk of increasing unemployment from an upward pressure on wages is zero. Nevertheless, Lipsey's theory should be considered one (not exclusive) explanation of inflation. It attempts to spell out the process of demand-pull wage increases, but does not deny that wages (and prices) may also increase as well from the operation of cost-push forces.

STRUCTURAL UNEMPLOYMENT AND THE EXPANDABLE LABOR FORCE. Lipsey's excess demand model depends heavily on the presence and extent of structural unemployment. The degree of divergence in sectoral unemployment rates contributes nothing to the Lipsey type of demand-pull wage increases and inflation unless there is also structural unemployment as well as structural imbalance. As was noted above, if all sectoral rates are above the frictional level, no matter how divergent the individual sectoral levels, with no excess labor demand in any sector, the aggregate wage change (decline) associated with a given level of unemployment is the same as if all rates were the same—abstracting from differences in weight among sectors in the overall labor force.

Similarly, when structural unemployment is present, the wage change for any given level of unemployment varies with the extent of structural

---

economic conditions and the direction of unemployment changes, wage increases, which are made less easily and frequently, will be made first, taking expectations into account, before workers are stockpiled or laid off in response to expectations. This argument is made by William G. Bowen and R. A. Berry, "Unemployment Conditions and Movements of the Money Wage Level," *Review of Economics and Statistics,* **45** (May 1963), pp. 167–168, and France, *op. cit.*, p. 174, n. 9. France also argues that the evidence that the unemployment distribution among sectors is wider during the upswing is not conclusive. Furthermore, in a study of local labor markets, Phillip Ross, "Labor Market Behavior and the Relationship between Unemployment and Wages," Proceedings of the 14th Annual Industrial Relations Research Association (1962), pp. 275–288, found no relationship between wages or wage changes and unemployment rates. But Ross' study covered only the six-year period, 1954–1960, when the aggregate Phillips relationship for all the localities was itself not significant.

Guy Routh, "The Relation between Unemployment and the Rate of Change of Money Wage Rates: A Comment," *Economica,* **26** (November 1959), p. 315, notes that the Phillips curve, which shows constant wage changes when the unemployment level is stable, makes the tacit "unwarranted" assumption that expectations then would be midway between what they would be with rising and falling unemployment.

unemployment, being higher the greater the amount of structural unemployment. This relationship follows from nonlinearity in the Phillips curve, with greater wage increases for a given reduction in unemployment, at low levels of unemployment.

As an example, if the overall unemployment rate is 5 percent and the (uniform) frictional sectoral rate is 2 percent, then if in three sectors of equal labor force, the rates are 4, 5, and 6 percent or 3, 5, and 7 percent, the aggregate average wage change would be the same as if each sector had a 5 percent level. If there is structural unemployment, though, such that the sectoral rates are 1, 5, and 9 percent, the aggregate wage change will be greater than that associated with a uniform sectoral rate of 5 percent or any combination of sectoral rates such that none is below 2 percent. Furthermore, the wage change would be even higher, with the average unemployment level of 5 percent, if the sectoral rates were $\frac{1}{2}$, 5 and $9\frac{1}{2}$ percent. This would follow from nonlinearity in the sectoral Phillips curve over the range 1 to $\frac{1}{2}$ percent level of unemployment. But this nonlinearity is a function of increasing excess vacancies over unemployment in the strong sector, which is simply another way of expressing the fact that a greater part of the overall 5 percent unemployment rate is structural.

Studies of labor force changes have noted a clear tendency for the labor force to expand as the economy strengthens.[37] If these new job entrants joined the labor force only in response to fresh job openings, then the rise in the labor force would permit a reduction in unemployment rates with no more inflationary effect than if the labor-force size were stagnant in the face of rising labor demand.

But this does not seem to be the case. These workers tend to form the "hidden unemployed," the labor reserve who enter the labor force in response to improved job opportunities in general rather than to specific job openings, but who are not counted among the unemployed at any time unless and until they actually enter the work force.

The "hidden unemployed," who enter the labor force as the overall unemployment rate declines, tend to swell the ranks of secondary workers—the old, the young, and dependent women. These are groups with chronically high unemployment rates.[38] Since there are rarely labor

---

[37] Alfred Tella, "The Relation of Labor Force to Employment," *Industrial and Labor Relations Review,* **17** (April 1964), pp. 454–469, Kenneth Strand and Thomas Dernburg, "Cyclical Variation in Civilian Labor Force Participation," *Review of Economics and Statistics,* **46** (November 1964), pp. 378–391, are two such studies.

[38] This tendency for labor force elasticity, with regard to overall unemployment rates, to be greatest for secondary workers has been found in statistical studies by Thomas Dernburg and Kenneth Strand, "Hidden Unemployment 1953–62: A

shortages for jobs that these primarily untrained workers can fill, their entrance into the work force retards the reduction in unemployment that takes place as the economy strengthens. With entrance of the "hidden unemployed" into the labor force, to reduce unemployment to a given level requires a greater expansion in aggregate demand than if the labor force did not expand with rising employment. If demand for labor increases more or less evenly among labor classes, then bringing about a net reduction in unemployment, which in effect means mainly a reduction in unemployment associated with jobs that the new entrants will fill, will lead to further tightness in labor markets already characterized by short supply. The inflationary aspect of the process stems from nonlinearity in the wage rise-excess labor demand relationship, which will lead to increasing upward-wage pressure in sectors of short-labor supply when demand is strengthening.

Expressing this analysis numerically, assume a two-sector economy of equal size with unemployment rates of 2 and 8 percent, with the frictional level at 2 percent in both sectors, and a stable labor force. If the policy goal is to reduce unemployment to 4 percent, then if expansionary steps are taken that increase labor demand equally, unemployment will fall to, say, 1½ and 6½ percent in the two sectors. (The differential in the unemployment decline is based on the fact that a given increase in labor demand for a sector already at the frictional level will take more the form of excess vacancies than reduced unemployment.) Inflation will tend to result not only because of higher wages

---

Quantitative Analysis by Age and Sex," *American Economic Review*, **56** (March 1966), pp. 71–94, and, on a cross-sectional basis for census years by Glen C. Cain, "Unemployment and the Labor-Force Participation of Secondary Workers," *Industrial and Labor Relations Review*, **20** (January 1967), pp. 275–297. Cain did not find, however, an inverse relationship between unemployment levels and labor-force participation of Negro wives among local labor markets. This finding is consistent with the tendency for labor-force participation of Negro wives to decline over time, as their wages and husbands' income have risen, noted in Chapter I.

As for younger workers, Beverly Duncan, "Dropouts and the Unemployed," *Journal of Political Economy*, **73** (April 1965), pp. 121–134, finds a significant inverse relationship between dropping out of school and unemployment rates for youths.

Jacob Mincer, "Labor-Force Participation and Unemployment: A Review of Recent Evidence," *Prosperity and Unemployment*, pp. 102–103, argues that because of the competition of nonmarket work with market work, and the lower percentage of time they normally denote to market labor, the net gain for moving into the labor force and net loss from leaving it by secondary workers is generally "quite small." Thus they will tend to enter when job-search costs are low and labor-market conditions "attractive," and will move out under opposite conditions, explaining their greater volatility to changing overall unemployment rates than that of primary workers.

associated with reduced unemployment but also because of nonlinearity in the sectoral Phillips curve at unemployment rates below the frictional level.

Assume now that the work force in the sector having 8 percent unemployment increases its labor supply by ½ percent as the economy strengthens. Then with the same increase in aggregate demand as before, the sectoral unemployment rates would be 1½ and 7 percent. To bring the overall rate down to 5 percent, unless policy measures direct demand specifically to the high unemployment sector, would require a further increase in demand, bringing increasingly greater pressure on wages in the tight labor market and, consequently, greater inflation than in the previous case.

What makes the inflationary aspects of the expendable labor force more serious is the apparent tendency for the elasticity of the labor force, with respect to unemployment rates, especially of secondary workers, to increase over time.[39] Mincer attributes this trend to the growth in the female labor force and weakening of permanent attachment to the labor force of young and older males—elements expanding the proportions of secondary workers in the labor force.[40] In any case, the entrance of the "hidden unemployed" into the labor market, who seek work when jobs in general become more available, adds to the inflationary problems that accompany expansion toward full employment and bedevil policy makers, who would prefer that measures designed to reduce unemployment would lead to as little inflation as possible.

PHILLIPS CURVE SUMMARY—BRITISH AND AMERICAN EXPERIENCE COMPARED. The discussion of the Phillips curve can be reviewed within the framework of a comparison of British and American wage change-unemployment level relationships. It is not suggested that the reasons offered are the only or even main explanations of international differences in the following Phillips curve aspects, but they serve to underscore the issues treated above.

1. The fit of the Phillips curve is much closer for English than for American data. In fact, Phillips found a stable English pattern for almost a century. This could reflect a greater and varying influence of cost-push

---

[39] Dernburg and Strand, *op. cit.*, and William G. Bowen and T. A. Finegan, "Labor Force Participation and Unemployment," *Employment Policy and the Labor Market,* pp. 146–148, have noted an increased responsiveness of secondary workers to changes in the unemployment rate, the latter study for the 1940, 1950, and 1960 census years.

[40] Mincer, "Labor Force Participation . . . ," p. 105.

forces in the United States. Wages can increase at a given (low) unemployment level from both demand-pull and/or cost-push elements in an additive manner. If the degree of cost-push, which may be considered more unstable, varies from time to time, then wage change, associated with any level of unemployment for a number of years, would tend to become scattered.

2. The Phillips curve for the United States is more stable for relatively shorter subperiods than for longer periods. This suggests that long-term relationships are not close in the United States because of a shift in the Phillips curve and because of increasing wage-push from institutional forces such as union-wage pressure, higher minimum wages, and/or an increase in structural unemployment.[41]

3. The American Phillips curve seems to lie to the right of the British curve. This tendency for wage increases, associated with any level of unemployment, to be higher in the United States than in England could indicate more wage-push here, greater structural unemployment, or a greater sensitivity of labor-force participation of secondary workers to changes in the unemployment rate.

4. On the other hand, there is less evidence of nonlinearity in the American Phillips curve, especially for low levels of unemployment. This might reflect that American unemployment rates have not fallen to the low level reached in England. But insofar as the Lipsey model applies, linearity in the American curve offers indirect support to the inadequate-demand-unemployment school by suggesting that structural unemployment does not comprise an important component of total unemployment even at relatively low American unemployment levels.

---

[41] Bowen and Berry, *op. cit.*, pp. 168–169, argue that the closer fit for American data of wage changes to the rate of change of unemployment than to the level of unemployment may be explained by growing structural unemployment. Year-to-year changes in wages would not be affected by this long-term trend in structural unemployment, but the wage changes for a given level of unemployment, which may represent widely spaced years, would be.

CHAPTER X

The Wage-Price Guideposts

Wage-push inflation results from an autonomous rise in wages, that is, a rise not based on an increase in labor demand. Conversely, wage-push inflation can be avoided if workers limit their wage demands to the degree of productivity growth. Thus, if wages rose in proportion to the growth in productivity, unit labor costs would remain unchanged, and there would be no upward pressure on prices exerted from the labor-cost side.

Alternatively, relative factor shares could be maintained in an adjustment to productivity growth that saw wages remain constant with prices falling at the same rate as the productivity gain. Under these conditions, of course, the adjustment would lead to deflation rather than price stability.

Much confusion has arisen over these wage-price-productivity relationships. Machlup, for example, contends that if productivity gains are taken by an equivalent rise in factor returns rather than in price cuts, cost-push inflation and not price stability will result.[1]

In a numerical example, he explains that if 90 workers can produce the output formerly requiring 100 workers, with prices unchanged, output would also remain constant, and 10 workers would be unemployed. The cost-push feature stems from the inflationary aspects of governmental measures to reemploy the 10 displaced workers.

But this analysis ignores the stimulating effect of increased productivity on production of the individual firm. As each firm strives to equate marginal costs with marginal revenue, this goal will be attained by maintaining its work force, if marginal product rises in step with the increase in wages under constant prices. This increase in output does

---

[1] Fritz Machlup, "Another View of Cost-Push and Demand-Pull Inflation," *Review of Economics and Statistics,* **42** (May 1960), pp. 125–139.

not result from a fortuitous increase in aggregate demand but from the increase in factor incomes.

Probably not all the rise in real income from the increase in factor returns will be translated into increased spending, making demand somewhat inadequate to restore the former employment level. But the resulting unemployment will undoubtedly be substantially less than the total potentially displaced by the productivity gain, assumed by Machlup. Moreover, the same unemployment problem results from the adjustment to the productivity gain along the path of constant factor returns at lower prices. Then, too, the total resultant increase in real income might not all be spent, leading to the danger of inadequate demand.

Thus, whichever the adjustment to productivity increases, whether through price reductions or factor-return increases, similar employment effects would ensue. Considering that the gains from increased factor returns accrue directly to the recipients while those from decreased prices are diffused throughout the economy, in the absence of policy directives to the contrary and, in view of the atomistic wage and price setting that characterizes American industry, the typical adjustment to productivity growth is through increased factor returns rather than through decreased prices.[2]

There are two possible noninflationary adjustments to productivity gains through the process of increased factor returns. Under the first method, using a microeconomic approach, wages (and other factor returns) can increase with productivity on, say, an industry-by-industry basis. Under the second method, all wages would increase by the same percentage, equal to the average overall productivity gain. Both methods will be discussed in turn, the second with reference to the Wage-Price Guideposts. The conclusion will be reached that the Guideposts are an ineffective means of achieving the twin goals of labor-market balance and price stability.

MICROECONOMIC WAGE-PRODUCTIVITY ADJUSTMENTS

If wages rose with productivity changes on an industry-by-industry basis, those industries with above-average productivity gains over a

---

[2] Alfred Kuhn, "Market Structure and Wage-Push Inflation," *Industrial and Labor Relations Review*, **12** (January 1959), pp. 244–246, claims that employers also prefer to distribute productivity gains in the form of wage increases rather than price reductions. He cites the ease in recruitment associated with high wages and the attraction to workers of a reputation as a high-wage firm.

period would pay above-average wage increases. Meanwhile those industries experiencing below-average productivity gains would pay relatively smaller wage increases. Thus, assuming equal wages for the same work previously, adjustment to the productivity gain would create a wage differential in favor of the sector having the greater productivity gain.

An obvious attraction of this method of adjustment is its automatic achievement of the goal of price stability. All prices would remain constant as productivity gains and factor returns increased proportionately industry by industry. Equally obvious, though, is the distortion that would result in the labor market. Wages would differ among industries inducing movement from low-wage to high-wage industries. This shift would probably lead to at least short-term disequilibrium in the labor market with a consequent rise in short-run unemployment.

To explain this negative unemployment effect, consider the influence on labor demand of a policy of constant prices, with wages rising in step with productivity growth on an industry-by-industry basis. Assume that the increase in potential overall demand would be sufficient to allow for the increase in overall productivity to be matched by an equivalent increase in total output to leave total employment unchanged.

Assuming, further, that the income effects from rising productivity were neutral, that is, not leading demand toward some industries and away from others, output would expand equally industry by industry, but labor demand would fall in the industry having the greater productivity increase,[3] where output increases less than the productivity change, and would rise in the industry of lower productivity growth where output would expand more than productivity.

Labor-market imbalance would result. Workers of the same type, attracted by the industrial wage difference, would move toward the high-wage industries, just those industries where fewer workers were needed. On the other hand, in those industries lagging in productivity growth, the demand for labor would increase.

Thus, from both the supply and demand side, the labor market would become tighter in the industries of smaller productivity growth and looser in the industries of greater productivity expansion. Considering the double impact of supply and demand forces, it is not unreasonable to argue that the climate becomes favorable for unemployment to increase, at least in the short run. Net unemployment would rise as the labor market

---

[3] Relative to the discussion at this point, for labor demand in the productivity-gaining sector not to fall would require that the share of increased expenditures out of higher income directed to this sector be equal to its proportion of the total productivity gain.

in the low-wage sector tightened to such a degree that labor shortages arose, and output fell short of demand in that sector.[4] In an illuminating article on the effects of productivity-related wage movements, Kelvin Lancaster emphasizes that the criterion of a good wage-adjustment formula should include neutral labor market or employment effects, as well as price stability.[5] To Lancaster, exclusive focus of a wage policy on the goal of price stability, without considering its employment effects, parallels an emphasis on banking policy toward the preservation of balance-of-payments equilibrium at stable exchange rates, without regard for the harmful employment effects of such a policy. In short, "wage policy is every bit as capable of giving rise to unemployment as is monetary policy."[6]

Only under two strained conditions would imbalances in the labor market be avoided. If the products for the two sectors were perfect substitutes, then production could take place wherever the resources were available. The presence of excess labor in one sector would allow for higher production there; in the case of perfect product substitutability, output would be determined by the availability of productive resources and not by the nature of market demand.

The second unrealistic possibility for maintaining labor-market balance would occur if labor moved against the current, generated by wage changes, from the high- to the low-paying sector. Although there is some question whether mobility between labor markets is influenced more by wage differences than by differences in job availability, it has never been seriously suggested that job availability would be that great a lure to induce workers to move in large numbers from high- to low-wage labor markets. In any case, a wage policy seems economically perverse that establishes tight labor-market conditions with low wages, and a labor-surplus market with high wages, for the same type of labor.

Thus, only in the unrealistic cases of perfect-product substitutability

---

[4] In this case, the increase in unemployment in the sector with the loosened labor market would not be matched by the fall in unemployment in the tightened labor market.

Should this new unemployment be called frictional or structural? It doesn't fit the standard of either case. Workers are of the same type, thus not conforming to the usual pattern of the structural unemployment concept. But the immobility, which would have to be overcome to eliminate this new unemployment, would be that of an unwillingness to move from a high- to a low-wage industry or location, not the typical frictional barriers that retard movement from low- to high-wage work.

[5] Kelvin Lancaster, "Productivity-Geared Wage Policies," *Economica,* **35** (August 1958), pp. 199–212.

[6] *Ibid.,* p. 200.

or labor mobility from high- to low-wage sectors[7] could a policy of matching wage gains with productivity changes on an industry-by-industry basis be implemented without leading to dislocation of labor markets and, at least, short-run unemployment.[8]

More realistically, the policy would not long be followed. The movement of workers toward the high-wage jobs and the tendency to accept wages below the productivity gain, as a means to restore employment, in the labor-surplus sector would tend to equalize wages, a process which, under competitive conditions, would lead to lower relative prices in the sector having the relative gain in productivity and to raise them in the sector lagging in productivity growth. That is, the tendency would arise to follow an adjustment path dictated by more competition in the labor market than the policy assumes. It now remains to examine the qualities of a policy that assumes perfectly competitive labor-supply conditions and that gears equal wage changes to the average overall productivity gain.

WAGES ADJUSTED TO AVERAGE PRODUCTIVITY GAINS— THE WAGE-PRICE GUIDEPOSTS

The problems arising from the arbitrary establishment of a differential wage pattern that cannot be maintained seem to be solved by adherence to the Council of Economic Advisers' macroeconomic Wage-Price Guidepost policy, first enunciated in the 1962 Annual Report,[9] and repeated subsequently. Under this policy, wage increases would be uniform throughout industry by a percentage equal to the national trend-rate of productivity (output per man hour) growth. As further adjustment, prices would fall in industries experiencing above-average increases in productivity and would rise in those industries for which the productivity gain fell short of the national average.

[7] Lancaster cites only the first possibility, but the second also fits his algebraic model. Nevertheless, his analysis would be strengthened by including the attractive force of job availability on labor mobility.

[8] Of course, if demand for goods shifted in line with productivity changes for the different industries, there would be no need for labor mobility. But the movement that would occur from low- to high-wage industries would in itself disrupt labor markets.

In a criticism of Lancaster's analysis, W. Peters, "Productivity-Geared Wage Policies: A Comment," *Economica,* **26** (May 1959), pp. 154–156, claims that Lancaster's implicit assumption of neutral or equal income effects makes his conclusions unrealistic. But in a rejoinder, Lancaster, *ibid.,* "A Further Note," pp. 156–157, shows that allowing for differential income effects would not alter his general conclusions.

[9] *Annual Report of the Council of Economic Advisers,* Washington, 1962, pp. 185–190.

What is the proper price adjustment for an individual industry related to the industry's productivity experience compared to the national average trend value for the year? The Council does not specify precise price movements, as it does permissible wage changes, but merely advises "price reductions" for the relatively strong productivity gainers and "appropriate increases" for the industries lagging in productivity growth. Nevertheless, the intent of the Council regarding these price changes is clear. In their Guidepost statements, the Council reserves to collective bargaining the right to alter the distributive income shares going to labor and other factors. Certainly the Council does not wish to suggest that its Guideposts should in themselves alter relative factor shares. Accordingly, the price changes in individual industries should be such as to relate to the uniform wage and individual industry productivity change in a manner not to affect relative shares. Thus, an industry paying a wage increase of about 3 percent, matching the overall productivity trend growth and with a specific productivity advance of 5 percent, should reduce its prices by about 2 percent.

To generalize, the percentage price change for a particular industry (i) should equal

$$\left(\frac{1 + v}{1 + v_i} - 1\right) 100$$

with v and v_i representing the overall and individual rate of productivity growth, respectively. For small changes in productivity, the percentage price change required to maintain relative labor and nonlabor shares would approximate the form

$$(v - v_i)100.$$

If every industry followed this formula, price stability would be maintained, at least superficially, at the same time that wages increased uniformly and factor shares remained unaltered.

THE GUIDEPOSTS AND COST-PUSH INFLATION. Despite the seeming wage-price harmony achieved by the Guideposts, even their strongest supporters acknowledge that they are of limited applicability. Specifically, the Guideposts can serve only as a deterrent to cost-push inflation and are operable only in an economic climate of neutral price and wage pressures from the demand side. As Solow states, the Guideposts can work only in a "zone of economic conditions, neither too tight not too slack, in which there is some tendency toward inflation . . ."[10]

[10] Robert M. Solow, "The Case Against the Case Against the Guideposts," *Guidelines, Informal Controls and the Market Place*, edited by George P. Shultz and Robert Z. Aliber, University of Chicago Press, Chicago, 1966, p. 45.

When times are too slack, there is no need for an informal wage-price control program.

"Too tight" economic conditions can be interpreted as signifying the presence of demand-pull elements. Under these conditions, management and labor cannot be expected to roll back prices and wages by following the Guidepost rules. If firms were to adjust their prices to the Guidepost formula, in the face of excessive demand for goods, price adjustments would lose their role as allocators of resources and production. For the Guidepost price formula to be maintained would require formal price controls in support of the informal recommendations of the Guideposts. In any case, some form of suppressed inflation would result.[11] Similarly, limitation of wage demands to the overall productivity-trend growth, in the presence of demand pressure on the labor market, would require more than informal wage controls.

Of course, cost-push and demand-pull elements may be present at the same time. Therefore, at first view, it might appear that under these circumstances the Guideposts could be at least of some value in eliminating the cost-push pressures on prices and wages. But this is not the case. Considering the effects on wages, Guidepost practices demand that wage increases be limited by the overall productivity growth. If demand pulls the price level up, then for labor to adhere to the Guideposts would require that workers suffer a loss in their income share. The same reasoning would apply to the effect on nonlabor shares if excessive labor demand pulled up wages, and prices remained stable. Cost-push elements are not inevitable, but the Guideposts refer to a total wage and price adjustment that cannot be carried out if wages and/or prices rise in response to excessive demand. If they do not rise when demand is excessive, then inflation must have been suppressed.

The inability of Guidepost policy to work while demand-pull inflation is taking place explains the folly of the Council's 1966 recommendation to use the past trend productivity growth of 3.2 percent for that year instead of the calculated 3.5 percent trend growth as the basis for the uniform wage rise. The Council explains its use of the lower productivity and wage figure on the grounds that the short-run productivity growth had been unusually high because of the cyclical trend toward full employment.

In any case, though, the actual productivity growth can be assumed to exceed 3.2 percent. The threat of inflation, which materialized during the year, could have been of the cost-push or demand-pull variety. If

---

[11] This shortcoming of the price Guideposts during demand-pull inflation is recounted by Milton Friedman, "What Price Guideposts?" *ibid.*, pp. 17–39.

it was to be cost-push determined, then there was no need to reduce the estimated productivity and wage growth arbitrarily. Adherence to the lower-than-actual 3.2 percent gain in productivity and wages would have led to deflation, not price stability.

On the other hand, if the inflation was to be inspired by demand-pull elements, Guideposts would not work at all. Furthermore, setting recommended wage and price changes too low would have only aggravated the suppressed inflation and misallocation of resources and goods. More realistically, setting a Guidepost formula that requires lower-than-standard wage and price changes when demand-pull elements are present makes doubly certain that the formula will not be followed.[12]

Thus the Guideposts can only serve to prevent cost-push inflation in an economic background of otherwise stable prices. Apart from this limitation to their usefulness, their application more often than not leads to harmful side effects of labor-market instability.

With equal percentage pay raises for all workers, initial disequilibrium in the labor market, a feature of the adjustment process that matches productivity and wage increases on an industry-by-industry basis, is avoided. Nevertheless, the Guidepost practice of differential price changes leads to labor-market imbalance, transferred from disequilibrium in the product market.

Demand will rise for the goods that fall in price and fall for the goods produced by the industries whose prices rise.

Recall that Guidepost policy calls for price increases in industries gaining less than the national average productivity growth. Output would tend to fall relatively in these industries of rising prices, but this negative influence on employment is compensated for to a degree by the decline

---

[12] Many studies indicate that during the years immediately following the formulation of the Guideposts, price increases were less than anticipated on the basis of prior relationships between price changes and unemployment levels and other economic variables. These studies do not claim that the Guideposts were necessarily responsible for the restrained price rise for the period, but do point out the association between relatively stable prices and presence of the Guidepost formulas. These studies are reviewed by John Sheahan, *The Wage-Price Guideposts,* The Brookings Institution, Washington, 1967, Chapter VII. Sheahan offers three alternatives to the Guideposts for relative price stability during the period—a lessening of inflationary expectations following two recessions that preceded the prosperous period studied, the stronger competition from imports, and the balanced nature of the economic expansion which avoided the inflationary pressure associated with differential sectoral growth.

Furthermore, it should be emphasized that the period studied was 1961–1966. It is doubtful, considering the sharp inflation of the years following 1966, that if the period were extended to 1968, price increases over the seven-year span would, on average, have been less than anticipated.

in productivity, which requires more workers to produce a given output in these industries. Meanwhile in the technologically advancing sector, output rises with lower prices, but the resulting tendency for using more labor will be offset, partially or totally, by the increasing productivity that makes less labor needed to produce a given volume of goods.

To find the condition under which labor market disequilibrium is avoided, it is necessary to specify the relationships such that the positive and negative effects on labor demand related to productivity changes just equal the opposite effects caused by differential price changes. Considering only the sector of declining productivity[13]—similar results occur in the other sector, *mutatis mutandis*—this would result if total sales remained constant. This means that the sector output would fall by the same percentage as the price increase. Since the price increase just matched the productivity decline, in accordance with the Guidepost formula, then the increase in sector employment generated by the reduction in productivity would exactly offset the decline in labor demand associated with the higher prices.

Thus, returning to relative comparison, in Lancaster's terms labor-market imbalance is avoided if the elasticity of demand substitution, defined as the ratio of the percentage shift in the relative quantity demanded for the two sectors to the percentage shift in their relative prices, is unity. Lancaster considers this case "not a trivial one," but nevertheless its conditions are quite unique. With any divergence from the special case of unitary elasticity, adherence to Guidepost policy of uniform wage increases equal to the average productivity growth would lead to labor-market imblance, except under the special condition of perfect response of labor mobility to differential job opportunities.

Before examing the maladjustments associated with other than unitary elasticity of demand substitution more closely, a great advantage of Guidepost policy when this elasticity is coincidentally unity should be noted. Strict adherence to Guidepost policy short-circuits equilibrating adjustments that would have occurred under normal competitive pressures. Without following the Guideposts, wages would tend to rise in industries enjoying above-average productivity gains and fall in those with lagging technological growth as firms were pressed to pass on differential productivity gains partially in the form of price declines and partially in higher wages. With a spread in wages, workers would tend to move from low- to high-paying jobs, and unemployment and labor market imbalance would, at least temporarily, arise until the flow reversed toward the job openings from which labor migrated, and wages

[13] For simplicity, in this discussion "declines ' stand for the more precise "relative declines" in productivity.

tended toward their former relative position. In fact, if the lure of higher wages were stronger than that of job availability in the lower paid sector for some workers, to a certain degree the unemployment that arose would prove difficult to reduce.

By short-circuiting the process of adjustment, by following the wage-price Guideposts, the long-run adjustments would occur immediately, and short-run disequilibrium would be avoided. Intersectoral wage changes would be equal, and labor supply would remain constant without the disruptive labor flows consequent to short-run differential wage changes.

Abandoning the unrealistic assumption of unitary elasticity of demand substitution leads to altogether different conclusions. One special condition (mentioned above) remains, however, in which adjustment in accordance with the wage-price Guideposts would not lead to labor-market disequilibrium. If labor were completely mobile in response to job opportunities, then whatever potential temporary labor market imbalance resulted from a uniform wage policy would be quickly righted. But perfect mobility is no more than a theoretical assumption.

The wage-price rules for the typical situation of non-unitary elasticity, which must be followed to maintain labor-market balance, are quite simple. With an elasticity greater than one, the sector with the greater productivity gains (and the price decline) would increase its demand for labor because the positive influence for additional workers to produce the increased output would more than offset the negative influence of increased productivity that reduced the work force necessary to produce a given output. In the other sector, the demand for labor would fall as the positive influence on manpower needs of a relative productivity decline was more than offset by the negative effect of relatively lower output. To maintain price stability and labor-market balance, this relative change in labor demand should lead to changes in relative wages in favor of the former sector, which would raise prices there above the Guidepost formula level, cutting back output, and lower prices in the other sector, raising output.

On the other hand, if the elasticity of demand substitution were less than unity, adjustment to a wage-price formula that maintained price stability and labor-market balance would call for higher wage increases in the sector with the lesser productivity advance. In this sector, too, prices would advance relatively more than suggested by the rigid Guidepost formula.

Adjustment would also begin in the labor market to restore labor-market balance as labor moved to the sector where wages and employment were rising. The spread of the wage differential that would be needed to satisfy the twin goals of price and labor market stability would depend on the interrelationship between the elasticity of demand substitution and the sensitivity of labor mobility to differential wage changes. The greater the deviation of the demand elasticity from unity, the less responsive the labor force to wage differences—and happily, under these adjustments, unlike those related to microeconomic industry-by-industry wage-productivity changes, labor shortages occur in the high-wage sector—the greater must be the differential-wage changes.

Die-hard adherents of some form of wage-price anti-inflationary policy might salvage the principle of the Guideposts while abandoning their formula. A wage-price adjustment could be designed to fit any combination of elasticity of demand substitution and wage-differential mobility sensitivity to yield stable prices and balanced labor markets. But from both a practical and political point of view, a policy that required the establishment of specific intersectoral wage differential changes that varied from time to time would be impossible to apply.

In the first place, the problems of calculation might prove insurmountable. The discussion here has been in terms of two sectors, but, in reality, elasticities of demand substitution would have to be calculated for a multitude of industries. Then, too, an index of labor mobility would have to take into account differences in attractiveness of a given change in wage structure among different locations and industrial sectors.

Further, how much bureaucracy would business and labor suffer? Even if appropriate individual industry wage and price adjustments could be approximated, it is unlikely that a long list of Guideposts to include each industry or industry group would be followed voluntarily. With its uniform wage increases for all workers, the current Guidepost formula has the charm of simplicity and a superficial semblance of equity, even if it doesn't work. In this connection, it is interesting to note that the original Guidepost statement allowed for modification of the rigid formula, permitting above-Guidepost wages in industries that could not otherwise attract sufficient labor and below-formula wages in industries that would otherwise suffer labor surpluses. It is the purpose of this section to show that these conditions describe the general rule and not exceptional cases. The Guideposts would not work with sporadic modifications. It must be acknowledged that a theoretically sound, but practically inadequate, policy would require differential wage adjustments built into the formula.

But the final formula, which yielded overall price stability and labor-market balance, would lie somewhere between the formula that has wages rising with productivity on an industry-by-industry basis and the Guidepost formula. Insofar as it led to differential wages for the same type of work, its operation would reflect the actual degree of imperfection in labor markets.

SUMMARY

Any policy that limits wage increases to productivity gains can be designed to call for price changes that will maintain overall price stability and the constancy of factor shares. The important question is whether wage and price adjustments can be geared to productivity improvement. If demand-pull elements are present, then to expect wages and prices to relate only to productivity gains is to ask labor and business to suppress inflation of their own accord or in compliance to an unenforced formula.

Assuming the absence of demand-pull inflation elements, factor shares can be kept constant while prices remain stable, as cost-push inflation is avoided if wage increases match productivity improvement on an industry-by-industry basis, all prices remaining constant, or if uniform wage increases match the overall productivity gain, price changes differing among industries. Under the former plan, differential changes disrupt the labor market, which requires a flow of labor from high-wage to low-wage sectors to avoid unemployment. The policy assumes a rigidity and degree of monopoly in the labor market far beyond the level that actually prevails.

Under the latter policy, that of the Guideposts, the disruption begins initially in the product market because of the differential price changes that result, even if overall price stability is achieved. Under usual conditions the demand for labor in one sector expands relative to that of another. With labor market conditions somewhat less then perfectly competitive, a differential wage change must occur to balance out the labor market. Individual industry-price changes must then differ from those of the Guidepost formula. Thus the differential wage and price changes permitted as "modifications" of the Guidepost formula are almost always required, and the formula become meaningless. The inadequacy of the Guideposts suggests that cost-push inflation must be tolerated from time to time, or direct wage and price controls be imposed,[14] or efforts be made to eliminate or reduce product and labor-market monopoly elements. But these two curbs to inflation might carry a heavy social and political cost.

[14] In effect the Guidelines, if strictly followed, establish a system of wage and price controls, which Arthur F. Burns, "The Effectiveness of Wage and Price Guidelines," *Harvard Business Review,* **43** (March-April 1965), pp. 59-60, calls "almost indistinguishable from an economy in which wages and prices are directly fixed by government authority."

Index

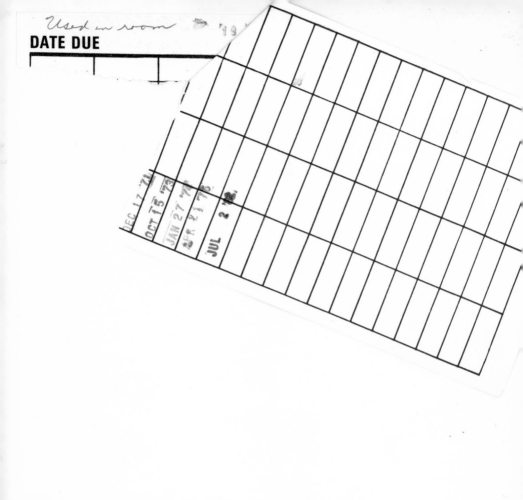